MORAL STRATEGY

MORAL STRATEGY

An Introduction to the Ethics of Confrontation

by

JAMES K. FEIBLEMAN

Tulane University

MARTINUS NIJHOFF / THE HAGUE
1967

PRINTED IN THE NETHERLANDS

PREFACE

No statement, except one, can be made with which all philosophers would agree. The exception is this statement itself. The disagreement has the advantage that it gets all the proposals out into the open where they can be examined, but it has the disadvantage that the cogency of any one philosophy must rely entirely upon that wide public which is unprepared to deal with it. Fortunately, ethics has a more immediate appeal than some other branches of philosophy; yet the history of the topic gives no indication that this circumstance has had the happy results we might have expected.

One peculiarity of ethics is that its problems are rarely settled on its own grounds. Ethical problems are for the most part referred to socially established moralities, and moralities are socially established not on the basis of philosophy but rather by some sponsoring institution, usually religion or politics. Such establishments, however, depend on the prior preparation of ethical proposals by philosophers. For it stands to reason that an ethics cannot be socially established if there is no ethics to establish. Thus philosophers provide the justification for socially-established moralities while seeming not to do so.

In the following pages I have undertaken to examine what ethics is, and how it works morally for individuals and societies. To see this clearly is to see also what theoretical ethics and its concrete moralities should be. If my analysis is correct, then what-ought-to-be is a natural development from what-is when what-is is sufficiently understood to enable inductions from it to guide the behavior of those responsible for change and direction.

New Orleans, La. – Chilmark, Mass.
June 1964 – February 1966

A SYSTEM OF PHILOSOPHY

TABLE OF CONTENTS

BOOK THREE – THE MORAL SITUATION AND ITS OUTCOME

BOOK ONE

INTRODUCTION

PART I

THE APPROACH TO ETHICS AND MORALITY

CHAPTER I

METHODOLOGICAL CONSIDERATIONS

(a) The Task of Ethics

The traditional meaning of ethics is the study of the good for man, the ideal of individual conduct; and the traditional meaning of morality is the study of the use by a society of a given theory of ethics. These definitions have been somewhat degraded in the popular account, so that ethics has managed to combine a lofty level of high and rather abstract consideration with a kind of smug moralism, neither having much to do with the actual lives and practices of individuals and societies. Morality has come to mean chiefly a reference to sexual ethics, more specifically a certain puritanical attitude toward indulgence. In professional circles these days ethics refers chiefly to the making of moral judgments on preferential grounds, emotive theories confined to the corrections of errors in the use of moral language.

But many developments in recent decades have combined to make us suspect that each of these interpretations of ethics while valid is too narrow when considered alone. How can individual ethics preempt the topic when the moral life of the individual is contingent upon the moral structure and concerted actions of societies? The professional version of ethics is perhaps where the theory of ethics ought to end or how it should conclude. But many agonizing questions must be interposed in the investigation before we are ready for such an eventuality. It is certain in any case that ethics is everyone's concern. For there is no human life which is lived in independence of all morality. Before the end of this chapter I shall propose definitions of both ethics and morality, but these must be considered tentative until the remainder of the study can expand their meanings sufficiently to offer evidential as well as theoretical support.

We owe to Camus the reminder that the understanding of human nature has been prevented by the prejudices of man in favor of his own virtues. Such attitudes have been inadvertently aided and abetted by those ethical theorists whose lives were so devoted to the good and the right that they were perhaps partially blinded to the extent of the participation in actual life of the bad and the wrong. It was not helpful to the development of ethics when approval of conduct was substituted for interest in behavior, so that inquiry came to be confined to what could be regarded as morally good. For in order to know something of the size of a topic its boundaries must be reached and crossed many times. Thus the man who enjoys inflicting pain on others, the Japanese follower of Bushido for instance who tortured his prisoners until death relieved them, is of as much concern to the moralist as the blameless man who in the course of a long life never did anything which could be questioned.

Before we make decisions on any ethical issue it might be better if we knew the truth about ourselves. But what is that truth and how could we recognize its limitations? Reality is always wider than our narrow schemes, a fact which Bergson made something of a profession of pointing out, though his work in this regard has been neglected. For life is both more wonderful and more terrible than it is usually conceded to be. Examples are not wanting of individuals whose total behavior could only be described as good, and there are even examples from time to time of societies which on the whole behave well in terms of a more general humanity. The other side, however, is more insistent. The spectacle of the treatment by Nazi Germany of minority Germans and of enemy nations judged inferior has taught us all that no progress had been made in human motives, and that people everywhere are capable of almost anything.

Conduct in accordance with the whole width of reality is all but impossible. For the individual, the society, the human species, there are alternatives and hence choices. Moreover, between any two of these levels there are demands which conflict; what a society requires of the individual may clash with what he needs for himself, and what humanity calls for may go directly against what society requires. And there is no avoiding these problems when they arise. Morality as such is inescapable. Any pattern of conduct pursued by an individual or a society is a morality. But one individual following such a pattern rarely approves of an individual following a different pattern, and strictly speaking we have come to think "immoral" any morality except our own. The code and customs of one society is often regarded with abhorrence by another.

The spectacle of the evils prevalent in our own time, not only the systematic evils of the Nazis but also those of the leaders of the Soviet

Union in Stalin's day, to say nothing of other and less organized bad behavior, such as the torture of prisoners and the sporadic resort to cannibalism, all have taught us how stupendous and difficult are the tasks confronting the ethical theorist and the practicing moralist. In order to achieve anything remotely approaching good behavior on the part of all, it may be necessary to adopt an indirect method and to address ourselves to the elimination of bad behavior.

What has happened has in any case opened our eyes to the necessity of recognizing the wide range of human behavior as a whole. Much is to be learned about the good from a study of the bad, including that absolute degree of bad called evil. The good is good because it is not bad, but what is bad cannot be explained altogether in negative terms because it has positive effects. The mere statement of the ideal may be meaningless, unless we first understand our situation fully, and work out a method for getting from the actual to the ideal. We need to learn more about how things are before we can afford to concentrate on how they ought to be. Only by recognizing the ugly facts can we hope to devise a strategy for transcending them.

The absolute surrender to the emphases of contemporaries is as inconsistent with the aim of the productive moralist as their neglect would be. Most novel moralities consist in selections and rearrangements of the elements of older ones, but even this is no condemnation of their novelty, unless organizations are held to be trivial affairs or wholes not supposed to be more than the sum of their parts. A new system at the comprehensive level of moralities offers a fresh perspective on the world. The current scene is supercharged with intensity, and this must not be forgotten. Ethical theories do not fail so much because of what is false in them as they do because of what is omitted from them. The minimum elements taken from rival positions would have to be included in any new and comprehensive formally induced moral scheme.

On the other hand, to see existence as a concrete unity requires the method of synthesis which philosophy undertakes. The present work offers an integral conception, and I fear not much can be done to put the reader immediately in the picture. Explanations must be accumulated little by little, and I can only hope that at some point the entire pattern will emerge. For (it will be contended here) an ethics is nothing more nor less than a system of ontology seen qualitatively as the organization of bonds between wholes, just as aesthetics is the same system seen qualitatively as the organization of bonds between parts.

The philosopher moves in a field of assorted concepts and among the battered remains of traditional systems. He tries to arrange them in the most suitable way. If he did not come to his task with a notion of how this could be done, he would have to devise one on the spot. His is more an act of discovery than of invention, though it requires some imagination to see how things could be made to occur together advantageously.

Where I have allowed myself critical remarks it is only to make the contrast with the extent to which some position seems to support my own. For I have tried as much as possible to adhere to Nietzsche's principle, "Where you cannot love, there should you—pass by." Accordingly, I have tried to see only what is valid in other proposals. Where too much has been claimed for them, or where I have thought mistakes were made, I have not stopped to argue; I have chosen to detour. My reason for this is that my chief aim is to present an original ethical theory and to offer as much explanation as I can in its support. At the same time I recognize that no philosopher thinks alone; each owes a great debt to his predecessors and contemporaries. We are engaged in a joint enterprise; and so the more it can be shown that we are joined, the better.

Every theory which has come to be taken seriously has made something of a contribution but also has proved to have its own limitations. It is possible to view a theory from the standpoint either of its strength or of its weakness. I shall take the former and more positive alternative here. I shall try to consider other ethical theories as in general true in what they affirm and false only in what they deny, and I shall ignore the falsity and the denial. If my theory of ethics is sufficiently large, there will be found within it a place for what each theory has affirmed. The rival schools of ethical theory are not on the same level of analysis. For instance the opposition of intuitionism and utilitarianism has been accepted; but intuitionism is individual, utilitarianism social. It should be possible to include both of them in a broader and more inclusive structure.

Whenever a system of ideas has to be presented, the question of the method of presentation immediately appears. To some extent any presentation other than the-whole-at-once is at least a partial distortion and therefore misleading. And to present the whole at once is obviously impossible. The reader has to imagine therefore as with music that the entire composition exists but that the performer has to run over it from start to finish in order to present it in the proper order. For the listener the effect is expected to be cumulative, and he should at the end gather up the total effect for himself. Then and then only is he in a position to evaluate "the-whole-at-once." So it is with any attempt to present a complete moral philosophy. I shall therefore begin at the beginning then move to the middle and from there to the end; and this is necessary, although the ethics presented here is not a developmental affair but what (it is hoped) the reader will recognize for what it is: a whole-at-once.

We shall be concerned in this book with states of affairs rather than with meanings. Meanings enter only in so far as we deal with the theory of ethics, that is, with possible states of affairs. I shall have some things to say shortly about the theory of ethics, but the theory of ethics is a theory and not an ethics. There is a theory *about* ethics and a theory *in* ethics. After this Part I shall talk only about the theory *in* ethics.

My primary purpose is to present an ethics, not to introduce or defend a methodology. An efficient medium of expression is one so perfectly adapted to its subject-matter that it makes possible a full disclosure while not itself being noticed. Nevertheless, something by way of an introduction will have to be said about the whole question of methods in ethics. We will look at this question and then move on.

I shall have just as much to say about morality, with its concrete features, bad as well as good, for while ethics must be pursued in independence of practice, as any theory must, at the same time it is equally true that no theory which lacks applications would be worthy of consideration. We are protected from such idle speculations by the fact that there are no inapplicable true theories. What we learn about possible states of affairs will be used as a canon of criticism of actual states of affairs.

(b) Methods in Ethics

In formulating an ethics I shall not begin by establishing axioms and then proceed to deduce theorems from them. Nothing that precise. Nor shall I start, as it were, from the other end of the spectrum and begin as Aristotle suggested in the *Eudemian Ethics* by advancing from "true but obscure judgments"[1] to arrive at clear ones. Despite the devotion of a first Part to the question of approaches to ethics, I will not trouble the reader with the method whereby the present study was formulated. Those who come to a book like this in the hope of discovering some enlightenment are entitled to find a finished product

[1] Book I. 6.

and not merely to watch a philosopher at work. Nevertheless, a few remarks about methods in ethics may be in order.

There are many methods employed in ethics but the chief ones among them are based on either reason or experience. I shall omit separate discussion of some of the other methods, such as the method of intuition or the pragmatic method. My reason for this omission is that they fit into the other methods as subordinate procedures. Intuitions are employed in finding axioms for rational systems; induction, for me at least, is the choice of axioms. Pragmatism is also taken care of in the usual derivation, for who is there among us who has had no experience and who therefore could not obtain his guide lines from his own living past? Whether one derives truth from workability (in James' sense) or tests hypotheses by means of experiments (in Peirce's), the considerations prompted by rubbing shoulders with the edges of the rough-and-ready world can hardly be avoided.

This elimination of intuition and pragmatism as alternative methods in ethics leaves us with two: the methods of reason and of empiricism. But the conception that reason and empiricism are alternative methods can be sustained only by misunderstanding them both. Such a misunderstanding requires a reason which operates on its own in the absence of the facts and an empiricism that is content with the facts alone without drawing any conclusions from them. But this conception is neither the only nor the preferred one. There is another conception according to which reason operates within the application of the method of empiricism to see that the facts are fairly selected and after the facts to employ them in the verification or falsification of hypotheses. Thus empiricism is the leading edge of discovery while reason pronounces the final judgments.

Aristotle perhaps is responsible for the emphasis on practical application from which the study of ethics has subsequently suffered. Such an emphasis is premature. He held that ethics is practical while metaphysics is theoretical. This would be true only if morals were the direct practical application of metaphysics. Metaphysics has many applications—all to theories of one sort or another, each of which has its practical applications. Metaphysics is high theory and applies to lesser theories. Ethics is a lesser theory and applies to practice. Ethics is still a theory and as a theory it is needed. We cannot apply a theory until we have a well-developed theory to apply, and theory to be properly developed must be worked out in some isolation from practice. We must determine what the good is before taking thought of one of its main subdivisions, which is human good. And then we must put the study of human good before the study of moral codes. It is true that ethics has a practical branch called morals, but ethics is no more intimately allied with practice than any other theory.

There must be something of the character of an assumption about a theory; otherwise it could not be used to help in understanding the connections between the disparate data of experience. A theory is not demonstrated by the situations to which it is relevant and which it is called on to explain. The theory at the beginning will have the status of an hypothesis, nothing more certain than that, until it has proved its usefulness to understanding. An hypothesis which has aided comprehension has justified its claim to be taken more seriously, and perhaps even to be considered tentatively as an ingredient of that world which experience discloses, but there is nothing final about it. Thus all understanding remains in the last analysis a conjecture.

Moral practice cannot proceed on any sustained basis without norms. The exigencies of experience compel the working formulation and immediate adoption of interim concrete ideals. Thus norms are matters of practical procedure even though how they are discovered may be theoretical and how they are introduced strategic. But ethics is empirical as well as normative. It deals with actual situations as much as with the ideals suggested by them just as physics does with its physical world and mathematical formulations. An individual's reasons for his actions and a society's rules for what is permitted to the individual are after all empirical elements; they exist and have an effect in the world of matter and energy in space and time. But the values which lie behind them are values in the same way that other values lie behind the physical elements. Whatever humans do it is human to do. No particular kind of behavior can be said to be more human than any other. The question is, what is it best for humans to do, best for them and also perhaps best for the world?

Moral values have been held to be normative and physical values empirical chiefly because moral values differ from society to society whereas physical values do not. But societies and everything they contain, including the moral values built into their peculiar constructions, are empirical also. The normative is the locally empirical. Morality is substantive, it is constitutive first and regulative only afterwards. The customs, traditions and laws of a society are intended to integrate that society with its immediate environment. The normative "ought," given the confines of a particular society, is entirely determined from what "is." It is conventional within a certain setup to assume a definite conception of what ought to be. The test of empirical values is not whether they are without exception and globally prevail but whether they enter into material things in space and time and influence them. This moral values do, and no less because they do so only locally.

Measurements cannot be allowed to make the difference between the normative and the empirical. We call what we can measure empirical and what we have not succeeded in measuring normative, chiefly because we erect our success and our failure into world conditions, which they are not. For (as Plato insisted long ago) what exists can be measured even though (he might have added) in some cases we may not yet have succeeded in working out the measuring techniques.

Perhaps the difficulty here arises because we have such a simple and naive conception of the methods of measurement. Look at the mathematics which has been invented to provide for the necessary measurements in physics and chemistry. A developing study always receives the mathematics it deserves. There has been no intense interest in the measurement of those emergent values which lie in the range well above biology. From the Greeks to modern times the quantitative linear method of logic and mathematics has prevailed, so that now we think of logic as mathematical. And yet all the while there has been a qualitative circular method struggling to be born. Hints are to be found first in Aristotle who introduced the importance of multiple definition, of opposites and especially of correlatives. It is to be found second in Hegel who read all opposites as correlatives, and who further emphasized circularity by making all things into parts of the whole. There are further hints available now, as for instance in the analysis of quality.

I shall not undertake to develop a quantitative science of ethics or morals, and mention one only to show what I think is involved in the position from which the present ethics was undertaken. I have in mind now only an ethical proposal. What is empirical exists to be measured and as we have just seen the moral is above all empirical. It has to do with a wide range of behavior: with the behavior of the individual toward his fellow man and toward himself as a person. The moral component is, as Dewey pointed out, an integral part of human life. The concrete nature of everyday behavior insures that the abstract consideration of morality must always to some extent falsify the proportions. But there is the little business of control. An adequate theory of ethics is one which can best describe moral behavior and offer proposals to improve it.

Morality has to do primarily with the rules of conduct which have been established in a given society. They are reflected in many places in the society, and particularly so if the society is a long-established one. The most obvious of these places is of course the conscience of individual members. Ethics has to do with the comparative study of actual moralities, and from this study with what the ideal morality could be and should be: with what moralities have in common and with how to establish by their aid the conception of the perfect morality for an ideal society.

If ethics is the theory of the good and morality is the practice of the good, then the good is empirical; and if it is empirical then it should prove to be not exclusively human. Human good is a definite part of the good but not the whole of it, for surely other things can be good in themselves. Human beings are animal organisms imbedded in the natural world, they are natural objects and their properties are natural properties. Morality at the human level may be an emergent quality and peculiarly human; but something analogous to it must exist at other empirical levels.

What is true of the physical level must be true of all other levels, because everything has at least the physical components. Then if I can show that quality exists at the physical level I have made my case for the empirical nature of the good and justified a generalization of ethics. The attraction between material bodies as called for by the law of gravitation suggests that intrinsic qualities exist in those bodies. Energy is quality at the physical level. All that we need to do in this connection is to recognize the qualitative kinship which exists between quality at the physical level and quality at the human level; the common quality of attraction which is found both in gravitation and in—say—friendship. The good, then, is not entirely human, though the human version is. In the next chapter I propose to fill in the details of this contention enough to construct a framework on which a theory of the moral integrative levels can be hung.

In traditional accounts of ethics the topic is divided in many ways. In at least one of these ways various species of the good are recited. I propose here to assume that a basic distinction can be made between intrinsic and extrinsic goods. The intrinsic good is qualitative and therefore does not admit of subdivisions into further distinctions and differences. The extrinsic is the useful, and so there are many sub-divisions. Among these are: the instrumental (the good as an implement), the functional (the good as a skill), the utilitarian (or social good), the hedonic (pleasurable), the voluntaristic (well-intentioned), the intellectual (the good as good reasons), the evolutionary (the good as an improvement of the species), the self-realizing (the perfection of the individual), and the linguistic (sentences conveying expressions of emotions or of prescriptions).

In the following pages I shall try to show that it is not necessary to choose between intrinsic and extrinsic goods, between the feelings of pleasure and the functions of utility, between, in other words, enjoyment and achievement. The greatest enjoyment is achievement itself, and the moral life a stage-process in which achievement becomes a matter of the capabilities of the individual exercised to their fullest: controlled enjoyment. The exercise of such energies as well as the constructions resulting from them are sure to be double sources of satisfaction. Hence the good life is life lived to the fullest and may be said to consist in the greatest enjoyment of the highest achievement.

Reason so far as ethics is concerned is the highest good because it orders goods. The goods which it orders are material goods: the integration of the individual's organic needs, the welfare of his society, the proper relations with all existing species. The good as intrinsic is the quality of a material. "Higher" goods are no less high because they happen to be material, for matter has many sorts of potentialities. For the survival of his body, the individual needs many things: food and water, shelter, clothing and activity; for the continuance of his species he needs other things: sex, a family, and for the evolution to a higher species still other things: a community, good government, knowledge, ultimate survival.

Most behavior is exigent and is aimed at the individual's immediate survival. No knowledge of fixed principles is required in order to seek the reduction of the basic organic needs, though such need-reductions (as it turns out) are accomplished by means of implicit regularities which we sometimes describe in terms of fixed principles. The question of morality, individual and social, arises because of the necessity for continuing need-reductions. Providing for future needs involves the establishment of rules so that individuals may assist rather than interfere with each other's efforts.

The various views of the good which have been advanced are not false, but they are not complete truths, either. It can be shown that each of them has to do with some part of the whole of the good. It is safe, then, to say that the good is not merely some one of the goods which have been claimed exclusively or primarily for it. Thus might is not right, unless it were to be the dominant good; intuition is not the sole guide to the good, unless it could be depended on to lead to more than knowledge; and duty is not the good, unless it mean also an obligation to secure ultimate survival.

(c) The Position of Ethics

People without professional training do not expect to understand modern physics. Therefore they find nothing strange in its technical vocabulary and habitual recourse to mathematics. But they do expect to understand philosophy because it uses ordinary words. Thus they are dismayed and even indignant when they find philosophy unintelligible. But philosophy, too, is a technical field, and when it employs ordinary words it does so in a special sense. In the hands of philosophers, such words become professional tools and are used in ways not available to those without special equipment.

The popular discontent with philosophy more often often refers to ethics than to metaphysics. Metaphysics is not counted, for by being assumed it has been thought to be abandoned. Ethics is a more familiar term, and this is chiefly because of the many kinds of morality ordinarily met with in a working day. Every state has an official ethics, usually embodied in a charter or constitution; every doctor is familiar with something called "medical ethics"; every religion has a formally authorized ethics, usually though not always divinely ordained. Every social institution has its professional ethics. And all of these are commonly encountered.

The effect of an official philosophy is to suppose that all philosophical questions have been settled and therefore that all further discussion can be ruled out. If an ethics has been chosen and is operating, why speculate any further about ethics? It was an advantage of the Greek culture of the fifth and fourth centuries B.C. that the established philosophy did not preclude the exploration of philosophies; philosophy was free. In the Middle Ages, philosophy as theology became the rational defense of religion. Now it is the voluntary slave of science or exists in virtue of the equally voluntary exclusion of science: the attempt to construct a science of ethics on the one hand and to escape from science on the other.

Ethics however can be investigated on its own, and the autonomy of such an investigation can be retained. Morality so far as it can be looked into must stand on its own ground and lie clearly within its own borders. In order to discover a theory of ethics sufficiently broad to include established moralities of whatever stripe and ethical ideals of whatever constitution, it is not necessary to refer to any question of divine origins or of supernatural causation, nor to claim scientific accuracy for the result. Such extra-ethical authorities are neither affirmed nor denied here, but they are not assumed, either. They are held irrelevant to the investigation in so far as it can claim independence for its subject-matter. The determination of just how ethics fits into a broader scheme is not one for speculative ethics nor is it an independent moral question. It involves issues which lie beyond ethics itself, which is to be my sole topic of consideration here.

I am not so much concerned in this book with making the right answers as I am with finding the proper questions. The art of discovery is at its best when it discloses new and hitherto unknown areas of ignorance, for then investigation can be directed toward fresh channels, usually with productive results. Thus every novel assertion may have probative value even though in the end it be proved wrong. For to be wrong is not always to be entirely misleading.

Philosophy asks the important questions, those for which no final answers have been found. Probably none will ever be found. But merely asking philosophical questions and finding supposed final answers can have the most important of practical effects. For on the basis of such answers institutions, societies and even entire cultures are built. Thus the efforts do not go for nothing, and even though the answers in the end prove wrong and are abandoned, they have in the meanwhile been put to the largest of human uses. Ethics as a branch of philosophy has a crucial part to play in the foundation of human life. What practicality could be wider and at the same time more concrete?

The history of philosophy is full of giants who can see into the depths of neglected truth only if they are allowed to subordinate all other truths. This has the advantage that it enables the giants to contribute to the sum of human knowledge, but it has the disadvantage of warping it. That is why a history of philosophy is necessary. It can be made cumulative only as philosophology, not the history of philosophy merely but the history of those ideas in philosophy which are worth saving. The sorting process is a prolonged and painful one, often calling for centuries of thoughtful scholarship. This is no less the case of course in ethics.

What I hope I have done, then, is to make a fresh appraisal of some very old ideas, and as a result rearranged them in a way calculated to render them more manageable. I claim some originality for the final product but I acknowledge also the influence of much in the history of moral philosophy and indeed of human culture generally, and especially of the works of those of my contemporaries who have speculated on the same set of concerns. I have not been uninfluenced by my own times, and feel very strongly the currents of thought which crisscross the world in which I live. The more the number of elements a book represents, the more it will be found representative by those who are in a position to pass durable judgments.

It might be illustrative to compare and contrast my approach to ethics with samples of others. Aristotle, for instance, divided ethics into the intellectual and the moral. The former was theoretical, the latter practical. The contemporary division most fashionable is the normative and the meta-ethical, the former being practical and the latter theoretical. My own division is somewhat different, though of course there are many similarities. I divide my study into the ethical and the moral. By the ethical I mean empirical ethics, or the study of those complex grades of the good which are ingredient in structured nature. The moral for me, then, would be the empirical good considered in its practical aspects.

After examining the good in nature I examine the ideal, a speculative field whose object is to study the theoretical good which exists as a kind of second story in a two-story natural world. What is the proposal which is best to be chosen as the ideal? Having decided upon this, I engage in a study of the obstacles to its attainment. The actual world contains in addition to the good the various grades of bad up to and including evil. The book ends with a discussion of the end toward which it has been working all along: what is the best strategy to employ in order to go from where we are to where we think we ought to be?

The book falls I should think under the general rubric of naturalism, although I am not sure that my version of naturalism is one other naturalists would be prepared to accept. The ethics of naturalism has been interpreted subjectively. For instance, morality has been thought to be based on the instinct of self-preservation and self-assertion by Hobbes, on the feelings of pleasure and sympathy by Hume, on the factor of interest by Ralph Barton Perry. Now the individual and his needs are natural enough and we shall be dealing with them. But there is another sense in which "natural" can be understood, and this is the objective meaning of the term according to which the good and the right are properties of material things as well as of persons, whether the individual is aware of them or not, and according to which anything which is "good for" anything else will have to be considered moral; and this is the meaning of natural to be employed here. "Natural" here also carries the implication that nothing super-natural will be introduced, and that too is the interpretation assumed in this book.

It is not possible to tell who has won until the race is over. A work is not proved substantial merely because it has outlived its critics. There must be something of substance in it that the generations continue to find solid and satisfying. About the fate of this work some readers will know, though certainly not its author.

CHAPTER II

THE MORAL INTEGRATIVE LEVELS

The investigation of ethics is conducted by and for members of the human species, but it must range in a far wider fashion, if only in order to indicate the particular setting of human ethics. We shall see that human individuals are tied to each other through the use of material tools. This is particularly true of the tools of communication: signs scratched on hard surfaces (writing) and sound waves modulated (speaking), for example. Human individuals are tied also to their immediate environment by other material tools, such tools for instance as buildings and bulldozers. It is important to remember that these signs and other tools (here collectively called "artifacts") are parts of the immediate material environment. They most assuredly are not parts of the human organism. But they have important human roles to play, and in some of these roles as least they have a high relevance to morality.

It is often true that an instrument designed to do one thing proves immensely useful at something else. Many human benefits have resulted from investigations not directly aimed at benefitting humans. Studies of radiation in physics is a case in point. The Curies and their successors were primarily moved by curiosity about the radiation of energy in the physical world. What they found has also been employed for practical human ends: roentgenology has been an important tool in the hands of doctors of medicine. The point is that the connection between human beings and the rest of nature is an intimate one, and no less so when the demonstration is inadvertent. It is often possible to make human advances through effecting changes directly in the environment.

The human being, then, has to be considered as a natural species and against the background of the whole of nature. Man is part of nature; and although this is not exactly a new idea, there are new features in our present conception of just what it means. The feature that will concern us the most is that the properties of man are to be found *mutatis mutandis* in non-human nature. The human is an extension of the natural, so that such properties as exist both in non-human and in human nature appear in human nature under different guises. That this is particularly true of moral features is what of course will especially concern us. Nature in this book will be called the cosmos and will be defined for this purpose as the sum of all natural species, that is to say, all species of material entities or material orders.

The cosmos is not uniform. It is split into cleavage planes, and when fractured responds with predictable striations. These are the natural joints. They have been given names, corresponding to the areas investigated by the experimental sciences, and their inter-relations have been studied. They are the scientific integrative levels, and they run roughly as follows.

The cultural
the psychological
the biological
the chemical
the physical.

There are of course a great many sublevels for each level, and there may be infra-physical as well as supra-cultural levels. Each level consists in a further complication of the entities at the level below, plus one emergent quality. There are many laws which hold between any two adjacent levels.[1] The situation is extremely complex. It is not made any simpler, either, when we consider the position of the human being within it. He is not an absolute isolate and indeed could not exist for very long alone; and even if he could he would be in no position to satisfy his most basic needs. But the situation is more intricate than this fact would indicate. For man exists at every one of the integrative levels. He is a piece of matter, having the physical properties of mass, density and dimensions; he is composed of a set of chemical compounds, chiefly organic; he is a biological organism, a psychological individual, and a part of culture.

As we might expect from these facts, he experiences confrontations at every one of the integrative levels. He must deal with physical objects, as when he digs stones out of a field; with chemical objects, as when he breathes in a gas, air; with biological objects, as when he

---

[1] See my "Theory of Integrative Levels," *British Jl. for the Philosophy of Science*, 5, 59–66, 1954; also "The Integrative Levels in Nature" in Barbara Kyle (ed.) *Focus on Information* (London 1965, Aslib, pp. 27–41), which is an expanded version.

goes hunting; with psychological objects, as when he talks with another human individual; with cultural objects, as when he reads Shakespeare's plays. For each of these confrontations there is a moral degree of involvement in which he is concerned with or without his knowledge.

We shall in this book be dealing with the integrative levels only so far as man is concerned in them. Thus we shall tend to ignore the lower integrative levels and concentrate on the higher ones, subdividing somewhat more as sublevels become for our purpose more important. We shall take seriously the level of the human individual himself, next his society, then the entire human species, and finally the cosmos as the sum of all species, from the physical species to those which may exist higher than man. Obviously, the choice of levels is weighted heavily on the side of human ethics. Our name for this selection will be "the moral integrative levels" or, in a more theoretical connection, "the ethical integrative series," and its considerations will dominate this study.

The moral integrative levels will read as follows.

> The cosmic
> the human
> the social
> the individual.

The differences between the scientific integrative levels given on p. 18 and the moral integrative levels given above call for some explanation. The scientific integrative levels and the ethical integrative series do not match. The cosmic is the sum of all material orders and so includes all scientific integrative levels, while the individual, the social and the human divisions are the elements of analysis of the integrative levels of the cultural.

The extreme naturalism of the position of man in the conception being advanced here will be evident. That man is part of nature means that his properties—all of them—are natural properties. It means also, then, that much of his constitution and behavior can be accounted for from this point of view. Thus ethics from this approach becomes a kind of moral cosmology since it considers the integration of the cosmos through a consideration of all its internal relations with respect to their qualities. In morality the qualities are substantive and the relations analytic of the qualities.

For each level, individual, social, human and cosmic, there are both broad considerations of that level *sui generis* and separate considerations for the human individual. Objectively speaking each level must be considered on its own footing and in its own terms, but we shall be concerned with the human individual primarily just because we are human individuals, and so it will be necessary also to consider each level from the perspective afforded by the existence of the human individual. That this is a legitimate approach follows from the fact that the human individual, too, is a cosmic material entity. And so we shall be traditional in emphasizing human ethics.

The fundamental difference between the traditional ethics and the moral cosmology to be developed here is that human individuals with their societies do not preempt the field of the ethical. For the astrophysical cosmology is concerned only with the physical species, whereas the moral cosmology, which is the moral side of the philosophical cosmology, is concerned with all species. And so there can be an ethical study of the morality of any species, of comets for instance as well as of man.

The time has passed when our knowledge allowed us to consider the human individual and human society as an absolute isolate or as an isolated affair in an otherwise hostile environment. To some extent it is true that the environment is hostile, but were it true altogether the human species would have become extinct long ago, as indeed some other species have. So we must assume that to some extent—indeed to the extent necessary for survival—the environment is friendly: man has not only survived, he has prospered and multiplied.

The human being, then, is a valid member of a number of organizations of increasing scope and complexity. He belongs to a society; through it to the human species; and through the human species to the cosmos, as one species of being among many. Recent developments in astronomy have assured us that there is considerable evidence for the existence of life on many other planets scattered throughout our own galaxy and beyond it throughout other galaxies in the intergalactic universe. The human species depends for its existence upon the earth where it interacts with other species, but the earth interacts with the sun and the solar system interacts with the galaxy. Now wherever there is interaction there is participation, and wherever there is participation there must be moral considerations: in our case not only how we behave toward the members of other species but also how we are involved with them.

Morality as such exists at many empirical levels. It exists for the individual toward himself, through his conscience (his self-respect, personal integrity, dignity). It exists for the society through its establishments (its laws, customs, traditions). It exists for the human species through its commitment to other species of beings. And it exists for the cosmos through the relation of all species in the material order.

This is stretching the term "moral" quite a bit, I will admit. Ordinarily it is conventional to think of morality only where there is choice and hence responsibility, and it is supposed that both choice and responsibility are peculiar to the human being. But consistent with our principle, announced in the foregoing pages, that there is nothing in human nature without a correlate in non-human nature, we may claim that we can look for—and find—the correlate for choice. Choice, it is usually understood, is made possible by freedom. Only where there is freedom to choose between alternatives can there be choice. Now some writers, notably Peirce, have seen in chance the external correlate of what is internally freedom. There is chance as well as law at every empirical level, and so there is morality, too; different moralities, admittedly, but all sharing a family resemblance; and so we are justified in assuming that something corresponding to what in the human being is called morality also exists in the world about him.

Human nature is continuously engaged at all levels. And although the various moralities are by no means the same, they may overlap. Moreover, the human individual may be at various times and in various contexts engaged with any or all of them. He is always engaged with himself, but he is engaged with others, too; and the prominence of the others and their challenge to the autonomy of the individual will depend very much upon the particular occasion. Ethical statements, then, can be true or false for the individual, for his society, for the human species, or for all species.

CHAPTER III

A SUMMARY PERSPECTIVE

It may be well to set forth as guide lines a sort of summary perspective of what further ideas the reader may expect to meet in the following pages, not presented in the order in which he will encounter them but more compactly so that the chief features will be prominent. We have already seen in the last chapter that the framework of this entire theory of ethics is to be built around the conception of the moral integrative levels. But further orientations should be helpful, for there are some ideas to be advanced here which could not have been predicted from the naturalism of the moral integrative levels taken just by themselves.

One of the principal ideas is the nature of the good as it exists equally at each of the integrative levels and justifies our description of this aspect of them as moral (meaning by 'moral' in this connection of course the entire consideration of the good and with it of its opposite the bad). What this means is that "values" will be assumed to exist at every integrative level. Among the values are to be found of course the moral values. But the fact that moral values exist at every level does not suggest an exact science of values. They are pervasive and they have vague boundaries, and so, as Aristotle said, it is well not to look for more precision than the nature of the topic admits.[1]

Ordinarily, values have been held to be subjective and psychological while the natural world with the exception of man is thought not to contain them. But values here (as with some thinkers, notably Reid, Peirce, Whitehead, Laird, Hartmann) are objective as well as subjective, ingredients of non-human nature as well as of human nature. We shall have to be prepared in advance for the way in which the case for this position is to be presented here.

The goals for improvement in a society are spelled out by its notions of the good and the beautiful. These values are not adjuncts to being, not chapters written in order to complete a philosophy, but essential

[1] *Nico. Eth.*, I, 3.

elements of philosophy because indispensable ingredients of reality.

Being is either quantitative (logic, mathematics) or qualitative (ethics and aesthetics). Reality, which is equality of being, is structured of wholes and parts. The beautiful, then, is the bond between parts in any whole, and the good is the bond between wholes. We are on this theory entitled to speak of the good as bonded wholes and of the beautiful as bonded parts. Any segment of being therefore must have its ethical as well as its aesthetic aspect. By "ethics" I understand all theoretical considerations of the good as defined above. By "morality" I understand the application of some particular theory of the good at a given integrative level. The moral domain is a self-sufficient one. That is to say, it is internally dependent in virtue of its intensive quality and needs no external reference. Morality is the property of a certain set of bonds between wholes at the levels prescribed by various types of wholes, wholes of various sizes of inclusiveness and of different degrees of complexity. The simplest wholes have their bonds (individual ethics) and the most complex have theirs (cosmic ethics).

The way in which any two things in the world are bonded together is their moral aspect. Thus when we speak of the good we are not confined to human values, even though we shall be primarily concerned with them because we are human. It is true also that the bonds are strongest between the members of any given type. The satisfaction of the organic needs of the individual must be conditioned by their social effects. In this way we find among humans a variety of type responsibilities. The attraction between individuals is partly at least the result of their interdependence.

If the good is what is needed, then there is more good involved when the bond is symmetrical, when what a man needs, for instance, also needs him. This is hardly the case when he wishes to eat lamb chops but it is the case when he needs a friend. There are socially-approved ways of accomplishing need-reduction, and what is approved and what not forms the content of the individual conscience. Thus the responsibility gets broken down still further to the members of a given society or culture.

The ordinary life of the individual, however, does not ever find him in direct contact with his entire society but only with some of the members of it. By sharing their morality with them, he meets them as though he and they represented the whole of society. And so he conducts himself always in consideration of all others, and this defines what in the society is regarded as good behavior. There are standard departures from this, in the direction of the individual's more narrow interests, in the direction of a wider membership in the human species, and, even wider still, in the direction of the cosmos.

In Book One I have sought to introduce the tasks of ethics as they appear from the orientation assumed in this work. In this effort methodological considerations are most prominent: how are the tasks to be approached, and from where? The answer is made in terms of level or grades of importunateness and importance. Finally, in a summary perspective I seek to bring the reader to the point where he is prepared to comprehend the main expositions.

Book Two is an extended presentation of the ethical integrative series, the four widening systems of involvement wherein the individual lives out his moral life. In Book Two, as the various Parts will indicate, we shall be dealing with the moral integrative levels, devoting a Part to each. We shall at each level have to deal with two very different (though of course related) considerations. We shall need to consider (i) the good and the bad which are at that level *sui generis* and (ii) the relation of the human individual toward that level, including both his privileges and his obligations.

For Book Three is reserved the final playing out of the drama of existence. We shall there seek to discover first of all what the actual moral practice is, then what such practice should be, and finally how to reach the ideal from the actual. In this Book, however, like the previous one, the investigation begins with the lowest level of organization, which for our purposes is the human individual, and ends with the highest, which is the cosmos. The ideal of morality is first considered, then the moral situation in which the individual can ordinarily expect to find himself, and finally the moral strategy which is necessary in order to reach ideal morality from the position of concrete morality. The last three Parts: ideal morality, concrete morality and moral strategy, it may be parenthetically mentioned, correspond to the three ontological domains of essence, existence and destiny.

BOOK TWO

THE ETHICAL INTEGRATIVE SERIES

PART II

THE ETHICS OF THE INDIVIDUAL

CHAPTER I

THE INDIVIDUAL GOOD

In the first section of this chapter I will introduce the good in connection with organic human needs, and in the second section I will argue that there is an autonomous level of the human individual, whereby his needs require no justification beyond his efforts at their reduction. In a third section I shall try to show that what is peculiarly human is the continuance of the drives to reduce the needs long after they have in fact been effectively reduced, the source of human achievements but also of bad behavior. Then in a fourth section I will try to show that the attempts to reduce the needs involve the individual together with his fellows and their tools in a society. In a fifth section I will argue that the content of the individual conscience is a product of the disapproval by society of the excesses of individual need-reduction.

(a) The Good as What is Needed

I begin with the definition of the good here as "what is needed." This definition can be said to hold throughout the universe and is true for all material orders and all species of physical entities, and thus for all existing things. In this chapter we shall be concerned with individual man and so we shall consider the good only in so far as it concerns him. The good for man, then, is what is needed by man. I shall postpone the discussion of the good in cosmic terms to a later Part. Here the only good considered will be human good. In so far as the term good does apply to man it is found in connection with his material needs. What does he need, or, in other words, what is his good? As we shall presently note, the basic set of material things which could satisfy the needs is the same for everyone; but there are also important differences. Although most of the values of human behavior fall within the Gaussian distribution, the range of human needs is enormous. One man seeks an orderly universe, but another collects rare postage stamps. Thus the simple definition which I have offered could be grossly misleading, and so a number of explanations are required.

In the first place, the good as defined is not to be equated with the need itself nor with the man who needs nor even with the relation between the man and what he needs. It is only the material thing needed in so far as it *is* needed. A certain trust is involved in need: the reliance upon a thing because of its intrinsic quality, which is to say its goodness. "X needs Y" means that Y as needed is good. We shall see shortly that the good considered from the side of a single material object is the quality of its external relations.

It should be stated at the outset also that the needs are unconscious as well as conscious. A man may or may not know what he needs. He may be in need of exercise without knowing what is wrong with him. He is often as ignorant of his needs as of anything else. We know as little about ourselves as about the world, and often the reason why we suffer remains a matter of ignorance. To know what is needed is of course to go in search of it; but how are we to search for what we do not know we need?

If the needs are unconscious as well as conscious, it is also true that they are involuntary as well as voluntary. A man may or may not want what he needs. We do a lot of things for our own good which at the time we do not want to do, such as taking medicine, paying taxes, or defecating. The will is not capable of making the distinction between what is and what is not needed. Often what we want is not what we should have; we will want what is bad for us against our better judgment.

The good is not necessarily a sensation of pleasure or a feeling of happiness. These often accompany what is needed, but when they do it is as a by-product, an indirect result of the reduction of the need for something else. Thus pleasure and happiness are often present when the needs are reduced, and they are goods in themselves, but in most cases at least they cannot be said to be what is needed.

I define a need as what something else requires in order to continue its existence. When what is needed is obtained, that is good; and so the good is a kind of completeness. When what is needed is not obtained, there is a kind of incompleteness, which is bad. An organic need is something an animal needs to continue its animal existence. What is needed is always something from the environment. The chief drive of the human individual is to dominate his environment in order to obtain what he needs from it. Thus his first and most exigent need is for domination and its drive is expressed through aggression.

The characteristic behavior of the human individual, then, is the drive to dominate the environment—all of it. For he needs it all in order to obtain the reduction of all of his needs. Such a generalized drive is properly called aggression, because it may be destructive as well as constructive, as we shall note later on in this study. It is what Schopenhauer meant by "the will" and Nietzsche by "the will to power," only where for these scholars the will was irrational it is not entirely so here except sometimes in its effects. It is fundamentally rational in being the attempt to reduce organic needs of one kind or another.

What is needed is the result of organ-deprivation. The individual acts as a whole but as the agent so to speak for the needs of his organs. For the human individual there are many needs, but they can be subdivided into a primary group characterized by importunateness and a secondary group characterized by importance. The subclass of human needs is marked by organ-specificity: primarily water for the kidney, food for the stomach, sex for the gonads, and secondarily information for the brain, activity for the musculature, and security for the skin. The reduction of such organ-specific needs benefits the entire organism. The primary needs insure immediate or short-range survival, the secondary needs ultimate or long-range survival. All of these are material goods, but they are not to be derogated by idealists. For as Moore said, "material qualities are a necessary constituent of the ideal" and "to exclude matter is to exclude the best that we know."[1] And yet the individual does not pursue The Good but only goods.

Marx and Freud were right in that hunger and sex are pressing immediate requirements; but in the long run a more permanent form of security takes precedence. Ultimate security is sought whenever the other needs have been satisfied or arrangements made for the continuing satisfaction. It is the feeling of beauty which promises security and it is the search for ultimate security which accounts for the great "world" religions. Freedom is of course necessary in order to pursue need-reduction.

The individual stands so to speak poised on the border between internal and external stimuli, between internal organs pressing for need-reduction through deprivation, and external stimuli promising the need-reduction. Ethics has always been thought of mainly in terms

[1] *Principia Ethica*, ch. VI.

of responses: what should a man do? But this is a question which cannot be fairly answered until he has answered a previous question: what is it that he wants done to him? And this last question can take many forms according as it is framed in terms of thought, feeling and action; for there is an ethics concerned with the brain (what should he think?), with the sense organs (what should he feel?), and with the musculature (what should he do?).

The needs stimulated by internal organs and by cues from external material objects promising need-reduction tie the individual to the external world through an intermediate set of material instruments, called here artifacts. It is difficult therefore to answer any of the above questions on an exclusively human basis. What he should think, feel and do cannot be decided without involving that considerable segment of the world with which he interacts and upon whose constitution he is so completely dependent. The interaction is conditioned by artifacts, and thus instruments form an important part of judgments.

Every need activates a drive, and it is the drive which we recognize as behavior. The change from a need to a drive in the process of activation involves the use of force. There is a definite element of aggression in all efforts at need-reduction. We may not always understand the source of aggression in organ-deprivation but we do recognize the aggression for what it is: an effort to alter some object in the environment—either a thing or a person—by means of the application of force.

Force, or power, as such is good because it enables things which need each other to come together and holds apart those which do not. From the point of view of the individual, then, the possession of power is good because it enables him to reach what he needs and in some cases also what needs him. Without power no need can be converted into a drive and hence there can be no need-reduction or goal-achievement. The individual's use of such power may have bad results, and this is what bothered Plato in the *Gorgias*;[1] but what may be either good or bad cannot be said to be bad in itself but only in some of its effects.

I lay down the two axioms: that
> existence is hazardous with respect to the values

and that
> existence is good in itself

and derive the important theorem that
> What can result in either good or bad, dependent upon its use, is in itself good.

[1] 466E–469B.

What results in good and is itself inherently good is therefore doubly good. But what results in bad but is not inherently bad is singly bad; what is bad is only the use to which the good has been put. Destroy power and you destroy the bad but also the possibility of good.

Drives have two dimensions: intensity and direction. The intensity is qualitative and is what in another context we call intrinsic good. The direction is quantitative and is what in another context we call extrinsic good. It is a mistake to oppose instrumental to intrinsic goods. The instrumental may also be intrinsic. This is seen at its clearest perhaps when intrinsic good is at its most intense. A great work of art is an instrument to the spectator, but only because it possesses an intrinsic quality.

We have noted that in the case of every need there is an activated drive, and a drive-reduction when that which is needed is obtained. In addition to the drive-reduction there is also a terminal goal-achievement. This can be constructive, destructive or neutral: constructive as when a picture is painted or a church erected; destructive as when a vegetable is eaten or a war fought; neutral as when there is identification with a far-away object.

If the good is what is needed, then in the case of every need described above there are corresponding goods. That portion of the immediate environment which is needed for the survival of man and which he makes over for his own uses constitutes a set of goods. And for such goods (in the sense of material objects needed by organs) there is in each case a qualifying good.

It is important to remember that the needs constitute a hierarchy and that corresponding to them there is a hierarchy of goods. The importunate needs are the most basic, but the important needs are the most productive. The former are the means *by* which, and the latter the ends *for* which, drives are activated.

In order to insure the continuance of need-reduction the individual has combined with his fellows in the establishment of social organizations; of institutions for particular needs, and of societies for the needs as a whole group. Thus there are families for sex and reproduction, city reservoir systems for water, agricultural projects for food, schools for information, galleries for art, etc. The unit of the immediate environment with which the individual has most of his dealings is a combination of other human individuals (social groups) and artifacts. Usually, in his encounter with single individuals, it is in the capacity of institutional functioning for one or both of them.

In the last analysis, institutions and societies, social groups and their charters, and all artifacts employed, are instruments in the hands of the individual, cooperating or competing with his fellows as seems advisable, in his efforts to reduce his needs. But the one important fact which has been overlooked in connection with such efforts is the one we have mentioned: the tendency of man to exceed himself. Thus human failing issues from an excess, not from a deficiency. It is caused by a superabundant appetite for the good.

In this way, triggered by individual needs, man is led first into becoming an integral part of a society and secondly into making of his society something of an end for himself. Thus it is that the good for individual man becomes the service of society. Of course this does not tell us what is good except in the broadest terms of social conformity, unless we know which society we are talking about and what are its values.

Drive reduction usually takes place by means of artifacts. There are not many activities taking place without either tools or signs (or both). Moral considerations are very much involved in the production of artifacts, and in their selection and operation. Is it good or bad that men should make engines of human destruction? In the very design and manufacture of nuclear weapons such grave moral considerations are apposite that the involvement is hardly one that can be checked out through technology alone. In the end perhaps all human activity —including thoughts and feelings as well as actions—are answerable to ethical theory. Now, what men do is not ordinarily done with their bare hands, and the more advanced the civilization the more this is true. The making and use of artifacts is very much a part of all human endeavor, and so what is to be made and used is primarily a moral question. Technology is a subdivision of ethics.

The large and continuous dependence of organisms upon interchange with their immediate environment is no less effective whether the need be for air, food, water, clothing, shelter, for the prolonged planning of a continual supply of these, or for more complex articles to serve more intricate purposes, such as knowledge, aggression or security. The fact remains that any direct intervention by man to obtain, and to insure the continuance of obtaining, what he needs from the environment will always be conducted by means of artifacts, the use, that is, of the appropriate tools.

Moore was right in supposing that intrinsic goodness exists in things (including of course material things) and that it is the same quality in all those things in which it exists. As Moore said in the summary of the first chapter of his *Principia Ethica*, ethics does not investigate human conduct but "that property of things denoted by the term 'good,' and the converse property denoted by the term 'bad.'"

Analytically, the good is the quality of external relations, and therefore the good at the level of the human individual is the quality of the external relations of those material things which are needed by the individual. From the point of view of another individual by whom a given individual may be needed, the individual's own good is that dominant inner quality which emerges from the integrity of his organization. The good as such is not good because others find it good but others find it good because it is good. Thus what is needed is needed because it is good. We have only to recognize by this that there is a universal of goodness and that it exists as the qualities of particulars. Artifacts are material objects altered through human agency in order to produce certain instruments for good. We tend to forget that the useful as well as the pleasurable is capable of having as its quality some particularization of the good.

But goods which have an intrinsic quality may also be useful—useful perhaps just because they have that quality. And so the good is what is needed in its several ways. But even so we have not yet described all that there is to a material thing. Anything may be and most things usually are needed by other things. Thus catnip, which has the qualities that it has regardless of its capacity for reducing hunger in cats, may serve more than itself and the cat by its existence. We do not know all of the needs in the round which may apply to catnip and thus not all of the good there is in it, but we do know some authentic parts of it, enough, that is, to disclose its intrinsic and extrinsic goodness.

Every good, then, can be subdivided into its intrinsic and extrinsic aspects. As we have noted, the former is Moore's good and the latter Mill's instrumental or utilitarian good. All goods are intrinsic in having the quality of a feeling and all goods are extrinsic or instrumental in being for something else, the quality as felt by the thing (or subject) of itself and that same quality as felt by something (or someone) external to it (the object). There is no inherent opposition between them, no "either/or." The good as what is needed presents both aspects. So far as the single individual is concerned it is the intrinsic aspect which counts, for he can feel it; but so far as society is involved it is the extrinsic aspect, for instrumentally it makes the functioning of society possible. Individuals become involved in the extrinsic good even though they are brought to it by the intrinsic good.

It may be objected that my definition of the good is tautological, that adding the notion of the good to the description of a need is like adding an explicit assertion of the truth of a proposition to a true proposition, when a true proposition implicitly asserts its own truth. But I reply that the need describes a state of affairs and that "the good" names the quality which emerges from it. Now all of the needs are not the same, and what is needed is not always the same for all men, not even for all those who are members of the same society; but the quality of the good is the same and that is why it is given a generic name and accorded a separate treatment.

The good is needed because it is good, not good because it is needed. The individual and his needs is a subject responding both to his own lack and to an object. It therefore is depicted from the subject but is not for that reason merely subjective. Something is lacking to a whole individual, some part which an external object can supply. That the object can supply the missing part is good for the whole of what it is a part.

The need itself is an empirical fact, and the good is an empirical quality which accompanies the need-reduction. From the point of view of a subject, that object which it needs is good for it. Physiological needs exemplify the principle. Thus information is "good for" the brain, fresh air for the lungs, water and food for the stomach, sexual intercourse for the gonads and ovaries. What is good is what reduces a need. So the quality of good in each instance exists apart from the subject and is felt by the subject. The feelings, unlike the perceptions, are passive rather than active, and report elements which exist in the external world. What is needed by the human organism exists as a material thing in the external world.

The good for the individual is always good because it is considered from the point of view of the need. Taken in a wider context it may be bad. It is true in the case of the human individual also that normative considerations always involve wider contexts. If a man is a drug addict and he needs a morphine injection, the fact remains that the morphine is good because it is needed. He may, for that matter, have good reasons for wishing to deteriorate in this fashion even though from a wider context others may suffer. Thus what is needed in this case ought to be done for him but ought not to be done if his family and my community are taken into consideration.

The limitations of purely individual good might have been foreseen by noting that as defined the good is not symmetrical. Individual good is good for and only for the individual. Whether it is a good which extends to others or not depends upon the good considered. Thus the morphine injection needed by the individual in the above instance is bad for his community, but if what he needed had been wisdom, say, instead of morphine, and he had needed it in a purely individual way, the incidental effects on his family and community might also have been good. Some individual goods therefore are transitive; they are extended beyond the individual to whom they are good to others; but some are not and are not extended in this way.

The minimal good is asymmetrical. X is good for Y. Most goods are minimal goods. Any complete good would of course have to be symmetrical, X is good for Y and Y is good for X. Symmetry and asymmetry as applied to goods depend upon the individual case. Most men need friendship as well as food; but one need is symmetrical, and the other not. If John's friendship is good for Tom, it may be also that Tom's friendship is good for John. But while catnip is good for the cat it is certainly not true that the cat who destroys it is good for catnip, unless the destruction of one thing for the good of another be considered in itself a good. If sheep could talk when a farmer walks down the road I can imagine one of them saying, "Don't look now, but here comes one of those fierce, sheep-eating men." For this is how men judge tigers in India though not sheep in Europe.

(b) The Level of the Individual

We shall have to consider at every one of the ethical integrative levels what the good is and what the privileges and obligations of the human individual are at that level. We have already said what the good is at the level of the human individual, but what is the human individual himself? We shall have to consider this first and next what his privileges and obligations are at that level.

The individual although usually considered as a highly integrated whole is actually a loose organization, a compromise of voices and of persons, in which the critical self settles with the impulsive self for what it must accept of what is available; that is to say, of what is offered and of what the individual of his own nature is capable of appropriating. Thus it is not entirely a matter of what he does regarded in itself but the extent to which he can be considered as operating within the framework of his own peculiar ethics. He cannot be identified with that ethics, for there are distinctions and differences: he is an organism and a member of the human species, it is a system of behavior to which he endeavors more or less to conform. What we have to deal with therefore is the posture of individual man confronted by himself; the self as a focus aware both of an external environment and of an internal environment in relation to the external environment, and behaving accordingly; the spectacle of man as a kind of arrangement arrived at *in situ*.

The individual incurs a moral obligation to himself to maintain himself, his own integrity, his own dignity. This is the individual level of ethics faced inward and *sui generis*. There are moreover inward sublevels: the level of the personality, with its obligation of the individual to himself as a whole; and the level of the organs, with its obligation of the individual to his parts. The individual incurs a moral obligation to himself to deal correctly with his environment. This is the individual level faced outward. There are many outward levels; beginning with the widest environment, there is the level of the cosmos, next the level of the species, and finally that of the society. But the individual is faced outward as well as inward, and when faced outward is at once confronted with both friendly and hostile elements in his immediate environment. As a matter of his own sheer survival, he must move toward the friendly elements and seek to encourage them, and he must move away from the hostile elements and seek to discourage them. He must encourage family, friends, and allies, and discourage enemies. He must encourage crops and farm animals, and discourage harmful body parasites, infectious viruses, and disease bacteria. In short, he must pick his way carefully, and neither accept nor reject his environment *in toto*. It contains the same ambivalence as does his own human nature.

The human individual is a whole to his parts. His obligations at this level, therefore, are those which he owes to his parts and through them to himself. Among his parts, for instance, are his organs, and for organs, as we have already noted, there are organ-specific needs and drives. Now, since the human individual can do only one thing at a time he can engage in the drive to reduce only one need at a time. Other needs must then be suppressed, even if only temporarily. Thus there is competition among the needs for opportunities to seek need-reduction by engaging in the requisite drives. There is cooperation as well as competition among the needs and among the drives. Increasing knowledge will often have incidental practical benefits. It is the task of the individual to determine a rank order for his needs and a procedural order for the consequent drives. Does he seek food first or a mate? Does he subordinate his hunger for knowledge to his desperate ambition to survive for as long as possible? Harmony among the needs and hence among the drives is an obligation which the individual owes to himself. He can hardly hope to lead a good life except under conditions of inner harmony.

The first order of business, then, for the individual at his own level is to seek harmony among his own parts. This is his chief obligation. It results in opportunities to exercise privileges. By means of self-knowledge there can be brought into play a large and powerful measure of self-control. And when the individual controls himself he is in a position to act integrally and with greater force to exercise self-determination. He can now exercise his effect as a whole, and pursue the good for himself and for larger organizations beyond himself which may also be of benefit to him. The individual as a whole achieves self-determination through a balanced control over his parts. The subordination of the interior self leads to the proper kind of interaction between the individual and elements in his environment on which he is able to exert his effect. In short, "learn to exercise self-control in order to do your best in the world" may mean simply "know what you need and should have and then see that you get it." Only he who is internally satisfied can be externally effective.

The hedonistic morality is the morality of the individual *sui generis*. To be a hedonist is to lead a life devoted to pleasure, and there is pleasure to be had from all of the organs. Thus the use of as many of them as possible would be the hedonist program. For the hedonist therefore the good life is the full life, the life whereby he comes into contact with as much of reality as possible.

It follows that it would be immoral for the hedonist not to use to the fullest any of the organs or faculties of which he was born possessed. This would apply to the gonads as well as to the brain, to the musculature as well as to the senses. Thus he who advises sensual indulgence alone is as wrong for the hedonist as he who recommends abstract speculation alone. The greatest variety of pleasures must go to make up the life of the true hedonist.

But the life of the hedonist is not easy. It requires training and special knowledge. For instance, it is important for him to have a weak character in order to be sure that he is equipped to yield to temptations. Beyond that it is necessary for him to know where the best temptations are to be found, for they do not exist on every street corner. Pleasures, he can argue, may be momentary, but so is everything else. Nothing lasts forever, not even the knowledge of eternal truths, only perhaps the truths themselves. But of what use are they to a mind which is preparing to perish? Before his organism wears out the hedonist resolves to enjoy it. It will wear out whether he enjoys it or not, so why then should he not enjoy it? An old prostitute is no worse for wear than an old virgin, but has perhaps a secret smile and greater knowledge of the world.

There are still other conditions imposed upon hedonism. If all of the organs can contribute to a life devoted to pleasure, then the difficulty arises that not all of them can function pleasurably at one and the same time. There must be an ordering of gratifications so that each drive-reduction receives its turn of attention. To be able to do everything pleasurable it is necessary first to arrange an order of precedence for the drives so that no one of them is able to interfere with any other. But this, as we shall see, requires a generalized morality, and so has taken us as far as hedonism can go.

This may sound primitive and anti-social but it is not; it is merely asocial. Individual morality *qua* individual has nothing to do with the morality of the society, only with that individual considered as a whole for himself. In short, individual morality is entirely individual and ends at the boundaries of that individual. In so far as it concerns his behavior that behavior is relevant in this context only in its effects upon himself: *his* needs, *his* goals.

Although it is far more important perhaps that the human individual is part of a larger whole—his society, for example, or humanity —he is at the same time certainly a whole to his parts, and it is within the framework of this latter structure that his integrity as an individual lies. Every level of organization has its own relative autonomy, its own integrity, its own values; and this is as true of the level of the human individual as of any other level of organization within the ethical integrative series. Here, it cannot be emphasized too much, the behavior of the individual is being considered only in its effects upon himself. In later sections we shall consider wider effects. But there is a private domain to be considered here for private reasons. It is helpful to recall at this point in the argument the intrinsic nature of goodness. The good is good, if it is good, because it is good. There are goods peculiar to every level. At the level of the individual which we are considering here the good is good if it benefits the individual, if it enables him to be a good individual or to remain one. And a "good individual" here means strictly one who is good for himself.

(c) Excessive Behavior

A crucial point about the needs so far as morality is concerned is that in many cases a drive is not stopped when the need is reduced. The accumulation of goods is sought beyond their possible use. Excessive behavior has its source in the fact that any drive can be generalized to dominate the environment in the interest of ultimate security. There are no territorial limits, as with other animals, to man's acquisitive ambitions. He would like to dominate and control the cosmos. Each individual man would if he could manage it incorporate the universe within himself and live forever. He cannot do so of course but his efforts to try to account for much of both his accomplishment and his failure. Men have accumulated vast fortunes they could not dream of spending, and in the east as recently as a century ago harems of a thousand women were not unknown.

Man is born neither altogether good nor altogether bad. He is born with needs but also with the urge to exceed the needs in his drives. This excess is what the ancient Greeks called hubris, outrageous behavior.[1] The needs are good and what they need is good, but the urge to exceed may be bad and its effects may be bad. The needs of the individual are in harmony with all other individuals, for after all the needs of all individuals are much the same. It is the individual's desire to exceed himself which causes him to clash with his fellow men. Such a desire leads to the demand for an excessive proportion of the goods which the community can provide, and thus tends to deprive other individuals of their shares. There is not room for all when each wants more than what he needs.

The two sources of immorality are, first, anti-social need-reduction, and, secondly, excessive behavior. The organic needs are the source of the morally good but when needs are reduced in anti-social ways they become the source of the morally bad. The urge of man to continue his drives beyond the point of need-reduction is another source of the morally bad. No book on ethics can be said to be complete until the bad has been thoroughly discussed, and so the bad should receive as much attention as the good. The reason for this is that the good rarely occurs in its pure form but usually mixed with the bad. What we

---

[1] Gilbert Murray, *The Rise of the Greek Epic* (Oxford 1934, University Press), Appendix D.

ordinarily call "good" contains more good than bad, and what we call "bad" contains more bad than good. We shall return to this comparison later. Here it is necessary to point out that bad behavior is the result of the continuance of the drives after the organs are no longer deprived. In most animals need-reduction leads to a temporary equilibrium in which there is inactivity; but in man the excessive behavior goes beyond and because of the foresight that the need will recur continues, or else simply shifts one drive over into the territory of another so that the aggression continues. Thus the alcoholic, the sex-obsessed, the super-rich, the over-scrupulous religious observer.

Excessive behavior, which is a source of immoral behavior, is aided and abetted by the inherently general nature of artifacts, the tools and signs which result when man alters material things for his uses. Artifacts are general in two ways: tools tend to proliferate, language is incurably universal. Individual needs are reduced by means of artifacts and very seldom without them, but the general nature of artifacts encourages the mechanism of need-reduction to be continued after the needs have been reduced and so reinforces excessive behavior. Thus after food has been found and eaten, more food is sought and stored, and man glories in the sexual conquest of women long after he has been satisfied sexually. The same provision for the future which has enabled him to be free of the demands of his primary needs and so liberated to pursue the reduction of the secondary, has resulted in civilization but has also produced the evils of excessive behavior.

Man's urge to exceed himself is responsible for much of what is most wonderful and terrible in human life. His monumental efforts to become one with the source of his feelings of sublimity, on the positive side, and to satisfy his frightful appetite for total destruction, on the negative side, both stem from it. He has total responses to cosmic tropisms which often are superb in their effects but equally often are ghastly and horrible. The sun led Plotinus to mystical flights of religious ecstasy in solitude. It led the Aztecs to the ritual performance of the bloodiest of human sacrifices.

The urge to exceed himself may in the individual take many forms. The usual form is an over-aggressiveness. He endeavors to impose himself and his will upon everything within his reach. At the other end of the social spectrum, however, it may lead him to sacrifice himself for the good of society. The aggressiveness of the individual is the commonest form, and we see it at wotk both constructively and destructively; constructively in his productivity, and destructively in his antagonisms.

(d) The Social Nature of the Individual

As soon as it is admitted that individual man has a set of organic needs which he endeavors to reduce by drives involving material objects, it must be admitted too that he is a social organism. For the drives involve him with his fellows in many ways. They involve him as a matter of cooperation and they involve him equally as a matter of competition. He cooperates with them in need-reduction, since they have the same needs and he and they together can render the drives more efficient. Also, other individuals themselves may be the objects of his needs; for instance he needs men for friendship and women for sexual love. In this and the next sections, then, I propose to show that the existence of needs is responsible for the social nature of the individual and for the content of his conscience. Thus he cooperates with others individually and through institutions. The individual competes with his fellows individually and in institutions. Most human aggression is directed by the individual against other individuals and institutions. He needs to guard the sources of his need-reductions against others, and often to appropriate theirs when he has none of his own or what he regards as not enough of his own.

It is well to recognize that there is no such thing as an individual in total isolation from his fellows. When undertaking a consideration of individual ethics, remember the weight which society brings to bear upon the individual. Habits of action, patterns of belief—customs and ideologies—reside within the individual. But although the individual holds them they rely very much upon an external reality, upon conditions in the world which houses society as well as upon the material components of that society. They can claim an existence outside the human mind—and a justification for their reality inside it—just because they represent paths which are amenable to the actions and conditions corresponding to beliefs. In short, what is true within the individual depends for support upon factors outside him—those in society and in the world which makes that society possible.

Morality in society consists in a possible set of intersecting actions of the individual as the result of his belief in what is out there. Robinson Crusoe took his language and a considerable number of material tools with him, and whatever he did on the island was of course similar to what he had done or at least known about before the shipwreck. The individual is permeated by society, its demands and facilitations; he is thoroughly saturated with social beliefs consisting in the principles and values established by his society.

Human behavior is indissoluble. Every human act has an effect both on the actor and on his society. Thus what we call "social ethics" and what we call "individual ethics" are merely particular aspects of the same total complex. For just as "social ethics" was the behavior of finite groups of individuals so far as such behavior was either similar or interactive, so "individual ethics" will be the behavior of the individual as seen in its effects both upon the individual himself and upon his society. Social ethics is the ethics of the individual as seen from society; individual ethics is the ethics of society as seen from the individual.

My definition of the good man, then, is neither individual nor social exclusively. But in my definition, as we shall shortly see in greater detail, humanity interposes itself between the individual and his encounters with other individuals, artifacts, or combinations of the two; and so in a sense all human ethics is social. The individual is always a person with a conscience and a will who can act with good or bad effects, in a right or wrong manner, and who as a consequence benefits from the good and suffers from the bad and the wrong. But the content of the conscience (as we shall see later in this chapter) is social, a set of beliefs engendered by society; and so any action taken within society is guided by society through the social elements which exist within the individual. Even when the individual behaves in a thoroughly arbitrary and purely individual manner, as he does when he is having a thought or a feeling or performing an act, it has an effect upon him. Thus he must consider himself as though he were another person, apt to be judged by its members in accordance with its standards, and, more often than not, also by him to the extent to which he is in agreement with those standards.

So far as the attitudes and behavior of individual man are concerned, however, he has to deal first of all with himself and only then with society. Let us talk about the terms and conditions of those dealings briefly here, for we shall be occupied with them throughout the length of this book in one way or another.

The individual has first of all to deal with himself, and such dealings are either direct or indirect. His direct dealings with himself are basic but minimal; they consist chiefly in receiving sensations, for what else can he manage without the mediation of language? He can perhaps scratch himself unaided, but only in front; in the back he requires the assistance of a back-scratcher. But he cannot think or act in exclusively individual terms and his feelings are limited to the lowest and simplest. All higher perceptions and emotions are mediated by social contacts.

Most self-dealings, then, are indirect. They do depend upon mediation, and the mediating instruments are either other human individuals and social groups or artifacts of one of the two kinds: languages or tools. We shall note the enormous role played by social groups in the individual's self-dealings when in the next section we come to discuss his conscience, and we will see the equally large role played by artifacts in the section after that when we come to discuss his needs. Here it is necessary to add only that he thinks by means of language, and everything else is accomplished by tools. In order to show that the individual is not a valid isolate we need only to point out that his awareness of himself is already a dualism, a dialogue. His thoughts are a form of self-communication, conducted in the terms of an ordinary language.

The greater part of the individual's dealings are with other human individuals, and such dealings are either direct or indirect, and if the latter then by means of institutions. We should have a few words to introduce each of these.

The dealings of the individual directly with other individuals is rare. It must be said to exist, I suppose, so long as there is such a thing as wordless love-making. But most dealings between individuals are indirect, that is to say, they are mediated by institutions. The institution is an established collection of social groups and artifacts together with the directions for the use of the latter by the former. We shall see that morality lies in these connections. Conventional ethics has been analyzed either as the ethics of the individual or as the ethics of society. Morality as a consequence has been thought of either in individual or in social terms but always as exclusively human. Now the conception of ethics as exclusively human cannot be defended if we remember that what has made men human is their use of artifacts. The morality of man is not confined to himself or his own kind but extends to that part of his environment which he has incorporated in his culture. Human culture includes artifacts as much as it does men. It involves them along with himself in moral considerations. I defined artifact as a material thing which has been altered through human agency in order to make it useful for human ends, and I find two kinds: tools and signs. Tools are material things employed to move other material things; they may be either moved by others or by self-movement. Signs are material things employed to refer to other material things. There are many kinds of tools. An implement or instrument is a tool. A spade is a tool but so is a violin, a street or a building. Similarly with signs, there are many kinds. Peirce has detected some sixty-four. A pointing hand is a sign, but so is a word or a combination of words: a language. Words as conventional marks on paper or as modulated sounds in the air are the most familiar kinds of conveyance of language. Individual self-dealings, we have noted, are in terms of language. Social dealings are in terms of languages or in terms of material tools. Material tools and signs can be good or bad instruments; also they can be used well or badly. They enter therefore into the domain of human morality. Thus what we shall have to regard as human henceforth in this book is not only the human animal himself but as much of his material environment as he has succeeded in organizing. Both men and their materials together constitute the body of society.

Ethics has been always thought of partly in terms of responses: what should man do. But this is a question which cannot be answered until he has answered previously the question of what it is that he wants done to him. For there is also an ethics concerned with the choice of stimuli: what should he wish to feel? And secondarily there is an ethics concerned with the association fibers: what should he be obliged to think? But since man is intimately connected with the material world through an intermediate set of material objects, the artifacts, it is difficult to answer any of the above questions on an exclusively human basis. What he should feel, do and think cannot be decided without the involvement in such judgments of that considerable segment of the world with which he interacts, and upon whose constitution he is so completely dependent. The interactions are conditioned by artifacts, and thus tools form an important part of the judgments.

Moral considerations are very much involved in the production of tools and in their selection and operation. What men do is not ordinarily done with their bare hands, and the more advanced the civilization the more this is true. The making and use of artifacts is very much a part of all human endeavor, and so what is to be made and used is primarily a moral question. Is it good or bad that men should make engines of human destruction? In the very design and manufacture of nuclear weapons there are such grave moral considerations that the involvement can hardly be checked out through technology alone. Technology is a subdivision of ethics. In the end perhaps all human activity—including thoughts and feelings as well as actions— are answerable to ethical theory.

The relation of man to the material tools and signs he has fashioned has not been considered in any way ethical. The efforts of man to alter his environment in ways favorable to the reduction of his needs is through and through moral (or immoral) because executed in terms of the concrete ideal of the society. The artifacts which result from such efforts could hardly be less moral (or immoral) for they are the instruments employed in striving toward the ends prescribed by the morality. How man makes and uses his artifacts is very much a moral question, for his social relations are almost always artifactually mediated. Then, too, there is a sense in which both he and his society are among his artifacts, for they, too, have been altered through human agency. This means that we cannot leave out of our consideration the moral role played by artifacts.

The account of the behavior of the human individual comes to an end, and that of social behavior begins, when the feedback from material artifacts makes them culturally influential. Strictly speaking, all behavior is individual, and what we call social behavior is simply the behavior of individuals organized into groups to accomplish a common end. What justifies the adjective, social, is the shift in location from one of intersubjectivity to the artifacts of the collective, the material objects of the institution becoming the social location. As an individual he accomplishes his ends only by cooperating with the group, and the good in this instance is contained in his responsiveness to the feeling of belonging to the group. The knowledge that he has sufficient intelligence and freedom to cooperate or not with other members of the group in its efforts makes him morally responsible and has the effect of a positive feedback on the character of his actions.

Thus just as we found that the individual was permeated with social elements, so we find too that society is permeated by individual elements, which are his rights and his duties. Society is after all composed of individuals and their artifacts. It is not possible to undertake a consideration of human ethics without retaining the weight which the individual bears within his society. Societies exist and change through the efforts of individuals. Man is in a sense self-made. His tools and languages are conventional and so are his established moralities. But in the end he has to be counted in all his singularity and just as himself. The individual is an autonomous unit and has to be reckoned with as such.

(e) The Conscience

Before discussing the conscience it might be well to say a few clarifying words about consciousness. Consciousness is awareness of objects. The objects are divided into two classes according as they occupy an internal or an external environment. The external environment is the world minus the subject. The internal environment is the reservoir of beliefs. Here we have touched the core of morality as it exists within the individual.

Morality is essentially social, but it exists within the individual also. It is how belonging to society affects individual man. When this affection is external we call it social ethics, when it is internal we call it the moral conscience. But it is the same in both cases.

The conscience has a structure and a content. The structure consists in the way beliefs are arranged which makes them available for conduct. The content is the beliefs themselves. The structure exists as part of the psychological nature of man and is more or less a constant. As such it is to be found in all human individuals with the exception of certain pathological cases, as for example the psychopathic personalities, in whom it is missing. The content varies, as we should expect it to, from society to society.

However, there is a constant to the content also and it consists in the origins of the content. The conscience is derived from social disapproval of the ways in which the needs have been reduced. It will be recalled that the individual always has the urge to exceed himself, to continue on with the conduct appropriate to need-reduction after the needs have been reduced. Excessive behavior leads more often than not to bad behavior, and bad behavior is anti-social behavior. Thus excessive behavior produces the social disapproval and hence inevitably the content of the conscience.

We have noted that the conscience derives negatively from social disapproval, but there are secondary aspects which are positive, and these are called "rights" and "duties."

"Duty" consists in the obligation to seek need-reductions in socially approved ways. A "sense of duty" is the individual's own recognition of this obligation in himself. The negative aspect of the conscience is responsible for the existence of the conscience and therefore is important, but there is a positive aspect of the conscience which in some ways is more important. For the conscience looks backward negatively, and looks forward positively. Duty affects behavior and so is concerned with the future. When the individual contemplates performing certain actions it is the conscience which he consults.

A "right" is the privilege of the individual to exercise a certain freedom. Thus rights involve dimensions of activity which are available to the individual. The enabling processes are provided for him by society, and so the discussion of rights in this sense must be postponed to the next Part of this book. Here we need to note that rights occur to the individual as the knowledge of what is available to him. He can exercise only such lattitudes of action as are familiar. And the lines of action permitted by the conscience are those which in his society are moral.

The content of the conscience is usually social but it may be individual also. For the individual may approve of his own behavior or he may disapprove and his disapproval could mean that he regards his behavior as anti-social or even anti-personal. He may behave toward himself in a way he condemns. If he fails to do something for himself with which society is not particularly concerned he may condemn himself for the lack. For instance, he may fail to keep down his weight when he thinks that he should.

In general, however, we see that conscience comes from the social disapproval of the way in which the needs are reduced. It is individual in origin, being based on the needs, but social in outcome, being the result of the effort of society to protect itself against the undue encroachments of the individuals who would scuttle it. Thus society is not merely a collection of individuals but of those individuals operating under rules of procedure: rules permitting good procedure and rules prohibiting bad procedure, including the good or bad use of the artifacts which have been designed for the explicit purpose of facilitating need-reductions.

So much for the conscience as a whole. We now proceed to analyze it, for the difference among its parts is crucial to our effort to understand morality.

What we call the conscience is made up of two ordinarily indistinguisahble components: the public retention schema and the private retention schema.

The public retention schema is occasioned by events in the external environment, and consists in all those beliefs which the individual holds in common with the other members of his society. Its contents arise from the exigencies of social life together with its institutions and artifacts, within the limits set by the available natural environment. The public retention schema is a sort of "community-consciousness" which becomes "modified by further experience" only with secular slowness.[1] Its solidity is rendered so by the repetition which is possible only through successive generations of the members of a given

[1] *Collected Papers of Charles Sanders Peirce* (Cambridge 1931, Harvard University Press), 1. 56.

society "for it has to become part of themselves and that takes time."[1]
It consists in the laws and customs of society considered as imposing
duties upon the individual. It is that mechanism within the individual whereby his participation in society is rendered obligatory and
altruism is secured on a firm basis. Because the individual contains
social elements from which he is inseparable he must be regarded in
the round as an incomplete system: there are elements within him not
deducible from his nature. To work out the ethics of the individual,
therefore, we shall need to examine the social level to which the social
elements of the individual inherently belong. The public retention
schema and the social morality are co-variants, with the schema dependent upon the morality.

The private retention schema is occasioned by events in the internal environment, and consists in all those beliefs which the individual holds as the result of his private experience with his own needs and
drives. Individual needs conflict with respect to their importunateness.
An ordering has to be arranged consisting in a sequence of activation:
only one drive at a time. This is usually done in terms of the private
retention schema. There are of course other elements: strains peculiar
to the individual, stresses peculiar to his particular situation. Along
with the private retention schema go all the subjective and selfish motives and a happy or unhappy temperament. But what the individual
does to or for society will influence what society does to or for him.
Thus he can have subjective and selfish motives for his moral concern
for society, but concerned with society he still is and his characteristic
happiness or unhappiness will depend upon what kind of adjustment
he is able to make between his private and public retention schemata.

Every individual thus has a moral code which he professes, usually
the established moral code of his society, and a code which he practices.
The first is imposed upon him by the other members of his society,
the second is imposed upon him by his own beliefs. To some extent
these two codes overlap, but rarely altogether and as rarely not at all.
What is effected in most cases is the best compromise that can be arrived
at under the circumstances. Each man lives as much as he can "according to his lights" within the framework of what is allowed by what
his society has come to recognize as good and therefore also right.

It would be plausible to suppose that a sort of structure of beliefs
consisting in the inter-relations of the two schemata could be worked
out to furnish an instrument of prediction as to the individual's moral

[1] Aristotle, *Nich. Eth.*, 1147a23.

behavior. We should need to know first of all, perhaps, what it is in the individual which makes him feel that he ought to conform as much as possible to the demands of the public retention schema. It would be necessary to know also of course the values of the variables in each instance, and this would vary from society to society and from individual to individual within a given society. It would also mean accounting within the calculation for continual changes in the elements of each schema as the individual reacts with his immediate environment, of which his society constitutes a large part but by no means the whole.

For the individual member of a given society the morality of that society is his reference system and its comparative invariants are to him of paramount importance. His conscience reflects it and he operates in terms of it. His behavior is in fact dictated by the following components which together determine his dispositional states: (a) the established morality of his society, (b) that segment of it which constitutes the laws of his society, (c) his conscience, and (d) his individual needs. We can see clearly the mixture of distinctions between individually-dictated and socially-dictated behavior. As Szent-Gyorgyi observes, individuals try to preserve themselves and grow rich, but at the same time they would die for their country and allow themselves to be taxed in a confiscatory manner.[1] In the former they have regard for themselves as separate wholes and in the latter only as parts of a larger whole. The former is individual and the latter social. The former arises from the need for individual self-aggrandizement and the latter from the need for social belonging. Don Marquis observed somewhere, "Whenever a man says, 'It isn't the money, it's the principle of the thing,' it's the money." And this is often true; but it is equally true upon other occasions that when a man says, "I am not operating from principles but only for money," it's the principles.

We have already seen that the individual's dealings with himself are mediated by society. What we intuitively know to be "right" is what the public retention schema has borrowed from the social morality. Thus beliefs which are the substance of the schemata are the most intimate of all individual elements and yet they are largely social in origin. They are not entirely social of course. A man's conscience is not altogether determined by the established propositions maintained as the truth by the community. In Thoreau's splendid image, he also hears a different drummer. "Morals," as Hume said, "produce or

---

[1] Gordon Wolstenholme (ed.), *Man and His Future* (London 1963, J. & A. Churchill), p. 376.

prevent actions,"[1] but whose morals? The individual rides on a two-fold philosophy: his own and his society's. They are seldom if ever identical. To the extent to which they are compatible he is free of conflict, but they seldom are, and so there may be a conflict and his choice in such a case depends upon what sort of man he is. But more of this later.

Here it is important to remember that most beliefs have a moral aspect; they are normative. They eventually lead through the conscience to prescribing what ought and what ought not to be done. The conscience is also permissive and regulative. Thus by means of the conscience beliefs lead to actions. Behavior is intimately linked to the beliefs through the conscience. The individual has reason to believe that what he pursues promises pleasure and that what he avoids threatens pain, and both promise and threat are beliefs arising from either custom or conviction.

It is aside from our present purpose as constituting too extended a speculation and a hazardous one, but certain structures of belief might be found indigenous to the human individual; what Santayana called "animal faith" may exist of necessity. Perhaps belief could be constructed on a kind of Kantian interpretation of the contemporary ethologists' conception of instinct, the array of folk beliefs outlined in Frazer's *Golden Bough* for example.

Waddington in *The Ethical Animal* calls man an authority-acceptor; he is also, though more rarely, an authority dispenser. All men have a faculty for good and bad, but unfocused. The criterion for focusing, that is to say the system of ethics or code of morals—the operative ideal—varies from society to society. Only the sense of good and bad is generally human. Conscience is the moral feeling, the "still small voice of conscience" which (it has been said) tells us that someone may be watching. Morality is the binding force between individuals which through the conscience holds society together by constituting a kind of social cement. This would in a sense make individual and social ethics one. Self-respect is a disguised form of social respect.

The conscience contains the social content of the individual so far as morality is concerned. But it is still possible to separate out the individual and set him somewhat apart, even from the social content which permeates him. There is a dimension of inwardness, a psychological distance between a man and his conscience. Some individuals live quite close to their conscience and in continual communication with

---

[1] *Treatise*, III, I, I.

it; others live with it somewhat apart. The Puritan in early New England maintained a state of constant reference to his conscience. Today the conscience seems much more remote. There are other subjective elements which usually are much more pressing than the conscience. These are the organic needs. And it is the organic needs which are much more intimately engaged with the good.

CHAPTER II

APPROACHES TO THE GOOD

In this chapter the discussion of the needs is continued but with the emphasis now on their moral aspects. First I will discuss the needs as motives, and then in the next two sections the mechanisms involved in type responsibility and moral confrontation. Then I will turn to the egoistic perspective, which is the basis of confrontation and its consequent moral equipment, and then I will end with the dispositions toward the good, in which all of this results.

(a) The Needs as Motives

Organic needs supply the motives for action. What moves the individual is the aim at need-reduction. What is needed is always the good, and the over-riding motive is therefore always the pursuit of the good. The individual is pursuing a good whether what is needed is a drink of water or a mate, an item of knowledge or a chance to exercise his muscles. Thus the good for the individual is usually something external.

Thus reason itself is never a motive. A man does not do things merely for good reasons, he takes action because it will reduce a need, and he goes about it in a reasonable or an unreasonable way. Reason provides the behavior by connecting the need with the goal-object of the good by means of belief. He finds his relevance in the schemata for the action toward an object which he believes will reduce a need. And it may, for whether or not there is such an object in some cases does not matter so long as he believes there is and is not sure whether or not he has reached his object. This may be the case, for instance, with religious invocation. But more of this shortly.

As I have drawn the picture thus far it seems a simple one. And it sometimes is, but usually the structure involved is anything but simple. For example, economics is not ethics, yet it would be foolish to expect a man with an empty belly to lead a moral life. The integrative levels are ranged upward as necessary but not sufficient causes: each makes the level above it possible but without compulsion. But let us consider a somewhat more complicated case. For most individuals friendship is a need; most individuals, we would say, "need friends." But what does this mean? How can we find it among the needs we have enumerated?

For the primary needs, we have already noted, cooperation is often if not always essential. In order to obtain food, water and sex, shelter and clothing, the individual usually requires the help of some of his fellows. But this is equally true of the secondary needs; in order to obtain knowledge, activity and security, he also needs social cooperation. The survival of the individual depends upon the community, the survival of the community depends upon a workable morality, hence individual survival is bound up with a workable social morality.

Now social cooperation in connection with organized religion usually furnishes security. But the security obtained from social cooperation may issue from other needs. For individuals whose living comes from serving a particular institution may find in the company of others in the same institution a companionship which furthers their need for social cooperation by reinforcing security. Thus through friendship the highest of the needs may be furthered by an association which has its point of origin as the lowest. It gives the individual some sense of security to establish an intimate communication with another individual who is not only in the same predicament but who senses that he shares it. The feeling of a common danger or a common dilemma, and finally the feeling of sharing a common experience however mixed, provides an informal institution of its own which we call friendship.

The factor of social cooperation which must usually be counted in when the individual is engaged in reducing his needs is thus essential. Here we have the source of social approval, which is also a private need. Belonging to the group is comforting, but the feeling is not always identified with the reason. For the feeling of belonging is an intrinsic good feeling and a property of the group, while the extrinsic good use is the group participation in the need-reduction of each and all of its individual members.

If the moral structure of the social group—the morality of the particular society—contains more bad than good from the point of view of the next integrative level of humanity, which it may and sometimes does, as was the case with Nazi Germany for instance, then social cooperation produces more bad than good for the individual. That social cooperation can be productive of the morally bad is a strange notion and one we shall not become accustomed to considering until we are more familiar with the workings of the moral integrative levels.

I have spoken at length about social cooperation because it contains the key to individual need-reduction. But competition is equally necessary and therefore equally prevalent. It functions in two ways: it serves to reduce the individual need for aggression: there must be something which resists for the individual to push against, and it serves to guard the resources of need-reduction against the incursion of other groups. Thus the social role of the individual is ambivalent; in some social contexts he cooperates, in others he competes. And as we have seen competition too furnishes need-reductions: personal contests but also economic struggles, and military adventures. That competition can be the occasion for good as well as for bad is as strange a notion as that cooperation can be a source for bad as well as for good. Yet both statements are true.

Thus whatever the need the good is always the motive for action, and reason always is the mechanism which insures that the need will be reduced in the way which has been designed for its reduction. But equally it may be said that the individual is always involved with some other individuals in his pursuit of the good. And since the individuals he needs need other individuals, the chain of individuals is endless and does not stop short before it reaches the whole of humanity. That man needs his fellows is not exactly news; only here I am trying to show the mechanism. It is not merely a sentimental affair, it is a need which goes as deep as the organism and spreads outward to include all of humanity.

To know the good is to follow it, Plato said. With the proper definition of the good this becomes a tautology: the good is what is followed; what is followed is the good. But there is an order involved which is crucial to the nature of the relation. For what is followed is followed because it is good, and it is not good merely because it is followed. If the individual follows what is bad it is not because he believes it to be bad but because he believes it to be good. The morally bad consists in the choice of a lesser over a greater good. Thus the bad is never a motive any more than the good is. The needs furnish the motives and the objects promising need-reduction always appear as goods.

(b) Type Responsibililty

Type responsibility does not depend entirely upon the similarity of the members of a given type; type membership does. In type responsibility there is an added factor which very much concerns the question of moral behavior. Type responsibility will be discussed at each level of organization in the ethical integrative series. Here we shall have to see it as it applies to the single human individual. The principle may be stated as follows.

All individuals of a given type are attracted to all other individuals of that same type in virtue of a common dependence upon type responsibility.

Let us look at the concrete exemplification of this principle first as it operates within the individual and secondly as it appears from the social point of view. In so far as one individual recognizes the similarity of another to himself he is to some extent recognizing himself in that other. In this way sympathy leads to empathy and empathy to appropriate activity. An individual in the long run can best promote his own interests by promoting the interests of others of his own kind. Hence type responsibility has a selfish base. If John sees that Tom is a man like himself he will feel that Tom should have good thoughts, feelings and activities like his own. And so also for Tom. Thus the effect of sharing a common type is to weld individuals together into something more than the type contains, more even than the type by itself can justify: the bonds of a social group and beyond that of a society.

Membership in a class means that the other members of the class impose upon a particular member those conditions which are conducive to similarity of behavior.[1] Seen from the perspective of the individual, class membership appears as an obligation rather than a privilege, although it provides both. The universal is more than a class name, it is the sign of an obligation. Thus the conditions for any individual are set for him by an environment of similar individuals.

Despite the distinctions to which we are committed between the four grades of moral integrative levels: the individual, social, human and cosmic, this is a unified work. Type responsibility, in a word, involves the individual with the cosmos. Types or classes are not locally confined but are identical everywhere and so involve universal spatial occupancy. What is true of a limited neighborhood is true throughout the whole of space. Thus type responsibility is an individual property which is coextensive with the whole of space, and from that comprehensiveness reaches down and does not stop until it applies to the single individual.

The degree of generalization involved in the principle of type responsibility is an important question. The function of generalization

[1] Cf. A. N. Whitehead, *Process and Reality*, Part II, Chapter III, II.

is no more peculiar to ethics than to any other topic. The degree of the generalization depends upon the extent to which it is intended to apply. What is good for an individual may yet not be good for a society; and what is good for a society may not be good for humanity; and what is good for humanity may not apply with equal impunity to the cosmos. There are ethical principles appropriate to each of these domains and they can be translated for other domains with appropriate changes for the extenuating circumstances, as we have seen; but they are not the same. It is clear that no generalizations are held in common except the cosmic; but this is a trivial tautology, it is in a sense what we mean by cosmic. In this connection it is possible, then, to read down the series but not up.

The variation among individuals being what it is, there is no condemnation implied in saying of a particular course of action that it suffers from the fact that it could not be generalized to all the members of a society and less so even to the whole human species; could not, in short, become an established principle of social morality. For instance virtue as moderation, as Aristotle defined it, may be an adequate rule of thumb but not an infallible guide. For I may benefit myself or my society by doing something extreme which it were well others did not do. I might have periods of overwork, I might have bouts of drunkenness; and both could be justified by their results in individual and social terms. My overwork might result in great social gains, and my overdrinking might enable me to clear the air for myself so that I see things more perceptively. Virtue is generalizable but not in such specific terms. It is rather the capacity to pursue appropriateness.

The individual is not a fragmented part of society closely resembling every other part so that his capacity to serve himself and society is identical in all ways for all individuals. He is if he is anything an individual, with his own individual differences. Thus society subjugates him in a sense and in a sense he represents a peculiar corner of it; by his personality and behavior, that is to say, he contributes to it what no other individual could, its own peculiar flavor as reflected by him. It is in the uniqueness of the person that his contribution resides and his duties appear, and it is in the similarities to others that his membership exists and his rights make themselves known.[1]

The loftiness of a morality is disclosed by the degree of generality of type responsibility: the more inclusive the loftier. Most men are

---

[1] Cf. Hegel, *Philosophy of History* (Eng. trans.), p. 107.

confined to a type responsibility that extends no further than their own persons, their own families, or at the most their own institutions or their own societies. They cannot represent anything beyond or extend themselves to the human species or the cosmos. But there are those others who feel their membership keenly and wish to elevate the species. To what extent in such a case should individual liberty be permitted? Should a man be allowed to starve himself to death if he wishes or indulge in severe self-flagellation? Should he be free to prevent his children from taking innoculations against poliomyelitis?

Type responsibility has been an empirical fact ever since through burial customs man linked himself with the generations. He has thought of the body and its tomb as a continuing bond between qualitatively different modes of existence.[1] The individual has always seen himself not only as connected with other living individuals but also as the bond between his ancestors and his inheritors, between his parents and his children. The recognition of responsibility therefore does not introduce new conditions but simply features some very old conditions which formerly operated without the recognition. Morality affects behavior, and men always do have to behave in one way or another regardless of the degree of awareness of their involvement.

There has always been a tendency to consider as moral or immoral behavior only that behavior of which the individual is aware through knowledge. A man, it is held, cannot be responsible for what he does not know. But type responsibility is responsibility which depends not upon being known but upon being. A man is what a man is and not what he knows, and he does what he does regardless of whether he knows what the consequences will be. His responsibility will be higher if he knows, and we shall see that species involvement requires such a description. Perhaps it is the ethics of the species which has led speculators into confusing the responsibility at that level with responsibility at the level of individual ethics. For with individual ethics only the feelings are involved, not the deliberate reason nor the will. Thus an involuntary act in so far as it has any form at all is an act involving individual morality. The prime ethical symbol is the single isolable individual conduct, in so far as it can be represented at all.

At the level of individual ethics type responsibility can be spelled out as responsibility (a) for thoughts, (b) for feelings and (c) for actions.

(a) Type responsibility extends to the limits of knowledge. The

---

[1] G. R. Levy, *The Gate of Horn* (London 1948, Faber and Faber), p. 70.

individual can be intellectually responsible only to and for what he knows, but also he *must* respond to what he knows. He knows of his own belonging, but he knows himself as human, and that is the source of his recognition of his type responsibility. The recognition of the existence of type responsibility furnishes a positive feedback which intensifies it. From the knowledge of such responsibility there is no turning aside without penalty. The criminal who has "gotten away" with his crime and lives a comfortable and well adjusted life under another name will give himself up to the authorities decades later "in order to clear his conscience." He thought that no one had known; but *he* had known, that's who had known. We are all our brothers' keeper just in virtue of a common humanity. Often such identification involves no recognition outside the society, but it is at least always society-wide.

(b) Type responsibility may involve awareness. Awareness has two dimensions: the intensity of the awareness itself and the extensity of the content of awareness.

First, then, the dimension of the intensity of awareness. The recognition of type responsibility comes to the individual not through analogical reasoning which recognizes in others behavior like his own and so perhaps everything else about them which is similar; nor through empathy, which projects onto others something of himself; but through feeling. There is between the members of a type a common feeling, and the feeling which compels the individual to share something which can best be described only as a type responsibility. Feelings are lower in the scale of human responses than perceptions; they are coarser but also more powerful. And they are not to be altogether denied.

Extensity is the dimension of awareness which involves the direction of behavior. There is a kind of superfluous caring for others through the effort to transform them in their own interest. Bad faith is faith confined to the individual himself. The individual finds that he owes to himself his own integration with other individuals in order to find his freedom in the choice of an object worthy of his dedication, and the choice proves to be that of those others. In this way dedication provides a kind of responsibility to others under the aegis of the type.

(c) Type responsibility for actions is what has traditionally gone under the name of responsibility. The reason for this is that actions may have important consequences for others. The point is large enough to deserve a more thorough discussion.

(c) Confrontation Theory

The theory of type responsibility in action is called here confrontation theory. It concerns the reduction of the needs, the encounter with needed objects or with cooperating individuals sharing the same needs and acting together in search of needed objects and possible participation in the same need-reductions. Ethics is not concerned then with behavior in all of its aspects but only with behavior so far as it involves confrontation; it defines the conditions under which confrontation is acceptable.

Confrontation as the term is here employed may be the outcome of any encounter conditioned by the specific stipulations of type responsibility. As conditions the stipulations are both material and formal. Their content is material: type responsibility is an empirical fact. Individuals never encounter each other directly but always indirectly. Confrontation is mediated by some artifact: a language or an instrument. Thus artifacts must always be counted into the moral situation and made a party to it. But in addition to the material content there is the fact that the stipulations *are* conditions, *a priori* conditions and so formal. The formality of confrontation is presented by the fact that the universal is a condition of the encounter of particulars, all men participating through the class, man, in every meeting of two or more human individuals.

Confrontation involves good behavior and may be defined as *conduct toward another, in consideration of all others*.

The moral quality is the quality of completeness. Confrontation represents the fact that in every moral act there is never a valid isolate but the entire involvement of existence is always represented through the operation of agency. Thus it is not legitimate to ask how many levels in the ethical integrative series are represented in any act of confrontation but of how high among the series is that level of which the individual is aware through his behavior (on the assumption that each includes all those below it). Thus confrontation involves a kind of theory of moral types. There is always in the individual a residue of humanity which has the effect of lifting him above the narrow standards of his society.

Confrontation and hence the ethical occurs at the individual-social interface where there exists between the individual and his society an interposition of type responsibility. Most of those whose interests are involved are not separately represented, but the collective representation is made through the individual because it is built into the very conditions under which the encounter takes place. For after all something more than a merely physical contact is involved.

Other varieties of confrontation exist. For instance, the individual may be confronted with his own conscience, either as nearby or at a distance; he may be (as already noted) confronted with society represented by its individual members; he may be confronted with the spectacle of the whole of humanity; he may be confronted with the spectacle of the universe. I shall in what follows mean by confrontation otherwise unspecified the confrontation of one human individual by another human individual, "conduct toward another, in consideration of all others."

An act renders concrete an abstraction. It makes the general into the singular, and dramatizes a proposition. It not only translates thoughts into overt behavior but the content of those thoughts. But there are qualifications attached to the transition. Ethics describes the conditions under which a moral encounter can take place; it must be always in the presence of generals: particulars conditioned by universals, individuals answering to type responsibility. The interposition of humanity between individuals in an encounter makes of it a moral confrontation, and as we have noted the interposition to be most effective must take place at least in terms of feeling, though thought intensifies it.

The study of complex relationships has yet to be developed to a point where it can apply in general to idem-level bonds and idem-level polarities. A few examples may be helpful. A theorem belonging to the axiom of confrontation recites that there is a law of minimum binary human relationships. Intimacy between two individuals can be increased from any level of intensity but cannot be decreased effectively short of zero. Those who have been casual friends can become close friends, but those who have been close friends cannot become casual friends.

Another theorem has to do with relative proportions in confrontation. In "conduct toward confronted objects" "all others" always constitutes a larger group than the group confronted, but they exist on the same integrative level of analysis. Thus there are definite "moral spheres" within which obligations and privileges can legitimately occur.

So much for idem-level bonds; but there are also idem-level polarities. For instance in confrontation there is the negative variety. Fellow feeling is not only or necessarily one of love. It may be love but also it may be hate. The attitude toward type responsibility can be equally effective in reverse. It is possible for an individual to hate his type and all of its manifestations, even in himself; hence the existence of the many forms of suicide. When confrontation involves the rejection of type responsibility, action becomes destructive. I have not said as much about it but it is as common as the constructive variety, and so I shall have to say more about it before we are done.

All individuals are opposed to all other individuals. This follows inevitably from that side of human nature whereby man endeavors to exceed himself. This is at least half the story of the drives. Men come into conflict with each other over both kinds of artifacts, for the very means of communication can themselves be the sources of differences. Language is a pathway but also a barrier, while instruments have both owners and those who wish to be owners. In cosmic ethics, I will talk about order and disorder; in human ethics, about congruence and collision; now in individual ethics it will be necessary to turn our attention to cooperation and competition. These are results of the drives to reduce the needs.

The aim of life is to continue living, the aim of every human individual, then, is to survive. For the primary needs it takes the form of immediate, or short-range, survival; for the secondary needs, it takes the form of ultimate, or long-range, survival. Immediate survival requires both cooperation and competition; cooperation with the hunting group and the family, competition with rivals for food and mates. Thus the idea of the good arose from cooperation and the idea of the bad arose from competition. It may be hazarded that gradually the abstract ideas of the good and the bad were separated from their sources and generalized. Thus it was that the good and the bad must have been discovered. It was a genuine discovery, like the discovery of all true ideas, for the good and the bad do exist if my conception of the good as what is needed is authentic.

The consequence of this development is the importance of the principle of polarity in all human affairs. Man has a deeply-rooted love of peace and war, of love and hate. It would appear from all we know that in all the millions of years since man first emerged from his pre-pongid and pre-hominid prototypes there has been no progress in motivation, only in intensification. He still wishes to help and hurt his fellow man, and he continues to do both with increasing efficiency. It may be a long way in civilization from the tribal shaman with his herbs and incantations to the modern physician with his equipped hospital, and it may be a long way from the tribal warrior with his bow and arrow or his club to the modern intercontinental ballistics missile with its atomic warhead, but the two games are exactly the same so far as the ends to be served by them are concerned.

The result is that cruelty and treachery are as common as kindness and fidelity. Extreme forbearance and ferocious brutality are often to be found side by side. But more on this topic in Part VII. The tendency of the individual to exceed himself continues to function. The individual will help or hurt his neighbor just in proportion as he thinks such actions hold out the prospect of helping himself. To measure individual morality it is necessary to consider who or what gets helped or hurt by a thought, a feeling or an action. Both are aggressive consequences of the need to survive, usually help for the in-group and hurt for the out-group (in ignoration of the interdependence of all groups).

In confrontation procedure the motives are pure. By the very nature of confrontation an individual will conduct himself toward another in consideration of all others. What can this mean except help; for it means that he knows himself to be one member of a type who needs the type to be the member, and the existence of the type is dependent upon the existence of others like himself. Man needs his fellows to be man.

But let us spell this out in an extreme case, which is the kind of case in which such principles are tested. Suppose that a man is confronted with a paranoid schizophrenic. He will have to attempt to turn him over to the authorities who will take legal action to insure that he is not able to murder his fellows, or failing that he will attempt to subdue him by force with the same end in view. Thus in confrontation conflicts and even the use of force is possible. But force will not be applied where persuasion is effective, for the schizophrenic is also a person. Under the principle of confrontation the individual is under an obligation to be true to himself, true to his institution, true to his society, true to humanity and true to all being. These obligations may and often do conflict and when they do he must take them in reverse order, the largest first.

It is always better for the individual if he feels rather than knows his type responsibility, and better if he knows it than neither, and better than either if he both feels and knows it. For the strong man to act under compulsion is painful, as Aristotle says,[1] but for the weak man it is a relief, something upon which he can depend and therefore pleasurable to be made to act in accordance with his type responsi-

[1] *Nico. Eth.* 1110b13.

bility. What men want and what they think they want is not usually the same. What they want is proportional to their energies. The strong man wishes to subdue the universe in order to make it a subordinate part of himself. The weak man wants a tidy order within which he can feel safe and protected.

(d) The Egoistic Perspective

Thus far in this chapter the argument has sounded as though the individual was in perfect agreement with society and so required no separate description. But this is hardly the case, for there is an egoistic perspective according to which the individual sets himself over against society and has regard only for his own needs. We shall want to devote some pages to this perspective.

The egoistic perspective has two aspects: the individual's moral view of himself, and his corresponding view of his society. I shall discuss them in that order.

I have been saying that ethics is essentially social and so it is, but it does have its individual legitimacy all the same. There is an authenticity to the domain which defines what the individual can expect of himself and what he owes to himself, and an autonomy in his duty to preserve himself, up to and including his right to a share in his society. An action will "feel right" only if it conforms to the conscience, and then only if in conforming to that portion of the conscience constituted by the public retention schema it does not conflict with anything in that other portion constituted by the private retention schema. The logical requirement of completeness cannot be met unless there is the richness of difference. Equality under the laws of society does not call for an homogenized society in which all individuals are alike. Thus the individual in preserving himself is preserving something of value which is unique.

"Self-realization" is the name given by Bradley to the moral attitude and behavior of the individual toward himself as a whole person.[1] "Self-realization" means self-perfection, and is the ideal of individual completion. The individual duty to himself as an individual is to complete himself in some way which shall be consistent. The needs and their activation in drives are efforts to obtain those materials from the external world which the individual must have if he is to complete himself. Thus from the point of view of the individual narrowly considered he leads a moral life only if his actions are consistent.

[1] F. H. Bradley, *Ethical Studies* (Oxford 1935, Clarendon Press), Essay II.

By self-realization he meant the aim at the self as a whole, but then he questions whether there can be any true whole except The Whole. Thus self-realization, Bradley insisted, must be infinite. His version of Hegelian morality (for that is what it is) seems more like a passive version of total aggression, in which an aggrieved world will be able to find consolation by having its own place in the self.

At the same time of course there is some element of truth in the conception. There is the authentic level of the individual even though it is not (as in Bradley's sense) absolute or even capable of becoming the absolute. There are important external conditions which are set for the individual if he is to strive for self-realization. There is no point in talking about the "self-realization" of an individual who is under-privileged and for whom the material goods to reduce his needs are not obtainable. Self-realization involves as a necessary (though not as a sufficient) cause a decent economic minimum whatever the political structure. Self-realization cannot be accomplished without a certain amount of freedom. To have freedom in the human sense an individual must not be entirely tied down to the task of earning an amount of money just sufficient to keep himself alive but must be so provided that in many respects his actions will be a result of his decisions made where alternatives existed and were open to him. Self-realization is a struggle of the individual to perfect his inward self by means of what he can accomplish when faced outward.

To be able to regard oneself as a person means to be an entire man, a whole containing parts rather than a part of some larger whole. The task of the individual which he must fulfill as an obligation which he has to himself is to maintain his integrity in the face of an established social morality. If he acts he acts in public but the public does not have to be the reason for his actions, this may remain purely private and individual. And its individual aspect is in a sense its unique aspect. What is unique about the individual ethically speaking is the peculiar perspective which each one possesses. Given a single social morality common to all the members of a particular society, there is still an angle of reference which is different for each individual member.

The existentialists have spoken well for the moral aspects of the egoistic perspective. A contrast with my thesis as advanced here may be helpful. The members collectively have provided us with a view of the world based on the fact of man in the world. Where according to Kierkegaard and his followers, Heidegger and Sartre, the view of the world based on the fact of man in the world calls for a prior understanding of man before it is possible to achieve an understanding of the world, the position advanced here calls for a prior understanding of the world before it is possible to achieve an understanding of man.

There is a difficulty, however, when we come to seek an understanding of society. The individual's egoistic view of society is of a world seen by a subject from his own perspective, colored by thoughts, by convictions, emotions, impulses, tendencies, inclinations.

Thus everyone regards his own reactions as standard for society. If he is shocked by some happenings, then he insists that what he is shocked by is inherently shocking. The end at which the individual ordinarily aims is to gain every advantage for himself. And if he does not seem to be doing this too well it may be because he does not understand too well just what is to his advantage, or because he is not able to grasp that a conflict may exist between what is to his advantage over the short run and what over the long.

It is easy after all for the individual to consider himself abstractly as a responsible member of a species; yet the notion of equality in this respect comes hard, and, when one gets down to cases, is in danger of being abandoned altogether. Thus a woman who does not understand the *Critique of Pure Reason* may not recognize that she has failed but instead may complain that Kant has failed her.

Integrity comes in many forms. From the perspective of society the individuals are merely conveniently sliced units in combination, easy to break up and reassemble in different societies. But that is what the individual is viewed from the perspective of society. From the perspective of the individual on himself despite the evidence to the contrary he appears to be sufficient unto himself. The individual in this perspective stands alone, responsible only to his own conscience for his being, and apart from all other considerations. Now there is only one connection in which this contention is not controverted by the facts, and that is death. Birth is a social occasion, but death is entirely individual. The individual is born from a mother, usually with the help of a midwife or a physician and attendants. But he is quite able to die all by himself and without any assistance, and usually ends by doing so whatever the circumstances. For help is needed in being born but assuredly not in dying.

There are three human faculties, three ways in which external reality can be apprehended. Each of them has its characteristic kind of response. Their names change through the millennia but the same faculties are always being named. Plato called them the three parts of the soul: the rational, the appetitive and the spirited element.[1] We should be more inclined today to call them thought, sensation and character (acting or refraining from action). We have been talking about sensation; but thought and action have their own effects upon behavior. As a man thinks things are, so he may behave accordingly; but his behavior will bring him up short if his thoughts with respect to the world have been misleading. Thus in the end action is the best corrective to error. For no man aims at pleasurable feeling directly. The aim is usually at some other goal, such as social influence, money, women, or fame, the attainment of which will yield pleasure. But these aims cannot provide for the whole person unless they are to some extent consistent.

It is important to remember that we are talking about the single individual, an organized man who must in some way act as a whole. Now a morality is a system of principles respecting behavior which renders that behavior consistent. Thus no man who acts consistently is lacking in morality. The man we call immoral may not conform to the requirements of the established morality but may have a morality of his own. That it may not be approved by the other members of his society is no indication that it is not a morality. Thus the actions of the individual can be consistent (or inconsistent) with his previous actions, as in the case of individual morality, or his actions can be consistent (or inconsistent) with the actions of others, as in the case of social morality.

But the usual situation with respect to morality is not as neat and clean as my description would suggest. Indeed it is far different from what it is usually asserted to be. For men publicly confess to desire the good both for themselves and for others, and they will readily agree that in the pursuit of such ends it is necessary to begin by following the established laws of the society, and yet in actual practice they will not hesitate to circumvent the law or even transgress it directly if they see a distinct advantage for themselves. And as a matter of fact, as things now stand their friends and associates will not condemn them for it but to the contrary will applaud although only so long as the offenders do not get caught.

So much for the individual's moral view of himself. I promised to say a few words about his corresponding view of his society.

To the individual intent upon self-realization, society presents itself as a prickly field of opportunities. The game here is one played for

[1] *Rep.* IV. 435B ff.

privileges and without regard for obligations. If he is careful it is possible to have all gains and no losses. Satisfactions of so many sorts are to be found in society; from the sexual to the prestigious. But there are also penalties for not playing the game correctly and these can be costly. So the individual develops a strategy in terms of which he can deal with his fellows entirely in terms of his own self-realization. Something of this attitude and approach is to be found in poets but also in gangsters, in scientists but also in bankers; it is to be found, in short, in those who seek the social good but also in those who seek personal advantage from it. In the last analysis the egoistic perspective is grounded in existence, and if because of excessive behavior the individual does not know where to stop in his self-preserving activity, taking it as he does well beyond its legitimate confines, at least it must be granted that without the attempt at self-realization the individual might not exist at all. As human the individual is delicately balanced between his own and his species' values. To devote himself exclusively to either is fatal, but it is difficult to know exactly at what intermediate point he is to find his true position.

(e) Moral Equipment

Man has needs, and the goods for reducing them exist in the external world. The conditions under which need-reduction can take place morally is plain. Man is not merely an individual but a member of a species, with responsibilities to his type which confront him upon every occasion when he is called on for action. That he both views the world and acts from a peculiarly egoistic perspective upon himself and his society, is well known. But what is his moral equipment for acting in the way preferred from an ethical standpoint?

In modern psychological terms, the individual has a set of organic needs. Drives to reduce the needs are activated when objects promising need-reductions furnish the necessary cues. But the individual has in addition to this equipment a character and an active will. By means of these he is able to be permissive toward the drives or inhibit them either temporarily or permanently. He controls his drives if not his needs, and makes choices concerning them, choices based upon an anterior scale of values which is part of his retention schemata. The moral equipment of the individual is thus exceedingly complex. The execution of moral (or immoral) acts depends upon more than merely feeling. In the last section we talked about the morality of feeling. Next, then, we shall have to say a few words about the character and the will.

Character is the structure of the person. A harmonic structure produces a strong character, as Plato noted in the *Republic*. It can be detected by the strength of the will. A man of character will have a strong will. Character is more than the adroit use of intelligence, it is a structure which functions under the terms of endurance. A man of character is one who can take a position with regard to any situation or set of values and adhere to it through any number of hardships. Housman was calling for character when he said, "Let us abide awhile and see injustice done."

A distinction with respect to the character of two types of individuals must be here recorded. We may divide all individuals into the demotic type and the heroic type. Demotic man is man steadfast in preserving the values of his society. Heroic man is man steadfast in his determination to replace the values of his society with better ones. The vast majority of men are demotic men, while only a very few are heroic. Yet the importance of the one class is as great as that of the other. Character is called out in both, and often equally; though sometimes a greater amount is required of heroic man than of demotic man; for heroic man is often compelled to stand alone, while demotic man usually has the support of a vast number of his fellows.

The will may be defined as the ability to act or to refrain from action. Usually, the will functions to make a union of aim and action, to conform to belief by matching it with action, but not always. Schopenhauer was correct in supposing that the will is a composite of emotional and often irrational impulses, but it can just as often be an arm of the reason. The will is an impulse, no doubt of that; but an impulse that may derive from any element of the character. Thus the will as often performs a service for the good as for the bad. The will itself in this sense may be a good will or a bad one. The goodness of the will cannot be measured by its effects. For as Kant properly saw, the will as such is good; it is good to be able to act. He was wrong in supposing, however, that only the will is good. For an act, for instance, may be good. If the good as I have defined it, is what is needed, then an act may be good because an act may be needed. Moreover, good actions are possible without a good will as with it. The rich man who gives large sums to the poor and underprivileged merely because this will enable him to associate with aristocrats is still doing a worthwhile thing even though for a bad reason. Thus action may have a moral (or for that matter immoral) effect which was not willed. Morality is not entirely a matter of the will, of consciousness or even of the conscience.

An "ill will" is a false conception. The will as such is good, though it may be put at the service of a bad act. Gossip for instance is always malicious. Bad news spreads faster than good and gives greater pleasure. In order to will the good for oneself it often seems necessary to lower the reputation of others by comparison. The effect of this on those who are thus derogated (and incidentally also on oneself), however, is bad. Success in life may be a tribute one pays to one's friends, but failure is a greater comfort to them.

Is the will, then, still always good? Yes; for the will is power and no good can be accomplished without power, and even though bad can be accomplished, too, the will is a power for good as well as for bad and therefore a good; because what is needed for the good is good; and though the power is neutral in itself because it is needed for the good it is good to that extent. Good behavior is behavior designed to bring about an improvement of some sort, and a good will is a will designed to execute good behavior. But if the behavior is bad the will still may be good merely because it is a will.

The subjective will presupposes an environment with a material object capable of effective resistance which it can strive to overcome. The will is the character manifesting itself through successive acts. A man thus comes to know his character only through the observations he is able to make of his own overt behavior. For no man knows what he will do until the occasion arises which elicits his actions. But he does not know this, either, and so he considers himself to be free and his actions the result of a free will. The will, however, is limited in several ways. It is limited by the character and it is limited by social restrictions on individual behavior. The will is not free individually, as Locke saw, but is constrained to choices made in terms of a set of preferences previously adopted; we live by means of values. Actions appear voluntary from outside; the confirmed alcoholic has no choice.

But this is not the whole story. Every man is capable of arbitrary impulses which he did not foresee and cannot control, and to this extent the will is free. But such freedom is not necessarily desirable, unless it be supposed (what is often true in many cases) that the impulses which derive from pure feeling untrammelled by reason are better guides to the values than reasoned action. Otherwise the will is a product of the character and limited by it and thus not free to that extent. On the social side, the will is not free because of social restrictions imposed by law or by the broader influences of social morality. The painter Dali once wrote that man has a right to his own madness, and this is true but only to the extent that the individual makes no demands on society. If a mad individual occupy more than his own living space and force, then his madness becomes a burden that society cannot afford. It comes to this, then, that the direction of any individual activity is the vector sum of the forces exerted on the will by all obligations and restraints, individual and social.

(f) Good Reasons

Perhaps the most popular element ever chosen as a basis for the construction of a theoretical ethics was reason. From Plato, who held reason to be a world condition, through those European rationalists who were talking about the human capacity for reasoning, especially Kant who thought of it in terms of pre-conditions, to modern advocates of "the rational temper," such as Blanshard, the importance and even the supremacy of reason in ethics has been recognized.

Off-hand such a choice seems, as one might say, reasonable. There can be no doubt about the necessity for the use of reason in leading the moral life. Reason makes itself manifest in the ordering of the organic drives. The needs conflict and compete for attention, and an appeal to reason is necessary in order to assign them a rank-order. This must of course take into consideration what is immediately available for need-reduction in the external world as well as the relative exigencies of the needs themselves.

But the very existence of a speculative study of ethics is also evidence. What is at issue is the definition of the precise limits of the function of reason in both ethics and morality. Two obvious interpretations will have to be dismissed at once as unworkable. The first of these is the supposition that reason alone is sufficient as a guide to the good. The second is that reason itself is the good at which all men aim.

Reason alone cannot be relied on as a guide to the good. The good is a quality, and we cannot be sure that quality will always be recognized by such a method. Then again deductive processes are always subject to error. There may be limitations in the axioms from which reason takes its start, and there may be errors in carrying out the deductive steps. Kant in endeavoring to base morality upon reason (understood as consistency) failed to give credit to the demands of completeness. A narrow rationalism can be worse in its effects than none at all. For a logical system will never of itself report that it is too narrow, that its axioms are insufficient. Reason usually gets the blame for bad reasoning, and the method itself condemned for the faults in its application. But reasoning is not to be equated with bad reasoning. Incomplete formal systems when taken as complete can have results as misleading as impulsive irrational actions, which they in fact greatly resemble.

That reason itself is not the good is shown by the nature of ethical ideals. Only for Aristotle in his *Metaphysics* (λ, 7) is reason itself the good at which human reasoning should aim, in imitation of God whose life is reason. But this denies all other goods. If the good is a quality as Moore asserted, then it is not reason; for we do not mean a quality by reason nor by reason a quality. According to the definition of the good adopted here, reason is the good only when reason is needed. That the human individual has need of reason cannot be denied; the brain is the organ whose specific need is for information, and information can only be retained as organized, and it can be organized only by reason. Some would argue still further that information can only be obtained by organizing it, so that reason applies much earlier in the process. But in any case there are other and quite different organs such as stomach, gonads, musculature and skin, with specific needs which are not precisely those of the reason; we have listed them already and they include such material goods as food, a mate, activity, and security, respectively.

There are no infallible capacities which the individual possesses and which he can exercise in his pursuit of the good. In general then it is best to combine as many fallible methods as possible. Reason, yes, but also feelings of intuition and activities involving trial-and-error. In the behavior of the individual there is no doubt a rank-order to the capacities. The individual acts as a whole, with as Plato said in the *Republic* his feelings and his character subordinated to his reason. Thus it may be that while feelings furnish the leading edge reason pronounces the final judgment in all matters concerning the good.

A judgment is a decision concerning the value of something. When that value is a moral value then the judgment is a moral judgment. Most writers on logic who have been concerned with judgment (and like Bradley or Joseph they would have belonged to the nineteenth century) consider it important but still distinguish it from reason. For both these men a judgment is an act of thought yet its rules of procedure are not deductive rules.[1] Thus elements other than reason are involved. Yet reason is involved, too, if not in the process then in the construction

[1] H. W. B. Joseph, *An Introduction to Logic*, ch. VII; F. H. Bradley, *The Principles of Logic*, Book I, ch. I.

of the judgment, for a judgment can be called good only when it correctly assesses a situation.

Thus there are judgments concerning the good and there are good judgments, judgments concerning the good which are ethical or moral judgments, and good judgments which need not be. In a work on ethics we will be concerned only with the former. But judgments concerning the good are subjective, and as subjective they are recognitions of objective values. In so far as a moral judgment is a recognition, there must be objective moral values to be recognized; there must, in other words, be goods. Often, of course, judgments are made wrongly, and these, I submit, are errors in judgment; something external was mistaken for something else external; but if there was nothing external then the judgment was purely internal, in which case it was either the indirect result of something which had been external or it was pathological and so beyond our ken in the study of the good.

(g) Dispositions Toward the Good

The individual views himself and his society from the egoistic perspective. In so far as he recognizes himself as human however (and that is usually pretty far), he is engaged in confrontation, that is to say, in conduct conditioned by type responsibility. There is, as we have noted, an ethics of feeling, and that is what I propose to discuss here. It has been neglected in favor of reason (as for instance by Aristotle and Kant) and in favor of action (as for instance by James and Dewey). Confrontation leads to feelings of approval or disapproval, and feelings of approval or disapproval lead to action. This makes of the moral feelings an important link in the chain of individual ethics.

Epistemology has suffered from drawing its inferences as to the derivation of knowledge from too sophisticated a sense: from the sense of sight. For visual perception is already influenced by anterior beliefs. But if we begin by considering the individual's feelings and work with these alone we get a different set of answers. For we find that the feelings are involuntary (and therefore more accurate because less interpreted) reports of the external world, often of something in the social milieu. Those aspects of the world which are encountered by the feelings are its qualities. Since qualities are either esthetic or ethical depending upon whether the bonds are between parts or between wholes, and since all parts are wholes to their parts, the ethical and the esthetic are simply the same qualities viewed from different directions in the series of integrative levels, and all qualities are, in one dimension at least, ethical qualities. The feelings are apt to encounter parts as wholes for it is the feelings that look down rather than up the levels. Other and more sophisticated avenues, such as perception and thought, look up and see things in their aspiration toward inclusion and perfection. Thus the feelings put the individual in touch with the moral qualities. It is in the world of other individuals and their artifacts that the feelings encounter objects. Thus the feelings tie the individual in to his society in a way more basic than his other faculties.

Both Scheler[1] and Peirce[2] have observed that the feelings are contagious and there is a tendency for them to spread socially. The feelings convey an unacknowledged and for the most part unexamined set of beliefs with them which the individual thus unconsciously accepts. (Later, those of the beliefs which come to his conscious attention are assumed to rest on evidence, on what seems to the believer to be true —whether it is or not—and on what appears to him to be adequate reasons—whether they are or not.) Thus there finally emerges within the individual a fully developed ethics based on the reality of values in the external world.

Let me conclude, then, that approval or disapproval is consequent upon the degree of conformity to type responsibility. From the perspective of the individual, it is necessary to consider his own sense of his obligations: first to himself, then to his institution, his society, next to humanity and finally to the universe. The problem for him is to maintain that degree of subjectivity sufficient to guarantee the integrity of the person while in pursuit of social reality as the individual's goal. To the extent to which he supposes a thing or event contributes to this, he approves; and to the extent to which he thinks it does not, he disapproves.

The individual's feelings of approval or of disapproval are the qualities which emerge from a whole made up of a complex of parts. His own state is a contributing factor, and his own state includes everything in the integrative levels in which he participates, everything, that is, from his physiological well-being (or its absence) at the lowest level to the conscious knowledge of his relevant beliefs resting in the effects upon it of the retention schemata. But there is also the contributing factor of the condition of the object which he is to approve or disapprove, its condition and its context, both of which range through two or more of the integrative levels themselves except in the case of

---

[1] *The Nature of Sympathy*, I, II, (3).
[2] *Col. Pap.*, 5.552; 6.151.

purely physical events which are confined to one integrative level. Finally, there is the third contributing factor of the interactions which take place in the apprehension of the object which is to be approved or disapproved. Its mode and the consequences which ensue from it are also contributing factors. How all this adds up to a single qualitative feeling of approval or disapproval is an exceedingly intricate mechanism, and it can hardly be studied by examining only its approbative side.

Now it happens that in recent centuries and especially in recent decades the approbative side has been considered so important that it has tended to block out the view of the other two sides. Ever since Hume in his *Enquiry Concerning the Principles of Morals* discussed the good under the heading of approval or disapproval as the kind of emotion which all people feel from time to time, there has been strong support for his views. I take it that Kant is on the same side when he asserts that the only good is a good will. Westermarck described ethical relativity as the relation of ethics to the individual through his emotions and through language.

The contemporary philosophers of ordinary language hang their conception of the good on what is approbative or emotive, prescriptive or preferred. Stevenson says "emotive" or "approbative," Hare says "prescriptive," and von Wright says "preferred." The position was invented by Hume, modernized in terms of a linguistic interpretation by Carnap, developed by Ayer, systematized by Stevenson and generalized by Hare.

There can of course be little doubt that these philosophers are engaged in exploring a genuine and important area and doing so in an enlightening and instructive way. The area is the area of ethical feeling or, as it is more commonly called, dispositions. Dispositions are neither good nor bad in themselves; they just *are* and it is necessary in every case to reckon with them. In this the philosophers of ordinary language have been right. One of the sets of phenomena with which we shall always have to deal is the native data of dispositions. Bentham called it "the principle of sympathy and antipathy" and considered it opposed to his own principle of utility which recognizes the governance of the individual by its two masters, pain and pleasure.[1]

The current effort of all ordinary language analysts to confine the domain of ethics to a description of dispositional states makes them, I think, right in what they affirm and wrong only in what they deny.

[1] Jeremy Bentham, *An Introduction to the Principles of Morals and Legislation,* ch. II, XI–XIV.

What accounts for such states, how were they arrived at, what caused them? Does not the theory of ordinary language confine the ethical to the conscious, to what is deliberate and psychological? But are not feelings responses, responses, in a word, to something outside the organism which caused the feelings? And don't responses echo also from deeper physiological levels within the organism and not merely from the conscious level?

The ordinary language analysts, Ayer, Hare and others, are talking not about ethics but about ethical judgments, and what they say is in large part true. There is only one difficulty. They speak as though there were no way to verify or falsify ethical judgments, and indeed they equate ethical judgments with ethical facts. The ethical judgment for them is the fact. And since such judgments belong exclusively to the individual then they are subjective elements and there is no way to determine their truth or falsity; they just are. But there are other facts to which the contents of ethical judgments refer (as distinct from the self-reference of the judgments themselves), and it is these other facts which have to be studied in order to be able to refer the judgments to something other than the individual who makes them.

To say that an ethical judgment or preference has only an emotional ground is not to say that it is arbitrary. There are reasons why one has this emotional preference rather than that. For emotions are responses, and the structure of the beliefs of the individual affect the stimuli to determine the responses. Let us suppose that John has a strong attachment to his mother who was an aggressive woman and possessed of an upturned nose, and let us further suppose that as a result of an early experience John is particularly susceptible to short brunettes. Then if there is a young brunette at the next cocktail party John attends, and one is aggressive and has an upturned nose, she may evoke strong desires in John or he may react strongly against her, but he will not be as neutral to her as he will be to a blonde or a tall brunette with a hooked nose.

A further clarification may come from the analogy with the epistemological distinction introduced by Carnap, between syntactics, semantics and pragmatics. Let us suppose that an individual makes a moral judgment. Ethical syntactics has to do with the ethical system by means of which his judgment is itself judged good or bad. Ethical semantics has to do with the individual uttering the moral judgment. Ethical pragmatics has to do with the practical situation which is being judged. Now dispositions toward the good belong to ethical semantics,

but there are two other valid ethical domains which are thereby neglected and which call for an equal amount of intensive examination.

An illustration here might be helpful. Suppose a man were to say,
"This food is good." Pragmatically, his statement refers, let us say, to
a particular dish which he has been eating. Semantically it expresses
something he has been tasting. Syntactically it must be judged true or
false according to the criterion of the good to which it is to be referred.
If to his own individual standards, then he alone is the judge and the
statement carries its own truth; what he says is true because he says
it provided only that he both means what he says and knows what he
means. But if the statement is to be referred to the criterion of his
society, then the truth or falsity of the statement might be otherwise.
For different societies have different standards of goodness in food
which sometimes overlap but are rarely identical. Finally, the statement could be referred beyond society to the species for validation so
that any member of any society would have to agree. And although
we lack the requisite knowledge no doubt the standard of reference
could be selected beyond the human species from the next ethical
integrative level.

Dispositions are, as Stevenson proceeds to show, based on beliefs.[1]
Now beliefs have to do with the external world when they are beliefs
about things outside the mind. In short, what the individual approves
he believes to be there for approval and what he disapproves he believes to be not there or at least not all there. Thus approval or disapproval is a manifestation of something more fundamental, something
which stands behind it ready to receive and to deserve it.

Men usually have reasons for approving or disapproving other than
their own merely arbitrary and subjective tastes, for both taste and
approval rest on anterior evaluations which in turn stem from beliefs
in objective existences and goals. A disposition to behave appropri-
ately can only be prepared by the acceptance of the right beliefs and
these in turn are dictated by the proper philosophy. Thus we are
driven back to the content of the retention schema in which such a
philosophy is maintained by the individual, equally whether he is conscious of doing so or not.

The emotive theory of ethics is not altogether in accord with the
connection, which Peirce emphasized so much, between belief and
action. A belief is what an individual feels is true, and what he feels

[1] Charles L. Stevenson, *Ethics and Language* (New Haven 1950, Yale University Press),
p. 136 ff.

is true is what he will act on, what he will attempt to carry out in practice. Thus his belief (which may have been private so long as it remained in the sphere of emotion or of feeling) is carried into the social world, for it is not possible for a man to act and yet not to affect his fellows in some way. Approval may be subjective but action is objective; feelings may be covert but behavior is overt; and so in the end approval does not stay mere approval. The individual must give his approval or disapproval with public moral seriousness, because its effects will be felt in society.

Ethics is not entirely a matter of awareness, responsibility or choice. If one man injures another inadvertently, the extent of the injury is no less. Dispositions have an ethical bearing but they do not exhaust moral content. Preference and choice belong to the psychology of value, but the psychology of value is not the only nor the governing area of value, for there would be no psychology of value were there no values to be preferred or chosen. Values are not brought into existence by the expression of a preference or the making of a choice but by behavior. And so it is to the action and conduct which are carried out in pursuit of individual goods that we must next turn our inquiry.

CHAPTER 3

THE PURSUIT OF THE GOOD

(a) Action and Conduct

We pass now from the discussion of dispositions toward the good to action and conduct involving the good. The first thing to note is the point which so much occupied Dewey; that every moral situation has an individual aspect and is to some extent unique. But what is the individual moral situation? We must be as much concerned with what makes it moral as with what makes it unique. The unique aspect is the individual aspect but the moral aspect is the general aspect. We shall find if my theory is correct that the analysis of any concrete moral situation discloses ramifications which are abstract and so must be considered apart from the concrete. There is more to a good or bad act than what appears to be local and particular; otherwise we could not consider it in a moral connection or characterize it as good or bad. All particulars are exemplifications of something general; there are no absolutely unique particulars. Action is intentional motion. A clear distinction must be drawn between the intention to act and the act itself; although of course a clear similarity connects them. The transition from intent to act is effected through decisions. We are in action concerned with overt behavior and in conduct with responsible behavior.

Conduct, then, is deliberate action. Its dimensions are intensity and direction. One thing which characterizes human nature and sets it apart from all other natures is that the human individual seems to have had handed over to him the responsibiity for the making of a great many decisions which govern his existence. This always may be of course because he is unable to read the fine print which announces that whatever is decided had been predetermined. He will never know. Perhaps he was destined to make the decisions he has made, but since he cannot be sure he must proceed as though the responsibility was his.

The major decision in favor of existence is made not by the conscious individual's deliberate decision but by his somatic organism. One thing is clear, if nothing else is, that life is intended to be lived. The individual may have the choice; he may, for instance, decide to live or to commit suicide; but that his organism itself has already been committed is evident from his needs. "Is life worth living?" someone asked, and Samuel Butler replied in his *Notebook* "This is a question for an embryo, not for a man."

Decisions are made by the individual respecting behavior, this much we do know. They are skimmed off the top of a large accumulation of influences which operate both from within the individual and from without. Those who make the decisions do so from thoughts, feelings or actions or any combination of these. Men act from decisions prompted in principles by means of thought, they act directly from feelings, and they act as they had in previous actions.

Decisions concerning behavior dictated by thought involves principles accepted and stored. Good behavior is behavior in response to the good. In the making of moral judgments concerning action and conduct the individual has at his disposal those capacities for reasoning which he has acquired from instinct or training (or both) but conditioned by his fund of knowledge, by his emotional set and by such needs as are uppermost at the moment of decision. The values selected in a moral judgment are those of the external world but the selection is internally conditioned. In other words, what is effective from a perpective is an object, but its effect is on a subject, in terms of the perpective available. There is something of a negative feedback here, for what the process of judging amounts to is the choice by the individual of just those elements in the external world which he has decided to have influence him.

So much for spontaneous judgment. The deliberate reference to convictions as a guide to actions has a predominantly rational cast. Those who act from principles do so on the assumption that the principles are true. And so they may be; but they may be false, and if they are false they may still serve as principles for the guidance of action. There is no such thing as ignorance, so no man acts from it, each thinking he has sufficient knowledge of the truth.[1] Nobody among the tribes of central India is ignorant of the nature of the airplanes which they often see moving overhead. They know that these run on very thin wires stretched across the sky and that the men in them are of a special kind who live only on air.[2] Ignorance usually

---

[1] Cf. Aristotle, *Nich. Eth.*, 1110b18.
[2] *The Tribal World of Verrier Elwin: An Autobiography* (New York and Bombay 1964, Oxford University Press), p. 172.

means false knowledge. Those who act from false knowledge act as well as those who act from the truth, for they do not know the false knowledge to be false.

Decisions dictated by feeling are the most prevalent. They are the most pervasive of the organism and hence the most influential. Valuation is a kind of judgment, as Dewey saw. It is the kind of judgment involving qualities and feelings, the feelings are responses to the qualities and deliberation holds them to a correspondence. Thus valuation is the result of the feelings affecting conduct. Everything we do is done as though it were done instinctively – including thought, and so it is, at least partly. For conduct has its reasons that thought knows nothing of. Indeed action itself is a form of thought; it draws the concrete theorems from the qualitatively vague and general axioms.

Decisions dictated by actions also exist, actions prompted by previous actions, but of a different sort. Bravery is often like this. When the Marine sergeant, Dan Daly, in the first world war said to his men in the trenches as he led them over the top, "Come on, you bastards, do you want to live forever?" he gave to the words by his actions a meaning they could not otherwise have had. He did not "suit the words to the actions" but the actions to the words; but they seldom suit either way. Action, the point is, has its own meaning. We can never predict what a man will or will not do under very special circumstances (or perhaps under any circumstances, for that matter); and, worse still, he cannot predict, either.

By an act I do not mean an act in Fichte's sense of an act of the will. I mean an overt act, something that happens through motion in time and space involving material bodies. Thus every act is a moral act whose moral antecedents are largely unknown and whose moral consequences are largely unforeseen. We act usually on the basis of insufficient knowledge (and we must do so otherwise we could not ever act at all) and from the moral intuitions prompted by a morally good will.

It has been supposed that ethics is concerned exclusively with practical action, and so ethics as a study is predominantly practical. This is not so. Ethics is concerned with the good and the bad, the right and the wrong, and not with action or practicality directly. But while morality may affect practicality by determining for the individual what he ought to do under given circumstances, it is true also that practicality may determine morality. For it happens that moral feelings for the good are affected by the moral qualities of actions; the individual often discovers in the heat of action whether what he is doing is what he ought to be doing. Then again activity may be a source of moral reinforcement; the more an individual does what he is convinced he ought to do the greater the degree of his conviction. There is a positive feedback involved in the practical application of moral principles; the more the individual does good the more he is inclined to do good.

An adult who is in a state of health is responsible for all of his actions. Morality is not entirely a matter of awareness or of knowledge however. Involuntary actions occur and they may be entirely free from compulsion. Some behavior is no doubt random or spontaneous, but that does not remove it from having moral or immoral effects. A wrong done inadvertently is no less a wrong, just as a good done in the same way is a good. Whatever X does that benefits Y is good for Y whatever X knows or does not know. Just as ignorance of the law is no excuse under the law, and a man is held responsible for his illegal actions, on the ground that it was his responsibility also to ascertain what the laws require; so ignorance of morality is no excuse, and a mature and healthy individual is held responsible for his immoral acts, on the ground that he should have ascertained just what morality requires.

The moral code for the individual is carried as part of his conscience. Properly employed it will insure that his actions will be consistent, that no two of his actions will be conflicting and therefore self-defeating. In this sense conduct is rational action. Insofar as a man's actions are not inconsistent they are rational. To be completely rational they will also have to follow deductively from moral principles which are defensible in themselves. This is the connection in which it is legitimate to claim that the actions of a good man are rational.

The good for the individual involves his participation in being. Any kind of behavior which can increase such participation is good insofar as it does, and so is good if it can do so without violating the legitimate participation of the individual in society. Thus we have for the individual beside his service to society his service to himself which consists in his participation in being. The dogma of affirming existence[1] asserts that when we act we exist. A theorem can be constructed by combining "the increase of participation in being" with "the dogma of affirming existence," to the effect that when we add to existence we reaffirm it. This is good behavior.

The dogma of affirming existence seems to have been known to that great sceptic, Hume. Hume himself observed that we act on the belief

[1] Cf. my Ontology, Chapter VIII, § 2, Axiomatics.

in practice as the best cure for all sceptical reflection. After spending many chapters to prove that the only reliable knowledge we have is that of our own impressions and ideas, Hume admitted that practicality revokes all his conclusions, for practicality puts us in the world of action, and the world of action is always objective, not subjective; we act outwardly and among other people and material things.

(b) The Pursuit of Individual Goods

The good is involved in action in two ways. It is involved with the subject in his own satisfactions, and it is involved with the object in his goal-achievements. I call the former a gratification appropriate to the short-range self and the latter one appropriate to the long-range self. Both are subjective in being gratifications, but the short-range self is more involved through the subject with his own satisfactions while the long-range self is more involved with his goal-achievements. A man who carves a statue has the pleasure of need-reduction in terms of activity; to possess an organ means to enable it to function, and there is pleasure in sheer activity involving the muscles. But that is not the only good involved in such activity, there is also the satisfaction of achievement; for it is a pleasure to make something and to take delight in the approval it brings from giving satisfaction to others.

So much for the good at the subjective end. At the objective end there is the addition to the society which a genuine work of art represents. For a society is not merely a collection of human individuals; as we have already noted, it includes artifacts, and a work of art is an artifact of a special class: the class of symbolic artifacts whose qualitative side is capable of supercharging society. This is a social good, and so the artist has achieved an objective social good as well as a subjective personal one. This can be well illustrated perhaps by the example of a productive artist.

We shall be occupied in this section with considering the subjective and personal good, which is individual. The individual pursues his own individual good through a number of objects. He may pursue his own good (a) through himself, (b) through society, (c) through the human species, or (d) through the cosmos. In each case, it should be remembered, however, that whatever the channels it is his own personal and individual good that he is pursuing, and no less so because the channels may be other persons and things, present or absent, or the whole universe. Let us consider them briefly in the order given.

(a) First of all, then, we shall consider the good as it is when it is involved in the individual's pursuit of the good for himself.

The goods at which the individual aims for himself may bc divided into the importunate and the important. The importunate good is physiological, the important good psychological. The physiological good is that of health. The achievement and the maintenance of a state of health imparts to the individual a sense of well-being, which is the quality of the good manifested at this level. It is good to "feel good." The bond between internal organs, the sense of well-being which comes to those whose body is functioning without disorder, is the good at the lowest internal level. It is the feeling of completeness. We are unaware of an arm when it does not hurt, but when there is no hurt anywhere in the somatic organism the good is not merely the absence of pain; it is the presence of a quality which enters awareness from the organism as a whole, and we can say that we "feel good."

Physiological good is not however a state which we attain and then maintain simply by being. Activity is involved. The physiological organism is built for action and its well-being can be maintained only by continued activity. Thus when the individual is healthy and active, it is legitimate to say that he is achieving physiological good even though by his actions he may not be aiming at this good but at some other. The only individuals who aim at physiological good dircctly are those who do not have it: the ill and the infirm. Those who have it as a rule maintain it indirectly by aiming through their actions at something else.

The psychological good at which the individual aims for himself may be termed solidarity. The awareness of solidarity comes from the explicit recognition that there is a condition of perfection prevailing within. The psychological good of solidarity is an aim, remember, and not necessarily a goal-achievement. Some activity is rcquired in order to work toward it. In this instance the activity involved may be one of intensive introspection. This is part of the ethics of thought; what is called consciousness is a special sort of searchlight playing over a large set of interior elements: feelings and thoughts. Consciousness conceived in this way is not a passive affair but rather one involving effort. The consciousness has its own terms and intentions.

The phenomenologists from Husserl to Merleau-Ponty have been much occupied with investigating the intentional consciousness. What the consciousness intends it does unconsciously; consciousness means awareness of its own content. Consciousness is conclusive evidence for the enormous capabilities of matter when highly organized (which means not only the result of highly complex and actualized forms but containing as its content the conceptualization of another and entirely different set of highly complex and actualized forms). The consciousness, understood in this way, works toward its own state of self-consciousness, probing itself in depth, seeking to discover greater sublevels of self-awareness, and a content of subtlety and sensitivity which will indicate progress toward self-perfection.

The good for individual man is made possible by his freedom, internal and external. Internal freedom is physiological. Physiological freedom is a matter of health. Only a healthy man is free from personal concerns and for the pursuit of outward goals. The individual is not his own goal except in the case of the ill who must concern themselves with gaining health. A well man does not think about himself but about those aims which his activities may help him to reach. Internal freedom, then, is the modulation of organic needs untrammeled by defects which might constitute obstacles from the very start; the will is free to arrange the needs in its own preferential order of importance: for food, sex, information, activity, and security, for instance.

Psychological freedom (a branch of the physiological) lies in freedom of thought, feeling and action; freedom of thought not excessively determined by official views or by mass agreement, freedom of feeling not excessively determined by official values or by mass agreement concerning values, and freedom of action not excessively determined by official views concerning what it is permissible to do or by mass agreement concerning conduct. By "excessive" here is meant that degree which would inhibit divergence or independence. The extreme of psychological freedom is fixed by the attitude toward death when it approaches. Death may be welcomed or met with surprise. Only the ill welcome it, in most cases, but to the well it comes as a surprise. If death comes early then the surprise. But to die at the right time is to be able to welcome death as a friend.

We have been discussing freedom, but what about determinism? The one cannot be understood without the other. The key to the understanding of freedom and its opposite, determinism, lies in not considering them on the same level of analysis. Determinism is always one analytical level below freedom, freedom always one analytical level above determinism. Thus the individual is bound by society, but his freedom is provided by the efficient working of his organs. The articulation of the parts, which are expressed by laws, make possible the freedom of the whole. This structural difference has its counterpart in function. All is determined but only after the fact; before, all is free. An individual for instance may think that after breakfast he has the option whether to drink a pint of whiskey or go to work, and he may therefore regard himself as being in a position of perfect freedom, with the responsibility his and the choice a free one to make. Afterwards, however, whichever choice he did make, it may be equally apparent that given his constitution and history he was destined to make the choice that he did.

The most familiar goods pursued by the individual when he aims specifically at the good for himself are called pleasure and happiness, the hedonic goods. (I shall reserve the term, utilitarianism, for social goods which I understand as social usefulness: the techniques and artifacts designed to produce the greatest happiness of the greatest number of individuals, there being no social organism which is capable as a whole of feeling happiness or for that matter anything else). Pleasure, and its opposite, pain, are parts of the axiological signalling system. They indicate approach and avoidance respectively.

Pleasure is the intense and usually short-lived feeling of good. Happiness is the pervasive and usually long-lived feeling of good. As a rule, pleasure is a by-product of means, while happiness results from the contemplation of ends.

The good for man is the pleasure accompanying need-reduction. He may be reducing a need who only stands and waits. For some ends it is necessary to have endless patience. The most intense feeling of the good, then, is pleasure. Pleasure usually accompanies the reduction of the primary needs: drinking is a pleasure for a thirsty man, eating for a hungry one, and sexual intercourse for the sex-deprived. The dimensions of pleasure are easy to discern; they are energy-level, duration, intensity, and frequency. Thus far however no method has been found for measuring pleasures.

The opposite of pleasure is pain. Pain is the intense feeling of the bad. Pain is not the absence of pleasure but something positive: a distinctly intense feeling arising within a mechanism reserved for it: its own nerve-endings. Pleasure and pain it must be emphasized, are opposites, not contradictories. Pleasure organizes, pain disorganizes. Pain always indicates a disorder, as pleasure always indicates an order.

Pain may lead the individual to look either inward or outward. When he looks outward, pain may compel him to participate in the struggle between good and bad, to make a decision in favor of the good and to oppose the bad. But more often than not pain is a signal of disorganization and so a looking inward, and when this happens it compels a concentration on the self. Pain initiates an activity on the part of the individual to restore organization. Thus pain calls the individual's attention to the self and this in itself is bad. Subjectivity is bad, objectivity good. For when the individual is well and has no pain he is able to mobilize his entire body toward its proper task of effecting accomplishments in the external world. He can attend to the object, in this way serving society and himself as an indirect object. But when he suffers, the pain forces him to attend to himself and as a consequence he makes of himself the indirect object he cannot afford to be.

It is well-known that pleasure cannot be pursued directly and is therefore not an end. It is too brief by nature, and it results from the pursuit of something else. That something else, as we have already noted, is a need; pleasure always accompanies need-reduction. It is good to reduce a need, and therefore pleasure of this sort is a good. Pleasure is always a good in itself, though what produces pleasure may or may not be. For the good of pleasure can be produced by bad things. Pathological conditions are capable of producing euphoria, which can be the result for instance of the elevation of the circulating adreno-cortical hormone level, but the same conditions can also produce aberrant behavior. A drug which is cumulatively harmful may be temporarily pleasurable such as cigarettes or morphine. Thus pleasure while itself a good is not a reliable guide to the good. Pleasure is a subjective psychological good and therefore not by itself a guide even to what is the good for the individual.

Happiness is the long-lived feeling of good. It has a better record than pleasure, having to do with ends rather than means. From Plato to Aristotle on, men have endorsed happiness rather than pleasure as the proper good for men to pursue. There is a relation of happiness to pleasure, however. Happiness may consist in the affective recognition either that one is having pleasure or that one has foregone pleasure and is perhaps even enduring pain for the sake of some more justifiable pleasure in the future. Happiness is more pervasive than pleasure because it arises from a sense of accomplishment. It is psychologically more inclusive because it reaches outside the individual to his situation and achievements. The reduction of the primary needs is accompanied by pleasure, but it is more likely to be the reduction of the secondary needs which is accompanied by happiness. What the individual has achieved for society, or even beyond society for the whole of humanity, is the source of his happiness. If the end of individual man is the service of society, the successful pursuit of this end is productive of happiness. The individual who successfully pursues information, activity or security, is involved with others engaged in the same pursuit and with them achieves happiness.

Unhappiness is the state of dissatisfaction which arises from the absence of happiness. As its name indicates, it is a contradictory rather than an opposite. It consists in the recognition that there is a cause for dissatisfaction. The good man will ordinarily have more pleasure than pain and more happiness than unhappiness.

The individual's urge to exceed himself is to be found in connection with all of his drives. The effort to attain to need-reduction does not necessarily have to come to an end with the attainment of the goal-object but may continue on. Hence any need may give rise to wildly superfluous activity. It is impossible to foresee all of the consequences of an action. But we do know this much, that it is a waste when an individual works toward conflicting ends, for then all of his efforts are self-defeating. Yet equally important is the need to avoid having aims which fall short of what they should be. However, there is such a thing as blind ungovernable impulse. Chance in cosmic ethics operates in individual ethics as impulsive action.

(b) The individual's pursuit of the good for society is in terms of utilitarianism. The individual usually does not serve society as a whole directly but through the medium of a institution. This is a social organization with a charter, written or unwritten, and a set of artifacts, organized around a central aim which is to furnish some particular kind of good or services to society. Many institutions correspond roughly to the organic individual needs, but only roughly. Thus agriculture corresponds to hunger, the family to sex and reproduction, and (as Hegel said) the state to reason or social order. A school is an institution, and so is a church, a post office, a hospital. The greatest good of the greatest number of individuals is furthered through the work of the institution; therefore its aims for the individual are social goods.

For the individual, then, the pursuit of social good means finding his place in a social institution and working through it for the good of society. Parts are the agents of wholes, and so long as there is a hierarchy of organization it is not possible to skip levels with impunity. Thus the pursuit of the good for society if conducted through the proper channels is next only to the pursuit by an individual of the good for himself.

Freedom in society means that the individual has such freedom of action as does not interfere with the freedom of others. This is the external freedom referred to earlier, and is what is usually meant by freedom. The individual thinks and feels that he is not bound in his actions except by those circumstances which are imposed by society in an effort to secure the maximum of freedom for all of its individual members. He is free to avoid the strictures of a society not run for the benefit of the greatest number of its citizens. A tyranny or an oligarchy, for instance, may be resisted by the individual in his pursuit of his own freedom as a good. For freedom issues socially from some accepted set of morals and the consequent rights and duties it entails. Freedom in society, then, consists in the greatest latitude of liberty which is consistent with a workable society.

(c) The pursuit of the good for humanity is for the individual a matter of achievement of the general kind which transcends cultural boundaries and local times and places. To discover a truth, to invent a technology, to produce a work of art; these are of the order of service to humanity. Mathematics, the wheel, animal husbandry, the works of Homer, Plato and Shakespeare, are examples of goods which certain individuals have contributed to humanity. Such productive achievements are the work of genius. Here, as Bergson has so well pointed out, the individual is able to step outside the closed moral obligations of society to make his contribution to the open moral aspirations of humanity.[1] In this sense, he says, the genius does not come to humanity through the stages of local organization but in a single leap.[2]

Freud inadvertently misled many by loosely assuming that the subnormal and the supernormal were both abnormal. And so they are; and society is unhappy with both. But their failure respecting society is for very different reasons. For the subnormal individual is unable to meet the demands of society, while the supernormal, the genius, is endeavoring to transcend society in order to meet the demands of humanity.

It should be remembered, though, that the genius is when he works an individual living in a society and somehow using it as a stepping-stone. His society maintains him however gladly or reluctantly and whether it rewards him richly or punishes him for his efforts. If he makes the leap to the service of the whole human species, it is as a soli-

---

[1] *The Two Sources of Morality and Religion*, R. A. Audra and C. Brereton trans. (New York 1935, Holt), pp. 12–37.
[2] *Ibid.*, p. 25.

tary genius and in a sense by standing on the shoulders of his society.

Ethical freedom is man's most valuable possession for it enables him to broaden the basis upon which he makes his moral decisions up to the limits of his capacity. The more he can feel the more he can know about. The more he knows about the more he can care about. And the more he cares about the more he can include in his ground for decisions. In this way the experimental sciences become high roads to an extended morality. We live the life of all humanity when we live life at its best, and we include among those to whom we are obliged for our position all those many who are absent as well as those few who are present.

(d) The pursuit of the good for the universe, how shall a man pursue it? That the universe is good in itself is something the individual feels and perhaps only more dimly understands. It compels him to the acknowledgment through religion and through astronomy. But how to serve it is another matter, and over this men have differed greatly and fought bitter battles, thus contravening the very good they wished to serve. All that is, is real, and all that is real is good. Yet what action is called out from the parts for that whole in which all parts and other wholes are parts lies beyond present comprehension.

All the same there is a sense in which the individual is not merely a part of society, or humanity, or of anything less than the cosmos. In this connection, paradoxically enough, the original ground of his absolute individuality is restored to him. The lesser connections have to do with existence; this connection has to do also with pre-existence and post-existence, and hence with the absolutely autonomous being of the individual as such. Thus the individual finds himself again, and a richer self, in the pursuit of the cosmic good. He has come full circle with his addition-groups of belonging. It is the individual as participating directly in the entire universe, an infinitesimal part but an authentic part, which he recognizes in his most cosmic speculations and yearnings. *Weltanschauungen*, home-longings for the world which find that world ultimately good and nothing less, is what a man can be at home with when he is most absolutely and entirely himself. The whole universe is the native home of entire man.

One thing appears certain, however, and that is the unity of the good at all levels. The quality of the good the individual feels when he is pursuing the good for himself may not be as much of the good as society contains, or humanity, or the cosmos, but it is equally good. For the good is a quality, and a small amount of quality is as much quality *qua* quality as a greater quality. There is in effect only one good but there are many levels of organization for dealing with it.

(c) Bad Behavior

When the individual acts to reduce his needs he does so in terms of the good for himself. This follows from the definition of the good as what is needed. Need-reduction is good and it is in most cases accompanied by pleasure. Thus behavior as such is good in itself. However, the needs are organ-specific, and what is good for a single organ may not be good for the whole organism. The urge of the individual to exceed himself is an extension of particular features of organs as the ends of the whole organism, often to its detriment. Thus drinking water is a good and not only for the kidneys but for the entire man, but pathological water-drinking is a well-known deviation and it is harmful. On the other hand, men die quickly of thirst. Thus behavior which is good for the individual in moderation may be bad for him in excess or defect. Aristotle's counsel of virtue in moderation applies to the primary needs though not to the secondary. Is it possible for instance to have too much knowledge or too much security?

Again, there is the good for society to be considered. What is good for the individual may be bad for society. A loaf of bread is good for the individual but bad for society if he steals it. The love of a woman is good for a man but bad for society if the woman is another man's wife. Only too often goods conflict, and the individual is compelled to a choice. As we have noted already, if he chooses the lesser over the greater good his behavior is bad; but it is not always easy to make the correct choice and so bad behavior is a common feature of human life. Finally (and alas most familiarly), societies conflict; and since societies consist in (among other things) human individuals, the human individuals get caught up in the struggle between conflicting societies and so once again involved with the bad. If construction is good and destruction bad, then wars are bad, and in wars between nations it is the individuals who do the fighting.

In this part of the book our chief concern is with individual behavior and I have only wanted to point out that the separation between the individual and the social is not always easy, and that much of what is bad as well as of what is good about the behavior of the individual is socially conditioned. With this preliminary extension behind us, let us fall back upon the examination of bad behavior as it is practiced by the individual.

I define bad behavior as action in conformity with the choice of the lesser over the greater good. The corruption of confrontation would mean in action, "Conduct toward all others, in consideration of oneself alone." In bad behavior there is a lack of the "consideration of all others" in the conduct toward confronted objects. Only human individuals seem capable of such a choice and its consequent action. All other organisms and objects are capable only of occasioning bad through accident. Extremely bad behavior is called evil, and so is the intrinsic quality of such behavior. Evil is the result of the individual's own limitations, his internal weakness making it difficult for him to live up to his own moral ideals. There is evil inherent in the shortcomings of the individual, his peculiar faults, which differ from individual to individual but of which all individuals are possessed to some extent. This is what Leibniz called "moral evil" and which George Meredith referred to in *Modern Love*, when he wrote

"We are betrayed by what is false within."

Evil is the qualitative correlate of the destructive effects of bad behavior. There is a quality of evil, and in this sense it is positive. Everyone has experienced it who has experienced the destruction of something valuable, say the infliction of pain. By the terms "good and evil" is usually meant the extremes of such acts and qualities.

How does bad behavior arise? To answer this question it will be necessary to return to the organic needs and consider them as a whole set. In order to reduce his needs, the individual must act in ways affecting other things. Need-reduction necessarily involves the alteration of objects, often even the extreme alteration which consists in their destruction. Goal-objects promising need-reduction are to be found in the immediate environment. In order to insure need-reduction, a certain amount of aggression on the part of the individual is necessary.

Aggression is the drive to dominate the environment. In the developing individual the drive is to make the environment over in terms of his own need-reduction. Given his urge to exceed himself, aggression has no limits. In the individual's efforts to insure complete need-reduction he endeavors to make the environment a part of himself. This is the form of ego-expansion. It means that the individual tends to like what is similar and to dislike what is different; to be attracted to what is promising of need-reduction and to dislike what is not. Since there is more in the world of what is different than there is of what is similar, his characteristic attitude will be one of dislike, antagonism, and destruction, rather than of like, sympathy, and construction. Bad behavior will be more common than good behavior.

I have discussed the good and bad behavior of the individual in terms of the individuals partly constituting a society. But there is good and bad behavior also in terms of the established morality. Good behavior in this connection is behavior in conformity with the existing morality. Bad behavior is behavior in which there is a failure to conform. Such a failure could mean for the individual a violation of his conscience and for society a violation of existing customs, laws or statutes.

Bad behavior could result from the inability to conform or the unwillingness to conform. The inability to conform would be the behavior of the subnormal individual. It could be a matter of ignorance or false knowledge, or a lack of will or character. Or it could be pathological: the decision of the psychotic or the habitual criminal not to conform.

The bad behavior which consists in the unwillingness to conform could be the behavior also of the supernormal rather than the subnormal, of the genius. The "bad" behavior of the genius in his unwillingness to conform might issue from a desire for individual improvement: merely the result of a decision not to conform but to follow instead a private morality deemed superior; or it could be because of a disagreement with, and a lack of acceptance of, the existing morality, and might represent a desire to work for social improvement.

In the case either of a public morality or a private morality, bad behavior might be the result of promoting an inadequate order as though it were an adequate order, and in this way of occasioning disorder. Good behavior depends upon finding the natural order under the circumstances. Bad behavior is disorder operating.

Bad behavior can be depended upon to continue to be mixed with the good so long as the individual's behavior is not entirely consistent. So long as the individual conscience contains mixed elements of the public and private retention schemata and so long as these overlap but may in part conflict, there will be no total consistency. Abstractly, consistency is good and inconsistency is bad, since the sole essential property of logical systems is their consistency. But if individual behavior could be consistent it could be consistently bad as well as consistently good. And so the saving factor is that the behavior of the individual is not entirely consistent. This may be a bad feature of predominantly good behavior but it is a good feature of predominantly bad behavior. For as it happens the corruption of the worst is the best. As the poet, Louis Gilmore, has it

> For Tannhauser
> The path to Heaven
> Lay through the Venusberg
>
> And Dante first saw Hell
> Before the sublime ascent.[1]

Inconsistency can take many value forms, and when it does there is an alternation of opposites in behavior. Human motivation is deeply ambivalent. The same individual is capable of acting both from pride and humility in turn. The need for aggression may issue from egotism or altruism. This may occur at different times in the same individual, as when for instance Andrew Carnegie amassed a huge fortune and then gave it away. Aggression may be destructive and constructive, it may lead to competition and cooperation. Love and hate always lie very close together; *odi et amo*, or, in the poignant phrase of Baudelaire *Hypocrite lecture, mon semblable, mon frere.*

Consistency is a virtue; yet men take so many wrong courses of action that it is fortunate they are not always consistent. Inconsistency becomes in this connection a safeguard against inevitably bad consequences when there have been equally bad decisions concerning what ought to be done. We have noted one example of this when we were discussing the class of moral decisions which are made on the basis of reasoning alone. An individual bent on destructiveness may accomplish some inadvertent good, as Alexander the Great did when he insured the survival of Greek culture by spreading it throughout the Middle East, and as Napoleon did by bringing an end to the feudal order and so making way for popular sovereignty and hence democracy.

What guide do we have to the choice of axioms from which we deduce those theorems we intend to apply? Only induction, intuition, insight. But this process (for it is all one) whose mechanism is thus far concealed from us can so easily go astray that if we were entirely consistent in deducing the proper consequences and putting them into practice much harm might be done to ourselves and others. Instead of this we have the protection which issues from our inconsistency: even though it prevents us from achieving perfection it also prevents us from

[1] *Vine Leaves and Flowers of Evil* (New Orleans 1959, Pelican Press), p. 5.

precipitating total disaster. Reason is supreme and must remain so; but it lies all the same entirely at the mercy of the axioms from which it operates, and we have no sure method of arriving at the correct ones.

We can be certain, then, that there will always be a reducible but finally ineradicable element of the bad in human life. A minimum amount of disorder is the price which has to be paid for not courting absolute catastrophe by acting in absolute consistency with axioms which may be false. In some ways chance is our only hope. We all work on the basis of the marginal departures from the type we know ourselves to be. We can hope to do better only because we know that types are statistically true and not absolutely true, and that chance makes up the difference. How else provide that freshness of novelty and that breath of life which comes from acting from impulse and from sometimes circumventing principles?

The good and bad behavior of the individual is concerned first with himself, next with the other members of his society, and lastly with artifacts. Morality is not often or usually (if ever) thought of in terms of inanimate and merely material objects, but that could be an over-sight. I will try to show in later parts of this book that everything in existence has its appropriate morality. Men tend to think of morality in terms of themselves for egocentric reasons which however under-standable are also crippling. For if everything that exists has its morali-ty, then artifacts have their morality. And there is another and perhaps more compelling reason for thinking of the morality of artifacts. As we have noted in an earlier chapter artifacts are integral parts of society. The individual communicates with his fellows and otherwise interacts with them chiefly by means of artifacts. Thus the proper use of artifacts is an element in the proper moral interactions with his fellows.

What, then, is the morality of artifacts? What does good and bad behavior of the individual mean in terms of artifacts? For just as we have seen that good behavior toward artifacts means using them for what they *were* designed, so bad behavior toward artifacts means using them for what they were *not* designed. In the former case, the artifacts will wear out eventually but not before they have been made to perform their function. In the latter case, the artifacts will be ruined and unable to be made to perform their function. Using a Stradivarius violin in a Beethoven concerto is an instance of good behavior toward the violin, but using it as a weapon is bad behavior. However, the substitution of the lesser for the greater good often in such cases depends upon circumstance. Using the violin say as a weapon to repel an intruder in a child's bedroom is good behavior; burning a chair in a fireplace for a man who is more desperately cold than weary is good behavoir. Sitting on an antique chair is good behavior toward the chair, but breaking it up for firewood is bad behavior. Respect for materials and for the objects which have been fashioned out of them is, all other things being equal, good behavior.

(d) The Incompleteness of Individual Goods

Almost everything we have discussed in this part of the book points to two apparently conflicting propositions. The first is that there is an authentic level of ethics at which the individual is autonomous. The second is that the individual is not an absolutely valid ethical isolate.

We have been cutting the integrative levels high in the scale when we chose to begin our analysis of ethics with the human individual. There are many levels below the level of the individual, levels of organs, of cells, of molecules, of atoms and of atomic constituents. Each is fixed in the series and each can claim its own autonomy. Thus when we argue for the authenticity of the individual we are claiming no more than that the level of the individual is an autonomous level. The individual is an organization, having an obligation to maintain himself. He is justified in this sense in pursuing the goods that he needs. Both himself and his needs are empiric facts, requiring no further measure of justification. If whatever is, is good, then the individual is good because he is an individual.

It is the second proposition which requires the greatest explication and which has been given it by points made in passages scattered throughout the entire part with which we have just been dealing. It might be well if we reminded ourselves of what these points are, bringing them together with a special emphasis and for greater effect.

The good is what is needed, and man, it must be recalled, is an animal with a great many animal needs. Other needs he has which are extensions or transformations of the animal needs. For all of them he must go outside his own body to accomplish need-reductions. What he needs is good for him but must be obtained from the world. He is in a constant state of interchange with it, and is in no wise independent of it. The good, then, involves connections and in order to establish them the individual is always in the position of reaching beyond himself.

In so doing, however, he is by his nature condemned to the committing of hubris. In the search for the good of ultimate security, his activities proliferate into what I have called excessive behavior, his drives to obtain need-reductions are in excess of any possible consumption. But excessive behavior on the part of many individuals would defeat the need-reduction of each of them, for the individuals themselves would come into conflict. What Hobbes called the war of all against all can be curbed only by means of social compacts. What Nietzsche called "self-overcoming" is what enables the individual to obey self-imposed commands and so to become a member of society. But social compacts lie outside the individual, and a society is necessary if individual life is to be possible. In this sense again the individual together with his goods is not a valid isolate.

The clearest evidence for the position we are maintaining is the social aspect of the individual himself. There lies within the individual that component of beliefs which is social and which I have named the public retention schema. These are distinguishable from individual beliefs, from the private retention schema. But where there are social elements such as this there can hardly be said to be an individual who is a valid isolate. The individual has thoughts, feelings and actions which may and often do conflict with the code adopted by his society. He may be immoral so far as concerns everyone but himself and yet be moral so far as concerns himself, and even so far as concerns considerations beyond his society.

The society determines what is good for the individual and enforces it as what is right. That the individual recognizes this state of affairs and accedes to it is attested by the existence within him of what has been long recognized as the conscience. Once again, morality is social, and if it is social then it cannot be altogether individual. The individual cannot live without morality of some sort and be an individual in the human sense, and so he must be to some extent at least social. He is not then a valid ethical isolate.

When the individual acts it is in terms of his needs functioning as motives. He has reasons now for going out into the world and endeavoring to change things so that they may the better serve him. He recognizes his own severe limitations in the similarity of others of his same type. Individuals are attracted to others in whom they recognize something of themselves. But those others are separate and they dramatize for him the extent of the world beyond him in which his species operates. Confrontation extracts from him a behavior in terms not of some others toward whom he is reacting but of all others to whom he is responsible. He is not alone nor a valid moral isolate.

Individual ethical norms consist in the best adjustment of the drives under the circumstances, but the circumstances themselves consist in the norms of society, so that given the usual conditions: cooperation with the in-group and antagonism to the out-group, individual norms tend to be partially (though not totally) determined by the norms of the society. Individual approval or disapproval, admiration or repugnance, is a matter of conscience, on the side of the public retention schema. In other words, morality remains personal to the extent, and only to the extent, that it does not have to be social. The evidence for this last statement is the phenomenon of altruism, which rests on the fact that the individual "needs" for there to be such a thing as a society with its established rules of need-reduction, its facilities for obtaining such reduction, and its stability, in order that he may be a member of it. Altruism has deep egoistic roots.

Thus the individual comes to know himself as both separate from society and obligated to it, and his society as a thing apart from him in which he can have certain privileges. Thus the very existence of an egoistic perspective underscores his dependence upon society. If he have the character to carry out his chosen program, and the will to act or refrain from acting when the program calls for it, then his very feelings, exhibited in his disposition toward the good, must remind him that he is part of a larger whole and not himself an independent whole, not a valid isolate.

The making of decisions, the execution of judgments, resulting in that kind of measured action which we call conduct, are based upon the existence of individual goods and also upon the good of existence itself. Since existence itself is a good, the things in the world which are goods are good by the very fact that they exist. The individual in pursuing them, although he does so for himself, cannot fail to recognize in them, in his pursuit of them, and finally in himself, elements of the world which are irrefrangibly bound together. That he is not a valid isolate he now sees but he does not regret it, for in sharing the goods of the world he is involved in a wider good than he would be if he were to be isolated at his own autonomous level.

We conclude then from the evidence that we are entitled to speak both of the ethics of the individual and of the incompleteness of individual goods. How is this conflict to be resolved? Before that question can be answered, we shall have to enter upon an examination of the entire commitment of the individual as well as upon the ethical nature of the world in which he is involved. He is involved with more than himself, with more than society, with more than his species, for that matter, with nothing less than the entire universe. But the next level of organization after the individual is the social. Of the ethical integrative series, the social level is in many ways the most exigent if not the most important. And so we must turn to it now.

PART III

THE ETHICS OF SOCIETY

CHAPTER I

MORALITY AS SOCIAL STRUCTURE

(a) Width and Constituents

We are ready to talk about social ethics, but first, a few definitions are in order. I define society as that social organization within a culture whose boundaries are recognized. I define culture as the works of man and their effects (including of course their effects on man). Thus "France" is a society within the culture of European, or "western" civilization. The elements of culture are loosely agglomerated elements swimming in a medium of less agglomerated similar elements. Societies are more organized; they may be equal in extent with a culture or contained within it as one member of a set. But a society is at best a partially-ordered system in which a definite structure has been put together from indefinite components.

In modern thought ethics is conventionally considered as equivalent to individual ethics. See for instance Sidgwick.[1] However, every individual lives within and is a member of a society. The aim of the individual is two-fold. His primary aim is the service of society. His secondary aim is to derive such satisfactions for himself as are not inconsistent with the primary aim. In moral terms, however, he does not deal directly with the society but with it through a common humanity which he holds with its other members. Humanity, in other words, is interposed between the individual and his society.

Just as there was for the individual the social view of himself and his view of society, so there is for the society the individual view of society and a quondam view which we can suppose society takes of itself. The individual view of society is the intrinsic view of society, and the social view of society is the extrinsic view. As we shall note, different aspects arise from considering what is available to these two different perspectives.

First, then, the individual view.

Social ethics may be defined intrinsically as the quality of the internal relations of a society. The social good is the dominant inner quality which emerges from the integrity of organization of a society.

---

[1] *Methods of Ethics* (Chicago 1962, University Press), Book III, Ch. V, p. 266.

It has a name, even though this has been used infrequently: the ethos. Many a visitor or stranger to a society has noted its peculiar atmosphere or pervasive affective influence.

The posture of the individual subjects him to it, generally without his knowledge. It is partly because of the power and prevalence of the ethos that the conduct of one individual toward another is never simply between them but is conditioned by all other members of the society. It should be possible now to state the principle of type responsibility as it applies to the short-range self in relation to society. *All individuals are attracted to all other individuals in a given society in virtue of a commom dependence upon that society.* This is type responsibility at the social level. Confrontation at the social level does not require of the individual that he consider anything beyond his society but it compels him to take into consideration all members of the society when dealing with any member. Thus there seems to be operating here a kind of theory of moral types, derived from the moral integrative levels, according to which confrontation is always one level higher in the series of levels than the individual confronted.

Thus we have *conduct toward an individual, in consideration of the society.* For more primitive societies it is possible of course to amend this to read "in consideration of all other members of the family (gens, clan)." In this way the bond between individuals, which always exists by embracing more than they do, constructs a community relation and community values, and accounts for the solidity of a society.

So much for the individual view; now the social view.

Social ethics may be defined extrinsically as the sum of the effects which a given cohesive group of persons and material things exerts upon the conduct of the individual. The aim of society is two-fold. Its primary aim is to contribute to the whole of which it is a part, in a word, to humanity. Its secondary aim is to enable its individual members to assist in its primary aim. Thus the secondary aim is to contribute, at least in part, to the welfare of human individuals. This it does through the establishment of rules of order, and through the enforcement of order, in so far as that order and those rules and their enforcement is consistent with the maximum amount of individual freedom possible. By behaving morally toward other individuals the individual himself helps to construct a society. Thus within the society there arises a morality, after which its members expect others entering into it to behave in the established way. The social good is inherent in the advantages which the society bestows upon each of its individual members. Social (or cultural) evil is inherent in the limitations imposed by the society in which he lives and of which he is a part in so far as he endeavors to transgress them. When the behavior of free individuals conforms to a pattern we know we are in the presence of cultural influences. There could be no cultural influences without a culture to exert them. The normative values of a society are the result of the cultural stamp which individuals willing and eagerly impose upon themselves because they identify it with the natural, the good and the right. The prospects of a moral life for the individual presuppose a society within which and by which such aims can be fulfilled.

The society with which the individual within it reacts is in the main inherited and thus exerts a formative influence upon him. He is molded by its peculiar structure, its productive forces and its unique properties. Only through a special effort, the possession of special talents and the exertion of an extra effort is it possible for a man to influence his society more than he is influenced by it, and this is the role chiefly of the originative genius.

One of the important problems in the social theory of ethics issues from the fact that there may be as many ethical theories as there are human societies. Does one ethical theory apply uniquely to every society or does each society in its differences require its own? Everything depends of course upon the extent of the society. And this question can be pushed back to two other questions: how wide does the society understands itself to be and how far do its communications extend? If the cosmological principle is to be accepted, then what is true of types is true for them throughout the whole of space. A society (it must be at least theoretically allowed) extends to others identical with it elsewhere in the cosmos. Locally, such relations may be safely ignored. There is always the local community but there is also that wider social organization of all living humanity with which at times societies have tended to identify themselves. Extreme examples are, on the one hand, those primitive societies which regard only themselves as people and consider all other people to be subhuman higher animals, and on the other hand, the western society which threatens currently to engulf all other societies. The current understanding of a society considers that it extends as far as its language reaches. It is tempting to add: as far as its tools are used as well.

The size of a society is then an elastic and vague affair of diminishing boundaries. But the constitution of a society is somewhat more definite. Here too however, a revision in the traditional conceptions is called for. The society to which the individual belongs is not merely the sum total of its individual members. It is that too, but there are other and equally essential elements. For men working together have constructed an artificial environment in the midst of the available environment. In his daily life the individual encounters other individuals and artifacts almost more than he does the non-human portion of the available environment. The artificial environment is composed entirely of artifacts.

Individuals within a society agree to use the same kinds of artifacts; indeed the boundaries of communication define the social boundaries and communication is chiefly by language but may be also by tools. Individuals rarely deal with each other directly but usually indirectly by means of artifacts. They speak to each other or they act toward each other in terms of conventions established by institutions and usually amploying the tools appropriate to that institution. Professional vocabularies color the language, and the adroit use of tools condition the interchanges.

The social term for artifacts is property. I am not using the term, property, here in the narrow sense of possession by an individual group, but of something belonging ultimately to the whole society. This would not exclude private property and would apply to the capitalist system as much as to the socialist. It is the moral aspect I want, and that is society-wide. Property may be defined as artifacts considered from the side of their social use. This may be individual, as with the individual possession of property, or it may be social, as with the Ashanti of West Africa for whom all land belonged to the ancestors via the matrilineal *abusua* clan; and while a living Ashanti may occupy a portion of it for life, he may not own it. But in the individual case it is social too though in another sense; for it is society which is responsible for safeguarding individual rights.

Property is the sense of society. Along with it go laws, sentiments, observances. There is a good and a bad way to use property. It may be used for society, in which case it is good; or it may be used against society, in which case it is bad. Plato spoke of it as the third good, after the goods of the soul (the Ideas) and the goods of the body.[1] Some of it is unconditionally free, as with the usual use of language, though not always; for there have been arcane languages, usually religious, which are reserved to those responsible for the society (priests, governors, etc.). Thus the laws of a society are its property as well as

[1] Laws, III, 697B.

its languages and other tools, just as much as the more conventionally regarded land and buildings. It is a common mistake to think of society as consisting merely of collections of individuals, for social properties furnish the necessary connecting links between individuals who otherwise would have no way of getting together.

All forms taken by a morality within a society change, but the morality is to some extent fixed. Indeed it is only in terms of a fixed element that change can occur at all. If everything within a society changed completely we should have to talk about rates of change, and it is the limitation of the classic Greeks that they failed to recognize this kind of stability. But as to the morality of a society, to some extent it is fixed and to some extent it changes. Both aspects are recognized and established under the form of established law.

Morality is the answer to the requirement that there be some principle of order which is society-wide. Societies are autonomous moral communities. I am not concerned here to trace the origins of social morality but only to determine its nature and function. My interest is ethical rather than sociological, and so I am concerned to show how conduct is ordered, not how it began. It is ordered by morality. For it is morality which governs the behavior of the individual members of a society to the end that they shall best function and survive.

We have noted before that the principle of moral order is a qualitative affair, that the good in this sense is completeness as the beautiful is consistency, and therefore the good is what brings wholes together. The society to which the individual belongs is a loosely organized affair, a partially ordered system in which he participates as one of the parts, only to a limited extent at his own disposition and largely at the disposition of others. But society itself can exist only on the basis of a socially established ethics, a concrete morality. There can be a society only if there is a morality. A moral structure to which all individuals must subscribe is necessary if all men are to control and order their drives. It now becomes necessary to limit the activity of the individual in any direction in which if he is not limited he may interfere with the free activities of his fellows. The hedonist must be somewhat constrained. Thus there are social limitations to individual activity though no individual limitations except the necessity for giving an order of precedence to the drives. Thus culture is possible only where there is moral order. This much Nietzsche certainly understood, even though he missed the role of artifacts.

Morality is established to preserve the community, it is reinforced through continuity until it gradually takes on the additional authority of custom and tradition and acquires sanctions, including social laws and the individual consciences. Ethics in this sense is *sui generis*. Every society has a morality, which can be the morality of every one of its institutions, but it is especially that of the leading institution. Thus in the Middle Ages in Europe the morality was that of the church supplemented by that of the nobility. What the individual can do is everywhere the same but what he should do is not. Thus there are local social and cultural determinations. Order is good, disorder bad. When there is congruence between individuals and between individuals and social groups and between social groups within a society, order is preserved; but when there is collision, order is threatened. The society therefore develops special institutions and instruments for dealing with such threats.

There are evidently no men without societies and no societies without moral orders of some sort. Therefore moral orders as much as men or societies are natural objects. What is called conventional is a subdivision of the natural just as much as what is human is. A morality is necessary because it provides the maximum degree of organization for a society, thus promoting the greatest amount of facilitation to individual behavior.

In trying to describe the stability of establishment I hope that I have not made morality sound too rigid. It is rigid to the extent that it holds, and in most cases it holds firmly, but there is also a plasticity about it which permits it to change. For change it most certainly does. There is nothing static about social morality any more than there is about anything else actual. Under the wear and tear of continued use, the morality of a society becomes eroded and changes, sometimes slowly, sometimes quickly. It has been shown by the philosophers of history, men like Ibn Khaldun, Vico, Danilevsky, Spengler and Toynbee, that societies are born, they grow and flourish, and then they die. Moral judgments rest on what is believed and practiced about the good and the right, but what is believed and practiced changes as the society grows or ages, and so moral judgments change accordingly. Nothing arbitrary is involved however. What is, is while it is; and when it changes it changes from what it then was to what it will become.

These are all in a sense absolute conditions; for while they exist, and to the extent to which they exist, they are fixed and authentic. And both moral beliefs and moral practices change in proportion;

and the relations between what is established as true about the good, and what is done to promote the good, remain the same.

The established morality of a society, then, is not an arbitrary affair, the result of some whim or question of taste. It is rather an empirical affair and could not have been other than it is given the set of determinants which were responsible for it. Starting with a social ordering of the organic needs, the morality is based upon how the majority thinks it can best cooperate with a view to achieving need-reduction. Thus rules and aims are interwoven, and this is Hobbes' social compact. But at the same time it is always made concrete in terms of drives which operate and by methods which are locally effective. Thus the laws of a society are designed to insure its own survival, but at the same time they make it dependent upon local circumstances. The society has an indigenous territory.

The governing moral force in a society is not love but determinism. Social cooperation issues from necessity: that individuals can accomplish more for themselves through a common enterprise than separately, is the source of social structure. If every individual bears in mind the need to further the interests of society and pursues this end unilaterally, society and consequently himself and his own selfish interests will benefit. Altruism is the principle that the individual recognizes the greater efficiency of voluntary over compulsory cooperation.

Good and bad are determined by reference to the morality of the society. True or false is relative to it, and the relevant "ought" is based on it. For statements are judged in terms of what its individuals believe in common, and actions are approved insofar as they are permitted. The social morality is employed as a concrete ideal.

Truth is culture-wide but it is also culture-bound. It relies upon the correspondence with the relevant elements in any given society. The moral code is often retained after it ceases to provide the most effective ways of behaving, because tradition proves such strong reinforcement. In time it turns out that what conforms to custom is good, what works against it is bad. Every society has had its moral code but not every society has speculated about ethics. In order to do this it is necessary to imagine how things could be other than they are. Social morality is falsifiable and thus the concept of truth is applicable. True moral action means action by any individual or group which corresponds to (or is allowed by) the relevant established morality (written or unwritten, codified or uncodified, legal or customary). False moral action means action by any individual or group which does not correspond to (or is not allowed by) the relevant established morality. Thus the good is also the true, and the bad is also the false. And the true is also the good and the false is also the bad. It depends upon which side of the same coin is being regarded or featured by the context, for instance whether it is one of judgment or of evaluation.

It is important to draw a distinction between the various divisions of the environment from a given society's point of view. There is the total environment, which consists in the rest of the universe; there is the available environment, that portion of the total environment with which it is possible for a society to interact; and there is the immediate environment, that portion of the nearby environment of a society with which it interacts. The results of such interactions are the artifacts, those material tools and languages which make social life possible and which therefore may be included among the elements essential to society. To be moral, which is to say, to exist as a society, such external goods are needed, "for it is impossible, or not easy, to do noble acts without the proper equipment."[1]

Is there a natural moral code for every society given its immediate environment and its population? It would seem so. A morality is an arrangement to provide the greatest amount of freedom possible in a society given the conditions of its immediate environment and the beliefs and customs of the people who came to inhabit it.

We are confronted here with the theory of ethical social relativity as advocated for instance by the French sociologists, Emile Durkheim and Lucien Levy-Bruhl. It has long been recognized that what is approved in one society may be condemned in another; suicide, for example, or homosexuality. But as Edel points out, there are more moral codes than there are ethical theories.[2] Ethical relativists who differ as to what constitutes the good may find common ground and a *modus vivendi* in recognizing its source as contained in the bonds between the needs of social groups and what is contained, and available for need-reductions, in their immediate environment. Relativism in ethics is not a negative creed, not simply a denial of absolutism, but a recognition of the necessity for adapting morality to local conditions. Absolutism in ethics could mean that one social ethics is right and all others wrong, that there is a common ground among social moralities, or that there are levels of consideration in which viable distinctions are validly applicable. The latter two are compatible with relativistic approaches.

---

[1] Aristotle, *Nicho. Eth.*, 1099a31. See also 1101a15.
[2] Abraham Edel, *Method in Ethical Theory* (Indianapolis 1963, Bobbs-Merrill), p. 215.

The conditions of the immediate environment must be understood to contain elements from every integrative level. For instance, the physical conditions (a cold or a hot climate, plains or mountains); the biological conditions (good farming, grazing or hunting country); the cultural conditions (other societies, hostile or friendly).

Societies, like individuals, react with their environment and interchange elements with it. No wonder that the state of the society is to some extent dependent upon the character of its environment. There is more to it than that, of course; for the environment is part of a wider nature and infinitely more abundant and complex than any of the limited demands made upon it by the finite requirements of a society. The environment determines to some extent what interactions shall take place because of its more prominent features, but the society inherits peculiarities from the interchanges which took place earlier in its history and which now determine the interaction from its side. We must now look briefly at some of these.

The beliefs of the people who came to inhabit the immediate environment in question contain as a foundation layer convictions concerning the nature of reality. These (although no one except professional philosophers would call them so) are metaphysical beliefs. Upon them the customs rest. For instance, the actions of those like the classic Greeks who accepted the primary reality of this world would be different from the actions of those like the ancient Egyptians who subscribed to the primary reality of the next world.

The situation is considerably more complicated than I have been making it appear. For some of the beliefs are traditional, but the conditions of the environment of the society also have something to do with the beliefs of the members of the society. For instance, a Puritan society in the tropics is unthinkable. The conditions and customs as well as the beliefs of the individual members of the society also influence it; for instance monogamy would be unworkable in a society which regularly produced more girls than boys or which because of its warlike customs repeatedly killed off a large proportion of its young men. The individuals in a society uniformly face the world from the perspective of the unified beliefs which comprise the retention schemata, made up of the diverse elements which enter it from tradition and the new challenges of the immediate environment, and it is this unity which is so deceptive as to the origins of its components.

(b) Needs and Norms

The validity of moral principles is to be found in the workability of the societies in which they appear. A good test for a moral principle is whether its opposite is unworkable. Insofar as a society exists at all, it is good. Insofar as any individual members tend to subvert it in their own selfish interests, it is bad. Thus the essence of social morality is contained in social organization. Some kind of organization is a social need.

The customs of the society are sufficient for the grounding of the social "ought." What is held to be good for a society is what that society endorses, and the endorsement is accomplished by the establishment of norms. This can be done formally or informally or by a mixture of the two. A good individual is a member of the society whose behavior conforms to the norms established by the society. Social evil is the result of the inability of an individual to live up to the moral code of his society, either through excess or deficiency. Competition is made acceptable by the establishment of rules whereby it is permitted to harm or take advantage of rivals within the society. Society itself rests on the practical exigency that the individual has more to lose than to gain by allowing his aggression to be restricted by the rules governing competition in favor of some kind of cooperation. Henceforth he agrees to abide by the rules for both competition and cooperation. He agrees because in most cases he cannot get around them; though certainly the only principle upon which all men can be got to agree is the hatred of compromise: each side wants all the advantage whatever the issue.

There are two kinds of intangibles: those which do and those which do not recurrently affect the tangible. The effect of morality upon a society is chiefly negative; it works effectively to make the society possible only by not working—and thus making the society impossible—when there are too many infractions. The morally bad is that which tends to reduce or cancel the effectiveness of a code of morality in its operation in a society.

Morality is in effect the workability of a society, established on the assumption that its opposite would be unworkable. Thus it is a short distance from the quality of the good to the relatedness of the useful. I hope to show that the good and the useful are two sides of the same entity; the good being its quality and the use being its relations. We have already noted that the justification for the morality of a society is the conflicting drives of individuals to reduce their needs and the necessity for some degree of cooperation in need-reduction. Morality exists in order to pursue goods by regulating competition and organizing cooperation in individual need-reduction.

A moral code exists, then, in the socially established ground-rules for individual need-reduction. It is established on the covertly assumed grounds that its opposite, or any other alternative, would not prove as efficient. (By "efficient" is meant "more permissive than restrictive" in terms of the chosen objectives of the reduction of human needs.) But there is a concealed difficulty here. Most moral codes are established in the expectation that the future will resemble the past. And it may; but also, of course, it may not. The need for novelty translated into moral behavior is capable of wrecking any moral code. If innovation is a necessity or even if it occurs by chance then the demands of tradition at once present themselves as immoral.

Workability as a criterion has been officially endorsed under the name of pragmatism. But there are several kinds of pragmatism. There is the pragmatism of Peirce, according to whom workability is a derivate from truth, and there is the pragmatism of James, according to whom truth is a derivate from workability. James said, what works is true; but Peirce (from whom he learned his theory) had said that what is true is bound to work in the long run. Jamesian pragmatism leads to moral chaos, from which James himself saw he would have to take "a moral holiday." Almost any kind of expeditious behavior, however selfish, however destructive, may work for a while. Peirceian pragmatism requires first the discovery of truth. For James workability is its own end, its own moral justification. For Peirce, there is another kind. The workability of social ethics as here defined has for its end not mere survival but survival making possible extension and improvement. Workability is designed to make possible the approach to an ideal society, for beyond workability lies the conception of the real.

The morality of a society is an immediately apprehensible structure of qualitatively-presented norms. The intangible and the pervasive is often the most forceful. Every established social morality has its practices, and these stem from its norms. The practices are approximations in action of the feeling of norms. Insofar as the empirical moral situation was formally established (and some are) it was aimed at a norm; the "is" is the imperfect result of the aim at an "ought." That one falls short of the other does not make any real distinction between them. In the case of deliberate activities, such as for instance the formal establishment here under discussion, no "ought," then no "is."

Thus the distinction between the normative and the empirical breaks down again, this time in connection with social morality. The aggregate of the norms of existing societies, together with those of societies which have existed and those which will exist, constitutes the empirical field of ethics.

The stability of the establishment of a social morality is furnished to it by the metaphysical theory of reality which supports it from its position in the beliefs of the individuals of the society. In this sense an ethics is an applied metaphysics and a morality is an applied ethics and behavior is an applied morality. Morality is firmly suspended by a tension which exists between the metaphysical theory which is more general than the morality and the experience of individual members which is more particular. The tighter the lines are drawn between very general metaphysics and very particular experience the stronger the stability of the moral establishment.

A moral code is an undertaking covert or overt as to how each member of a given society is to conduct himself toward others with respect to the establishment of the society within its immediate environment. The set of undertakings constitutes a moral structure which functions covertly or overtly. Covertly it manifests itself as the implicit dominant ontology and as inter-personal beliefs; overtly as the state and as institutions. It will be best to deal with these separately.

CHAPTER II

THE COVERT MORAL STRUCTURE

(a) The Implicit Dominant Ontology

We may detect through the study of the pervasiveness of the morality of a society the foundation upon which it rests. This what I have called elsewhere the implicit dominant ontology. The theory of reality of a society is what makes the society possible by holding together in a single comprehensive scheme all of its articles and endeavors, its persons, their beliefs, skills and techniques, and its artifacts, including languages and tools—everything as well as everybody contributing to the composition of the society. It is implicit because seldom recognized as such by the members of the society, it is dominant because it determines everything else in the society, and it is an ontology because that is the name for the theory of reality. Since the implicit dominant ontology determines everything else in a society it determines among other things the morality of the society.

The origins of the implicit dominant ontology are obscure. No doubt such a complex and hidden affair of profound significance was not planned but grew slowly by accretion as a result of the accumulated experience in a new environment. The elements of the environment are telling, since they usually include not only physical elements, such as mountains or plains, a hot or a cold climate, a productive or an unproductive soil, but also neighboring societies.

The force of the implicit dominant ontology in a given society, however, is without challenge. It rarely lies upon the surface, but there are places where its existence can be detected more easily than at others. I shall enumerate a few.

The written and advocated professional philosophies of a society are overt. They exist in the books and lectures of the philosophers. But underlying these there is a meta-philosophy which is covert. Those assumptions of a metaphysical nature which are found to be held in common among a group of philosophies said to be typical of a society, however much those philosophies may differ in other respects, is the meta-philosophy of the society and best reveals its implicit dominant ontology.

Another place, which we will discuss at greater length in the next chapter, is in the order of institutions of the society. The hierarchy of institutions determines which is held to be more important, and although the charters of those institutions are explicit, the arrangement of the institutions among themselves is seldom official and is more likely to be covert.

A third place where the implicit dominant ontology shows itself plainly in a society is in the set of preferences of the society. Styles in everything, from the fine arts to the fashions in clothing, are revelatory in this sense. What the individual members of the society tend to like, as evidenced by the selections of food and the introduction of new customs, trends in contemporary literature, all of the ways, in fact, in which tastes can express themselves, tell us something about the values which are prized, and hence about the principles which exist undisclosed behind them.

The government of a society always in a sense stands outside institutions, and therefore will receive separate treatment here. It is of course the province of politics rather than of ethics. But ethics stand behind politics in a covert sense, for it was appealed to in the determination of what form of government was chosen by the society, what laws were enacted and how they were to be administered.

Ethics is more general than politics because it touches upon and influences both individual and social life at more points. Consider the force of social disapproval, for instance, where morality is apt to apply more pressure than law in some cases and over a wider front. It is not applied by some individuals who are duly constituted to act for the government for instance but by any citizens who come into contact with it or even by all citizens should they become involved. This is seen more dramatically perhaps in the case of an individual who incurs moral disapproval without actually breaking a law. Thus the overt government and its explicit machinery which is political has a covert justification which is moral.

(b) Inter-Personal Beliefs

A fifth and—for our present purposes—very important place where the covert implicit dominant ontology rises to the surface and can be detected is in the inter-personal beliefs of a given society, the implicit dominant ontology of the society here presenting itself as the set of inter-personal beliefs is what I have called in an earlier chapter the "public retention schema."

What the individuals of the society agree to do discloses what they believe real. Like the Christians of the European Middle Ages if for example their lives are devoted to prayer, it is clear that they believe in the reality of intuitive communication; but if like the Americans of the mid-twentieth century their lives are devoted to the invention, dissemination and use of the products of applied science and technology, it is equally clear that they believe in the reality of facilitative material instruments. The hosts of presuppositions which surround each of these schemes like vast clouds of enveloping atmospheres point to very different kinds of moralities.

It is of much concern to us that what is real is also what is chiefly good, and that morality is concerned with it. The life lived in accordance with the belief in what is real is also the life lived in accordance with the good, the good life. There are many refinements and subtleties of distinction among the beliefs which are to be found at the inter-personal level, any of which will constitute the morality of the society. This is what I have earlier called the public retention schema, and it is the same for every member of the same society. As the governing part of the conscience it accounts for most of the conduct of the individual insofar as that conduct affects and is likely to be judged by society.

The inter-personal beliefs are not within the control of the individual. Indeed as such they may be without either the knowledge or the consent of the individual. He assents to them as a matter of hidden compulsion, wrung from him by the circumstances of his existence and activity within a given society. Not all consistent efforts are deliberate, and that is why such a conception has been included within the present chapter. It is covert; but it is no less an effort to frame a workable schema in conformity with type responsibility within the limits of the immediate environment given the prevailing convictions, customs and traditions.

CHAPTER III

THE OVERT MORAL STRUCTURE

We have been discussing the hidden moral structure of society in an effort to discover its nature and power. Now we shall turn to an examination of the exposed moral structure as it lies in full view of the individuals who have established it and in this way indicated their expectation that they shall follow it. In this and the following two chapters we shall be dealing with the overt moral structure. For the state and its institutions, the rights and duties of individuals, and the legal structure are well recognized, even though the moral ground on which they stand may be more obscure.

(a) The State

The covert morality of a society is society-wide. It enters into and forms part of every segment of a society. It constitutes the chief (although as we shall see not the only) element of the individual conscience, it stands behind the law-making and law-administering procedures, and it governs politics and everything internal to a society. It is perhaps mostly overt in the established law. Thus it concerns overtly one institution: the state.

Politics, it can almost be said, is formulated morality. What interactions between individuals, between individuals and social groups, and between both and property, are allowable it is the business of the law to decide and of the state to control. The state is social law brought out into the open and recognized to be what it is. Under the governance of the state rights and duties are stipulated by the law. Thus the laws are derived from the state, the state is derived from the morality, morality is derived from exigency. No state, then no order; no order, then no hope of need-reduction because no cooperation and no regulation of competition, only unrestrained competition resulting in frustration for all the needs of all the individuals within the society.

Morality as the socially accepted theory of the good and politics as the endeavor to establish and administer the accepted morality show the clear dominance of ethics over politics in importance while conceding the dominance of politics over ethics in importunateness. Morality determines how a man should conduct himself as a citizen of a state, but politics is the structure of the state. An ethics which calls for total social surrender is encroaching upon the area of politics, as for instance the ethical precept that a man should be prepared to sacrifice his life for the good of the community. Similarly a politics which says that a man should be given over entirely to ethics, as for instance in the theory of nihilism when political anarchy is called for and all that is left is the ethics of the individual, in encroaching upon the area of ethics. Each should have its own autonomous area and see to it that such autonomy is preserved.

Politics is morality made official and operative. It is in effect the largest form taken by overt social morality. The state has two functions; one internal, the other external. Internally it has to do with the maintenance of order and the facilitation of the activities of its individual members and social groups; harmony in the state. Thus we can speak of the moral posture of a society toward its own institutions and individuals. These aims it accomplishes by making and administering laws and regulations.

But it has also an external function, and this has to do with the relation of the society to other societies. In this case we speak of the moral posture of the society toward other societies. States have a tendency to exceed themselves. They do so by extending their territory through war and annexation or by seeking in diplomatic and economic ways to increase their influence. When the state comes to be regarded by its individual members as an ultimate whole, it seeks to subordinate other states as parts. For what appears to be bad is so only from the point of view of another and in terms of asymmetrical relations. Taking now the position of a given state, insofar as its external relations are orderly they constitute a morality, and insofar as the same state administers that morality it overlaps with the internal morality of the society. For it can be said of the morality of the state and of the society that they are neither exactly the same nor altogether different.

Societies have as ingredients human individuals, artifacts, social groups and institutions. One of the artifacts takes precedence over all other ingredients, and this is the charter. Every state has a charter; a declared conventionally established set of ideas based on beliefs, customs and traditions for the guidance of its procedures and its members.

The charter of the state contains its morality. Often this is written but just as often it is unwritten. The written charter may contain a moral assertion, as for instance the one at the beginning of the Constitution of the United States. The charter written or unwritten sets forth the guide lines for individual behavior; it establishes what has been agreed upon about how individual needs are to be met, it prescribes the penalty for meeting individual needs in other ways held detrimental to the society, and it serves as a concrete ideal to be used as a model in conducting all affairs. A concrete ideal is one which has been adopted explicitly as an ideal and employed as such in practice.

The charter is one of our chief concerns in this connection because it contains the morality of the society. But there are two more elements which are equally important. These are the customs and traditions which prevail in the society. They are usually less well organized and more pervasive than the effects of the charter, and they change imperceptibly and informally, whereas the charter must be changed decisively and formally. Custom is the social prescription of the manner in which the needs can be reduced. Laws prescribe the limits according to which the individual is impelled toward or restrained from need-reductions. It is the beliefs of the individuals and the customs of the society which determine the moral content of the charter and the laws. In short, the morality exists as a pervasive force and receives concrete expression in manners, ritual, customs, tradition, charter and laws.

(b) The Institutions

The state is the political arm of a society. Societies themselves are by and large self-sufficient communities of individuals organized around their joint efforts at survival. The first level of analysis of organization in societies is institutions. An institution is an organization of individuals and artifacts brought together to serve a single human need directly, or in some more indirect way contributing to survival. Primary institutions are those organized around the needs of immediate survival: a waterworks or an agricultural practice. Secondary institutions serve the primary institutions: post offices, railroads and telephones. Finally, there are the institutions for which the individual exists, serving his ultimate needs; institutions for knowledge, for activity and for survival; universities, country clubs, and churches.

Ordinarily the individual's relations with his society are mediated by institutions. He belongs primarily to the one in which he earns his living and secondarily to many, if not all, of the others. The more advanced the society, the larger and more complex it is, the more this is true. Civilized man is in the main institutional man. In so far as the moral duty of the individual is to serve his society, it will be done through the medium of institutions. For the good life, however, it is not enough that the individual adopts the proper attitudes and practices self-discipline. What help are these without the requisite instruments? Property rarely refers to unimproved natural resources. Buildings are erected upon land, and instruments are complex assemblages of treated materials. Marx has recognized the human value which accrued to a material product because of the labor power expended in its manufacture. When a material is altered and shaped to further human ends it becomes incorporated as part of the social resources and enters, so to speak, into the moral domain. A tool represents a human and usually also a social intention to take the society in a certain direction, one having a moral bearing. As we have seen, the individual is not an independent isolate and social cooperation is a necessity. Men need therefore to devise the most subtle institutions and to construct and use the most complex tools and languages. Institutions are standing arrangements to service the needs. The good life becomes one with life itself if individual survival hangs as it does upon social morality. Thus the necessity of individual morality leads to the construction of social institutions.

The moral order is the highest and most pervasive form taken by social law. Generally unwritten and often unacknowledged, the moral order is in fact not the property of any one institution, though its terms and conditions are often carried by the leading institution. These terms and conditions are promulgated in many ways but chiefly through the members of the leading institution, their beliefs, behavior and life-style. Indeed there is a tendency among leading institutions to adopt and make official a particular ethical theory and a specific morality which is proclaimed as absolute. Traditionally, religions have been the favored institutions in their capacity as guarantees of the truths of social ethics; but there are others: states, for instance. It is easy to find examples; the most obvious are: the Roman Catholic Church, with its creed and approved philosophy of Thomas Aquinas; the Soviet Russian state, with its official philosophy of Marx, Engels and Lenin. Such official moralities are usually turned against further ethical speculation and deviant moral practice in an effort to suppress them. The more channelled the conventional behavior the more stifled are all the attempts at innovation in behavior theory.

Ethics is *sui generis*. Every society has a morality which comes from the morality of its leading institution. It often happens that some institution other than the state gains the highest prestige in the society and by becoming the leading institution dictates the morality of the state, its own morality becoming the social morality. This has happened most often perhaps with a church, but there have been instances of other institutions dominating the state. The Mongol Empire of the early thirteenth century was established for the sole purpose of making war, and in so far as it could be called a state it was dominated by the military. When there is an established church then the church which the state endorses becomes a kind of moral addendum to the state morality. There is usually only one legal system endorsed by the state and it marks the attempt to establish a particular morality. Other moralities, even other religious moralities, must conform to the established variety. The Mormons were compelled to drop the plurality of wives which their code permitted when Utah was incorporated within the United States.

CHAPTER IV

RIGHTS AND DUTIES

We have now to consider social rights and duties as they appear to the individual. Morality is a matter of having one's preferences governed by principles, one's own or another's; and such governance may be by oneself or another. Thus it is true as Reid said that when actions are regulated (and I would add also when thoughts are induced and feelings generated) always either interest or duty is involved; although the distinction between them is not usually so clear, since it is possible, for instance, that on some occasions if not on all one might want to do what one has to do; might, in short, be drawn toward something toward which one would otherwise be compelled. In the pursuit of preferences under principles, expedience turns into prudence. However, it is not prudence which can be expected to bring interest and duty together but, because the governance is by principles, reason; the prudence should have operated earlier in selecting the principles. In the course of pursuing the moral life (inescapable for the individual in any society) there are goods which may be expected and rules which must be observed. The former are called rights and the latter duties. Rights are the goods which the individual can conventionally expect to receive from society. Duties are the goods which the individual can conventionally be expected to give to society. The use of words here is not entirely consistent, however. Rights are often spoken of as though the term covered duties also. I will use the term, rights, here in both senses. Both rights and duties are meant to indicate certain actions which the individual can perform and which he in fact will perform if he wishes to behave morally. In most studies of ethics duty has traditionally been accorded more attention than rights, but rights stand on an equal footing.

Rights—and wrongs—may be spoken of in connection with the established morality of the society or in connection with the codified law. I shall deal with the first here and with the second in a later chapter.

(a) Intrinsic Rights and Wrongs

The right is not a primary factor but a secondary one. Right is secondary to good, the good determines the right. An act is right only if it conforms to the good as established by the morality of a society. Thus by the right is meant what is formally in accord with an established social morality. "Right" thus means also "appropriate" or "suitable." If we did not know what was good we should not know what is right. Moreover, there are many good things not involving action, but right is always concerned with conduct. The right is broader and more inclusive than the good. It is good that John feels sorry that Tom died, but no rights are involved. The good applies to existence apart from as well as including behavior, while the right applies to behavior only.

Since right is action designed to promote the good, it can hardly be held independent of the consequences. However, here as usual in the case of values, we find an intrinsic and an extrinsic or instrumental aspect. Right as intrinsic is good if it is intended to promote good consequences, and right as instrumental is good if it does promote good consequences. The former is psychological, the latter social. But in the end and on balance it is the behavior which counts for the most because it has the largest circle of effects.

Intrinsic individual right is the impulse to right conduct, conduct in accord with the individual's conscience or with the morality of the society to which he belongs. A man who "feels right" about things is apt to do right, but the feeling is independent. When Kant said in the First Section of his *Foundations of the Metaphysics of Morals* that there is nothing in or beyond the world which could be called good without qualification except a good will, he was referring to the intrinsic individual impulse toward the good. The will is a quality and all qualities are both positive and simple. It is not difficult to see how any of them (including the will) could be called good without complications introduced by further distinctions or differences; for that is what simplicity means: having no parts.

We owe to Kant much of our knowledge of the intrinsic right. For him it was the only kind of right that mattered, and he tended to ignore or neglect the instrumental right. But the difficulty with the intrinsic right is that it may have no validation beyond the individual. "Right is right" often means "I feel this is right and nothing can sway me from considering my feelings absolute and therefore authoritative." But the individual can be wrong in a larger context.

What he feels he feels, no doubt of that, but while his feelings may be right as feelings they may be wrong as indicators. For they do point beyond the having of feelings and toward action in a society. And there they may be misleading. There is no such thing as "wrong" feelings, but there are misleading feelings based on the mistaken reading of just what the feelings mean.

It must be admitted, however, that there is such a thing as an intrinsic individual wrong. This is a feeling (which in itself may be positive and good) which is not in accord with the individual conscience. The impulse to steal a great painting from a museum so that the enjoyment of it could be privately prolonged at will is a good insofar as it is a feeling; but if the individual has a conscience in which the public retention schema reflects the morality of the society and the private retention schema does not depart too far from the public retention schema, then the impulse to steal will not be in accord with the conscience and is therefore a wrong impulse. But let us consider another case in which the individual is at odds with his society. He feels that it has wronged him and that his anti-social actions are therefore a rough kind of justice, righting what would otherwise be a wrong done him by society. Then the private retention schema will dominate his conscience and his impulse to steal the painting will be in accord with his conscience. It will be right for him as he sees it, but whether he sees it or not it will be wrong for society.

Individual rights include not only what the society permits to the individual but also how it safeguards him. The individual thinks of his rights in addition to what answers to his conscience and what his fellows approve as the protection which is due to him under the statutes as a member of the society. "Enjoying his rights" means expecting society to enjoin others from preventing him in the enjoyment of his rights.

(b) Extrinsic Rights and Wrongs

So much for social rights and duties viewed from the individual, but what about these same rights and duties viewed from society? This is a larger consideration and the one properly belonging to the term, right.

One of the chief reasons for the existence of society is its necessary relations to rights. It may take a number of positions toward them. It may for instance allow for them, encourage them, or in extreme cases command them. Thus the right to work is allowed for in a democratic state, provided for in a welfare state, and commanded in a communist state. It is questionable whether the extreme cases are entitled to the term "rights," for a right which commanded—or prohibited—is hardly a right. The excessive use of alcohol may be allowed but not encouraged, or it may even be prohibited, but there are few cases where it has been commanded, though these no doubt exist. In European countries drunkenness is tolerated while in some Asian countries it is prohibited.

The extrinsic moral rights are laid down by the morality of a society. What is right is what the social morality approves. By a like logic, what is wrong is what it disapproves. The morality of the society is designed to facilitate the need-reductions of its individual members. But this does not mean that it is always successful. If it is not run for the benefit of its members but only for one of them, say a tyrant or a dictator, then the morality will require the repression of many needs rather than their reduction.

The generic need of the individual is to survive in his environment by dominating it in order to obtain from it whatever is necessary to his need-reduction. His aggressive instincts compel him to use force to reduce his needs and to exceed them in the effort to dominate. Thus a fundamental aggressiveness activates drives which in themselves may be extrinsically good or extrinsically bad just according to whether the actions which result from them are allowed by the society or prohibited. The individual is then naturally both good and bad. He has biological needs and these cannot be reduced without loving women, cooperating with his neighbor, and opposing his competitors.

Now, whether his resultant actions are right or wrong depends upon the composition of the society. For instance, we ordinarily think of cooperation as right, but some forms of it which are deemed to be in restraint of trade are considered wrong and in the United States condemned by the Sherman Anti-Trust Act. We ordinarily think of loving women as right, but loving women who are the wives of others is considered wrong. What is right and what is wrong extrinsically is a function of the morality of a society as expressed by its laws. These endeavor to tread delicately between distinctions which serve to indicate the moral values upon which the society has settled as its own.

(c) Duties

I have said earlier that duties are the goods which the individual can conventionally be expected to give to society. Usually the duties of the individual are specified for him by the institutions to which he belongs. Thus he has duties to the state (paying taxes, performing military service), duties to his family, to his church, and so on. Duty, then, is the obligation to transform a right into an action. To do what is right means to perform a duty and thus to increase the good. Coming down in the scale from the more general to the more particular, the good prescribes the right and the right prescribes specific duties. Thus duty is the particular case under the more general rules prescribing the right and the good.

Duty is an obligation to act in accordance with the established social order, to conform to the concrete ideal as embodied in the individual conscience, the established morality or the law. In the case of disorder, duty becomes the obligation to act so as to promote or restore the established morality. Here confrontation becomes the archetype of responsibility. "Conduct toward another, in consideration of all others" turns into an obligation or a duty when it is seen as an act which ought to be performed. Duty is the dynamic aspect of the appropriate good.

Kant was right in insisting that the greatest moral acts are those performed without hope of reward simply because they are duties, but this is simply the recognition of a social obligation by a responsible individual. Duty for duty's sake is another way of saying that duty is good and that no further reason need be found for it. Kant again is impressed by the qualitative nature of intrinsic duty as felt by the individual. But the obligation to conform to the established morality issues in conduct which collectively makes the very existence of the society possible. If a majority of individuals were to refrain from doing their duties, the society would become disorganized and cease to exist as a society.

But as duty has minimal limits of obligation which it imposes upon the individual to perform acts which are appropriate under the social dispensation of the good, so it has maximal limits too. These are in fact recognized when we say of an individual that he has committed acts of heroism "beyond the call of duty." Duties ordinarily are such as apply to demotic man. Heroic man who characteristically engages in excessive behavior does not stop when he has done his duty but goes on to help others or in different ways to do more than is normally his share.

The hierarchy of relationships running from the individual through society to the human species and the cosmos insures that the opportunities for performing one's duty shall be many. Duty is an open-ended affair, with no ceiling to the size of the organization to which conduct can conform. Duty to the self, the society, the species, the cosmos, are all encompassed and included in confrontation theory. Everything is present at once that concerns morality; entire man, as it were, condensed into particular man who is in this way made to represent the species, or even beyond that, the good in the world.

That is what is so very special about the individual, that his responsibilities do not end when he has discharged his duties to himself and to his society. They extend beyond his immediate environment to that unseen attachment to his species, under the dispensation of type responsibility; and for his species he carries an obligation beyond it to the world of other species: to the cosmos. This obligation is what is recognized in the conventional religions in which such concessions are not only asked for but demanded in a wide sweep of excessive deontological acknowledgment.

CHAPTER V

THE LAW AND LEGAL PROCEDURES

(a) Levels of Application

The difficulty in the path of the application of ethics is the very abstractness of it. From the speculations concerning the good and the right, which occupy the theorist, to the immediate problems confronting the judge and jury seems a fairly far cry. Yet the fact remains that the more abstract the theory the wider its applicability if it have any validity. Ethics at this level is not intended to be applied cold so to any concrete instance of behavior. Ethics has first to be treated as jurisprudence which in turn has relevance to the law.

Here we encounter two genuine difficulties. In the first place we are faced not with a plan for action which is to be put into effect but with an ongoing society with its traditional and customary procedures. The morality of the ongoing society requires study in terms of some speculative ideal. In the second place, in terms of which ideal is the society to be evaluated? It is not without its faults if it is an actual society; it can be improved only by adopting a strategy aimed at achieving an ideal. But the principle of consistency requires that we shall choose only one ideal. On what ground is it to be selected?

The concrete ideal which is already operative in the society implicitly or explicitly makes the direction of improvement a matter of common sense, that being the surface way in which deep principles make themselves felt. Thus we are compelled to rise above the concrete at least by one abstractive level in order to consider how jurisprudence can affect social practice. Jurisprudence is the study of how the concrete ideal of the established morality can best be implemented in the legal procedures of the society.

The laws result from the establishment in a society, through the process of enactment and promulgation, of the morality which has been accepted by the beliefs of a majority of the individual members of the society. They can be sustained only if a majority of the individuals continue to believe in them or if the maintenance of order requires them. In this way they are informally authorized. Further authorization may come from some other institution, such as the state, when a sovereign power decrees them, or from a church, when they are said to be authorized by a deity or deities.

In the adventures of individuals in search of need-reductions, inevitably infractions of laws arise. There are bound to be conflicts of various sorts: between individuals, between individuals and institutions, between institutions, and between individuals or institutions and the state. These have to be adjudicated in the pursuit of the maintenance of social order.

(a) The Law as Enacted Morality

The laws of a society represent its attempt to codify its morality, for, as Aristotle said, "it is through laws that we can become good."[1] It is the task of the legal establishment both to codify and to enforce conformity with the prevailing social morality. Law differs from morality in two ways: in the first place, it is deliberate and it is known; and, in the second place, it changes slowly. The morality of a society is an informal affair and enters into all of its structures and activities. What may be called the implicit dominant morality of a society as we have noted is to be found in connection with the public retention schema in the conscience of individual members, in the hierarchy of institutions, and in the pervasive qualitative atmosphere of the ethos. But it also exists formally in the law. A particular morality lies behind the enacted laws of a society; which explains why those rather than others.[2] The legal structure of a society is the formalization of its morality. Thus for example a contract is an agreement between persons to engage in the joint pursuit of a symmetrical good. A tort or delict is a violation of civil right and hence a civil wrong or a moral bad. Law is codified and enforced because it can in this way guard the morality of the society. By means of the law its institutions become protected enterprises. Infidelity is bad, theft is bad, murder is bad, because they threaten the society. If you wish to examine the exposed morality to which a society lays claim, examine both its legal procedures and the actual cases in its courts of law. Morality changes faster than law and so some differences between them are inevitable.

When we say that an individual has a "moral right" to such and

---

[1] *Nico. Eth.*, 1180b25.

[2] Writers on jurisprudence call the implicit dominant morality of a society "positive morality." See e.g. G. W. Paton, *A Text-Book on Jurisprudence* (Oxford 1946, Clarendon Press), p. 59.

such, we do so in terms of his conformity to the morality of his society. This distinguishes it from legal right, which is his conformity to the established laws of his society. The two overlap but they are by no means the same. The morality changes faster than the established laws and so there could easily be a conflict. The use of alcohol was at one time prohibited legally in the United States but it was not morally disapproved, and so eventually the law had to be repealed in order to keep pace with the morality. In the end a bad law, i.e. a law completely lacking in conformity to the existing morality, cannot be enforced. Only a law which does conform to the morality of the society can be. The law spells out the morality and prescribes penalties for infractions. By "law" then I understand the legal right; by "wrong" any infraction of the legal right. Justice is the righting of a wrong.

The laws of the state are based on the requirements of the society. They spell out its rights and duties. In this sense they are absolute while they prevail. The function of reason is not to repress the drives but to insure their orderly reduction. The laws are reason operating in society toward this end through the regulation of the drives. In a well-run state the social goods, at least as Plato, for instance, saw them,[1] of freedom, harmony and right reason, issue from the correspondence between morality and the laws. The morality of a society is based on the interests of that society as the society itself conceives them. The laws insure that the society will be able to survive as a society. Thus the purpose of the laws is to facilitate the maintenance of the morality of the society and hence of the society itself.

(c) Material Goods

Material goods take on a new relationship in the ethics of society. In the second part of this book when we were discussing individual ethics we spoke of artifacts, those material tools and signs which have been altered through human agency in order to make them useful for human ends. The alteration gave them a new meaning for the human members of society by turning them into property. Even where a material thing has remained unaltered it may become a property, but here it is still in connection with human use. Virgin forests are sometimes owned by the state and valued just because they have remained unaltered, but here again it is because they make pleasurable areas of hiking, camping and picnics. Hence the discernment of English law which has long held property to consist in possession or in action.

[1] *Laws*, 701 D-E and ff.

I define property as material goods under ownership. And here ownership entitles the owner to exclusive use, which means either the right to use it himself or to keep others off. The chief function of equity has been to protect property. Equity reaches through the law to appeal to the morality which underlies it. But there is rarely any absolute ownership even in capitalist countries. The distinction made by the Romans between *dominium* and *possessio*, the former designating absolute possession and the latter merely physical control, would be meaningless today, with the exception of the Marxist countries where the ownership by the state of the means of production does appear to be a true *dominium*. The usual case is the right to ownership for the duration of proper use. "Proper use" here meaning use which will not be prejudicial to the morality of the society.

Dewey's complaint that lofty ethics seems thin because it leaves out all economic considerations is certainly justified. The truth of the situation requires that we penetrate further than the economic level of society, however, to the greater generalization involved in the assertion that all material things have a moral bearing, not only in their economic relations but also in their legal and political ones. We shall omit all but the moral bearing here because this is a study of ethics, and we shall go on to claim that all things have a moral bearing in so far as they have a human one. In this connection we are not entitled to speak any longer of material things but of material goods. Not only is it true that material things have a moral bearing which renders them goods, but also that all social goods involve a minimum of material things. It would be difficult to consider the ethics of society without bringing in the part played by material goods. Of Hume's "three fundamental laws of nature" governing property: stability of possession, transference by consent, and the performance of promises, only the last is not necessarily involved with material goods and it of course could be.[1]

I am not here concerned with the political question of who should own property, or with the economic question of how much he should own, but with what the function of property is in society, and I am contending that although material goods may not always be an end in themselves they always are *at least* the means to an end. I cannot conceive of any moral end a society may have which would not involve the use of material goods, and so I am trying to underscore the function of material goods in considering the ethics of society.

A society establishes itself as a state, and recognizes that establish-

[1] *Treatise of Human Nature*, Book III, Part II, Sections III–V.

ment in setting guide-lines for the individual's relations with his fellows and with the material things which are to be found in the society. He is henceforth a citizen of the state and cannot be allowed to pursue the good life for himself except within the limits laid down by the state through its laws. Similarly, material goods are henceforth properties and cannot be used by citizens except within the limits also laid down by the state. And since the former aim involves the latter material, we are entitled to two conclusions.

The first of these is that societies, for moral purposes or any other, cannot be described as consisting exclusively of persons. The second is that social laws which are intended to facilitate the achievement of the good life by the members of the society do so only provided that they move toward it in a certain prescribed direction. Thus there is not only a definite morality involved in the relations of the members of the society with the material goods in the possession of that society but a particular one at that. The existence and the use of property is a moral question.

(d) Justice

Laws are by their nature universal, and universal laws are at least partly blind; they do not introduce differences in particular cases and it is not contained in them that they do not apply necessarily beyond particular societies. If the law is enacted morality, then justice involves conformity to morality and may be defined as the restoration of good. "Good" is to be understood here as including material goods, rights and duties, for instance restitution for theft, and for mayhem, and the enforcement of contract. Justice has to be more flexible than laws, tending to conserve them on some social occasions and to reform them on others.

It may be remarked parenthetically that unjust laws can exist and still be laws, because the enacted morality of a society is not always identical with the morality of that society, as is the case for instance when the morality is changing faster than the laws. The distinction which is sometimes recognized between laws and morality, based on the fact that laws flow from a sovereign power whereas the morality does not, is not viable where the sovereign power is sensitive to the morality. It is not viable when the sovereign power is an elected body answerable to the popular will but is viable when that power is a divinely appointed King or Emperor who does not hold himself answerable.

The complete theory of justice has never been written. Anaximander used it to explain death, Plato used it to explain religion and politics as well as ethics. We shall be concerned here of course chiefly with its ethical use. In this connection justice may be informal or formal. Informal justice has to do with the proper or moral use of persons and things. To deal justly means to behave in a manner calculated to preserve or replace the due proportionality of goods and services. Formal justice is administrative morality and has to do with seeing that the proper observances are carried out, that the procedures are conducted by due process of law, and that conventional covenants and agreements are respected.

Here justice will mean primarily formal justice: the restoration of the moral social order, the return to the conditions imposed by the concrete ideal. There would be no need for the application of justice were there no social disorder. Hence the correctness of Cairns' definition of jurisprudence as "the study of human behavior as a function of disorder."[1] Justice thus becomes a sort of methodology of the application of morals. In society there is always more congruence than collision, otherwise there would be no social order, but justice is concerned with collision. Judicial decisions are based on goodness of fit: finding the facts of the case and fitting to them the appropriate laws. Moral judgments made informally by society have the effect of conveying ill-defined but definite social sanctions. Social disapproval can in some instances be very hard to bear. Moral judgments made formally by society through its agency in the courts of law have the effect of imposing legal punishments. Thus justice is only one more example of right and wrong, of seeing the good as put to its proper and therefore highest use, an instance of appropriateness, the adjustment of a situation or an action to a principle.

(e) The Incompleteness of Social Goods

In this third part of the book we again encounter two apparently conflicting propositions, and they are similar to those we encountered in the second part. For there is an authentic level of ethics at which society is autonomous. And yet society is not an absolutely valid ethical isolate.

Below the social level lies the individual, and the individual enjoys a certain autonomy. The autonomy of the individual is felt by the

[1] Huntington Cairns, *The Theory of Legal Science* (Chapel Hill 1941, University of North Carolina Press), p. 1.

society in connection with those rights which the individual possesses over against the social pressures of duties. It is felt also in those incursions into the social order which are made, and often made successfully, by exceptional individuals who wish to seek and to impose social improvement, those exceptional individuals who are super-social rather than sub-social. The social level lies above the individual level but is not entirely independent of it.

Above the social level lies the level of the species, the level of humanity. Society is an organization within the greater organization of humanity, with privileges from it, but also with obligations to it which argue against the absolute autonomy of the society. A close examination of any moral code established by society discloses weaknesses within it; inconsistencies, perhaps, and a certain degree of incompleteness. The laws will not be entirely compatible and they will not cover all possible moral issues. These shortcomings suggest the necessity of going beyond the moral code as it exists, more specifically to a more comprehensive and better integrated morality which could apply to the whole human species.

Then again, as we have noted in this part, workability in a society implies an ethical ideal, and thus points to a condition of incompleteness in any local and immediate sense. In a word, no individual seeks to become tantamount to society but every society does seek to become tantamount to humanity; to embrace the rest of the human species within its organization either as equal or under its control as a subordinate subdivision.

The two levels by which the level of society is surrounded in some ways join hands across it. The individual has connections with his species in ways which transcend his membership in a particular society. What is ordinarily called a moral man is one whose actions are approved by the society to which he belongs. But this mistakenly identifies morality with the approved or established morality. Men are considered moral only if their actions are loyal, which would mean that if a German was a loyal Nazi he was moral. But there is a morality beyond the local society and often even is in conflict with it. This necessitates a search for a wider morality. For there are many societies but there is only one human species; and when the individual recognizes his membership in his society he does so against those who belong to other societies, but when he recognizes his membership in the species he does so with all other individuals regardless of their social differences. For while individuals have social differences they have at the same time species similarities. For instance, what the individual *can* do is everywhere the same but what he *should* do is not. Thus there are local social and cultural determinations which blind him to the moral demands of a common humanity.

The autonomy of the social level is genuine and authentic, however, and there are rules against skipping levels. The hovering existence of, and hence the ever-present possibility of confrontations with, the ethics of humanity is sufficient to remind the individual that while he is for all immediate purposes a member of a particular society and obligated to work for it because of the goods which he derives from it, he can also work through it toward the next integrative level. The individual, then, not only derives benefits from society which are both of an individual and a social nature but he also aspires beyond it toward the ethics of humanity. Society for the individual is not only a goal and therefore the site of his prospective goal-achievements, it is also a ladder whereby he is able to climb higher than his own petty, short-range self and aim above him in the ethical integrative series toward humanity and farther.

We conclude then from the evidence that we are entitled to speak both of the ethics of society and of the incompleteness of social goods. How is this conflict to be resolved? Before that question can be answered we shall have to enter upon an examination of the entire commitment of the individual as well as of the ethical nature of the world in which he is involved. He is involved with more than society, with more than his own species, for that matter, and with nothing less than the entire universe. But the next level after the social is the human. With the level of the species we began to look at the problem of the individual as he examines his being apart from the specifically social, in an effort to gain an insight into what it means to be an human individual and in the world. So we turn now to examine the ethics of humanity.

PART IV

THE ETHICS OF THE HUMAN SPECIES

CHAPTER I

FROM SOCIETY TO HUMANITY

In this study of the moral nature of man I have treated first of individual man and then of society. Continuing the policy of enlarging the area of consideration, I undertake next an examination of the ethics of the human species. This is the largest consideration possible if the study is to be limited to the human, but as we shall see it is not. Still larger vistas open up before us as we undertake to review the little which is available to us of the study of the ethics of the cosmos. Cosmic ethics is the ethics of the universe of existence, but there are still other universes, such as the universe of essence, in which is found the ethical ideal, and the universe of destiny, in which are found ethical strivings. Each of these will be treated at sufficient length to give a comprehensive view of the whole field of ethics.

(a) The Domain of Humanity

I begin, then, with a definition and description of the level of the human species. The domain of the human species is the aggregate of the qualities of all social relations. The ethics of the human species is the ideal of the aggregate of all social relations. It includes all individuals, all social groups, all artifacts, all institutions within societies but only as those societies are related to each other. At the species level we are concerned with these elements of analysis only in the bearing they have on the totality of humanity. From Antisthenes to Shaftesbury there have been ethical thinkers who have wished to deny the ethics of any and every limited society, in favor of linking up the ethics of the individual with that of the whole human species. The recognition that the demands of humanity take precedence over all other demands whether individual or cosmic was much later conventionally labelled humanism. Humanism has been an attempt to preempt for the whole of ethics the ethics of the human species. It suffers from certain limitations. Notably, its adherents have failed to recognize the ferocity as well as the civility inherent in the species and therefore has failed to make provision for it, in what begins to look as though it may prove a disastrous omission. Then, too, its adherents seem to suppose that the human species is a viable isolate. Yet in violating the rights of other species, as we shall shortly note, it commits an irrefrangible evil.

The difficulty is greater still, however, and must be faced. For there are local considerations which have a bearing on moral conduct, and which cannot be erased merely by riding over them with a consideration of a common humanity. The human individual in this connection, then, is defined in terms of his relations direct or indirect to other individuals. Thus his characteristics are the products of his peculiar place in the collectivity and not merely of his own private consciousness.

What is common to all men and all societies may be (a) identical with what one society practices, (b) a part of what every society practices though not identical with the whole in any one case, or (c) a morality which lies altogether outside all known societies and all known social practices. The usual thing is an example of (a), namely the identification of the moral code of one's own society with the absolute morality. But the truth probably belongs with (b) or more likely still (c) or both. These last two may be combined, as for instance by considering a part of what every society practices to be an element or the elements of a whole morality which lies as a whole outside all known and practiced moralities.

Ethical relativity is a phenomenon which has been known since the Greeks. Xenophanes refers to it, and it was certainly part of the doctrine of the Epicureans.[1] It is not without modern adherents, from Spencer to Peirce, who see in tribal customs an evolutionary theory.[2] Social and cultural differences are not purely arbitrary nor are they accidental. They derive from a people's heritage and from its environment. The heritage itself, however, is the history of its adaptation to an environment and so is an environmental influence once removed. A people's heritage, like the people themselves, ultimately derives from the environment. Nature admits of a large variety of choices in the institutional orderings of customs and artifacts. Every instance of the variety is natural; indeed all that exists is. The artificial is simply a working over and hence a further complication of the natural. Cultural relativity is simply the recognition of the variety of choices admitted by nature.

But one fact must immediately be noted. Ethical relativity does not mean that what is considered good in one society would be *considered*

---

[1] See *Diog. Laert.* II, X, 151.
[2] Peirce, *Col. Pap.* 8.158.

bad in another. It means, as Stace points out, that what is good in one
society might actually *be* bad in another. Monogamy, which works so
well in a society where there is an equal number of men and women
and is therefore good, would work badly in a society having a great
predominance of women. Polygamy would be a good in the latter but
not in the former.

(b) Cultural Limits to Ethical Speculation

Cultural relativism is a fact and must be admitted. The membership
of an individual through his society in a particular culture is highly
determining. He cannot easily (if indeed at all) get over the perspective from which his culture appears as furnishing the norms of all
human behavior, so that all other cultures are judged by their similarities to or differences from it. From time to time men are aware that
a wider world of humanity exists, but they consider this a less pressing
fact than their own involvement in the details of the culture to which
their society belongs and in whose goods they participate. Judgments
of good or bad are culturally conditioned and are not the same for
individuals who are members of different cultures.

We are interested in this book in the *structure* of ethics, in the sense
that it is the same for all cultures even though in each case the cultural
contents be diverse. Cultural relativity applies only to the contents of
cultures, and it has to be admitted that there is a sense in which it is
possible to transcend particular cultures. A common humanity exists
among men and can be studied. It is the task of this book to undertake
one such study. Cultural relativists will charge, however, that the
present attempt to find a structure for an ethics which is trans-cultural
is itself an effort conducted by a member of the western society whose
efforts are no doubt a product of the culture in which he lives. In
other words, the very effort to discover a trans-cultural ethics is itself
culturally conditioned and might not have occurred to the members
of another culture.

This charge cannot be effectively refuted. It can be partly answered
by claiming that a trans-cultural project undertaken for cultural
reasons may yet have trans-cultural results. If for instance I try to look
outside my own culture I might in this way demonstrate my cultural
affiliation (it being a characteristic of the western society to seek out
the knowledge of other cultures), but I might also obtain results which are
not culturally determined. I might, in short, however briefly and furtive-
ly, obtain some glimpse of a wider perspective than is ordinarily my own.

We can look over into other cultures, removed in space or time (or both) from our own, and in most cases, ours as well as theirs, we can find behind the morality the exigencies of survival. For instance, it is said that the only trans-cultural social law is the prohibition against mother-son incest. This is the only form of incest likely to be unfruitful. With father-daughter and brother-sister incest children are more likely to result. At the age when sons are becoming potent, mothers are more often than not reaching the menopause. The species has long ago forgotten the reasons for its morality. There is a reason in the survival of the species for permitting all forms of incest except one. Society is the source of morality as that topic is ordinarily understood. Ethical relativism is the evidence. Societies in which marriages are arranged by parents differ from those in which individuals choose their marriage partners for themselves. But in each case where the custom has been established and has prevailed for a great number of years, the arrangement whatever it is is felt to be right by everyone and recognized as the only natural way of doing things.

The charge of cultural conditioning can be further answered by claiming that those who try to see their own culture as one among a number of cultures, each with the viable qualities and relations peculiar to it, is already to that extent outside his own culture and able at least in a small way to share the perspective of that larger organization which is a common humanity. There are as many social ethics as there are societies, but there can be only one ethics of humanity because there is only one human species. The ethical relativists concentrate on the former fact to the exclusion of the latter, while the ethical absolutists insist on identifying one of the former with the latter. The relativists are sure that there is no ethics of humanity, the absolutists are equally sure that the ethics of humanity is identical with the ethics of their own society. Both are limited views and neglect the structure of the ethical integrative series. The human individual is not entirely a member of his own society or his own culture, not entirely even (as we shall see in the next part of this book) a human limited to his common humanity. The individual has larger links and gets his own back only in the widest of organizational circles. Religions exist because individuals have cosmic affinities; and this remains true however naive and crude the religions.

The charge that the ethics of humanity is itself culturally conditioned can be defended in the ways specified above, but in the end it cannot be defended with total success, and so the issue must remain unsettled.

When it is left open in this way, at least the strong winds from other quarters are recognized for what they are when they blow through the tight consistency of any small society, and so the claims of a wider completeness are in this way maintained.

The best example of a narrow (though deep) cultural view is that of Plato in the *Republic*. The limitation of Plato's ethics is that he considered individual man both as himself a whole and as a part of society, and he considered society too, but only as the state. He did not go beyond that to extend his theory to the whole of humanity. In this way he was thoroughly Greek. His conceptions of the harmony of the parts within the individual and of classes within the state is masterly and a model; but it leaves out the last consideration without which the earlier one becomes impossible to carry out as a concrete morality for very long. Plato's theory lasted but not Greek society. In the end, which came shortly, the Greek state was overthrown, cast into a condition of disharmony and with it the individuals who composed it, by the hostility of other excluded states. Without humanity—all of it—the ethical ideal is faulted, limited and even undesirable.

Individual man belongs to humanity in virtue of being human. But this is something he is, an inescapable condition of his being, not something he does. In order to discover the ethical nature of his behavior as well as of his existence, we shall have to step up one integrative level from society to humanity. That we have special reasons for making this selection rather than another seems obvious, and what they are; but the analysis would have been the same in any case. How valid an isolate is "humanity," however? The validity of fixed types has been seriously challenged ever since Darwin discovered the process of evolution. Plato is credited with the theory of fixed types, and contemporary biologists have declared the theory discredited. If this had been Plato's claim then the biologists are right. But the theory may not be after all so simple. The criticism fails to take account of the separate and independent existence of the types. If the types are intelligible things, then they are fixed and permanent; and this could be true without committing sensible things to the same rigid and uncompromising structure. For, as Plato pointed out, sensible things change, they come and go, and when they return they are not essentially the same things. Thus the types could remain fixed while sensible things changed in type. Ape became man, and for all we know man will become superman; but in the meanwhile he is man, and while he is man we are entitled to consider him a member of a type.

What is said about ephemeral things is no less true because the things are ephemeral. *Australopithicus* is one type. *Pithecanthropus* another, Neanderthal man another, and *Homo sapiens* still another. Between them there were many gradations. That in the course of several million years the same animal has evolved through thousands of successive generations does not alter the fact that at any given cross-section of development he is either a member of some type or of an intermediate type. But the intermediate type is also a type. Indeed it would be hard to discover an individual that was not a member of some type. We have seen that so far as our limited knowledge goes this is true throughout the cosmos.

(c) For and Against Cultural Relativism

It will be recalled from an earlier chapter that the good has been described as the quality of completeness and the beautiful as the quality of consistency, and that the only difference is one of direction in the whole-part series, the good bringing wholes together and the beautiful bringing parts together. From the point of view of the good of humanity there are good and bad aspects of human societies. Speaking generally, the good aspects are those which operate in favor of the logical requirements of completeness and the bad aspects are those which operate against the logical requirements of consistency.

First, then, the good aspects which operate in favor of the logical requirements of completeness.

The most obvious of these is the gain in values which results from diversity. The enlargement of the scope of humanity is made possible by a great variety of exemplars. For instance, in a single world society there would be only one kind of dance for each relevant occasion, but with the diversity of societies there is a wide diversity also of dances. Anyone who has attended a world dance festival will testify to the enrichment which results from the fact that each society has developed its own characteristic set of dances.

The principle involved here can be generalized to all of the arts and indeed to all of the enterprises of a culture. Morality has to do with the quality of relations, with bonds between human units, and if there are few such units then there will be an impoverishment of morality. Strait is the gate only if many must pass. Every element of culture has its moral aspect, in the broad definition of morality entertained in this work; and so the abundance of societies will mark an abundance also of what is to be morally included. The small and the good is not as good as the large and the good. The intrinsic good may be developed under narrow and exclusive conditions but the extrinsic good there cannot be; intensity may be developed but extensity never.

The morality of a society whether established through mode or charter or only implicit in practice is in a sense an experiment. How good is the society which is operated on such and such lines? What has it to teach other societies in how it operates this or that particular moral element? Obviously, the more societies there are the more such experiments will be kept going. All can be considered efforts to solve the human predicament with respect to its organization of values. In a world where the unknown is more common than the known any effort to gain knowledge should be encouraged, and all doors which promise to lead to usable information, moral or otherwise, should be kept open.

A second favorable aspect of a variety of cultures is the opportunities for departure it affords originative individuals. The originative individual does not function in a social vacuum nor start from the beginning. He takes off from the accepted values of his culture and adds to them. Occasionally he operates against them but always in any case in terms of them. In a word, he needs them. Now the greater the variety of cultures the more originative individuals will be enabled to contribute to the net gains of humanity. Discoveries are angled through the gains of societies in which they are made, and so the societies must exist if there are to be discoveries. Despite the novelty of discoveries they all bear distinct relationships to particular societies. Mozart was a great composer but despite the immense originality of his music it bears a distinct family resemblance to the music of his European contemporaries, chiefly German and Italian. It would be hard to think of Phidias' work as anything but Greek or of the Chartres Cathedral as anything but Gothic. The English talent for social order would make of any morality other than that which underlies the common law unsuitable.

Societies provide the unit for individual existence. The individual lives within as well as on and by his society. His maximum personal contacts determine its boundaries, and with the increase in material efficiency in the construction of tools and languages the contact is widened to include more individuals. Every society maintains social classes, and these are not always determined by economic considerations as Marx insisted. What happens is that some individuals are more talented than others and can therefore contribute more to the society. They are accordingly rewarded by the society and as a result of this constitute a privileged class. The talented individuals I call heroic men and the others who constitute the vast majority demotic men. In older societies the privileged class becomes heritable, thus freezing a situation which existed at one time but perhaps exists no longer, so that talent in the privileged class is encouraged but among others only sometimes encouraged and more often discouraged or stifled for lack of opportunities. Economic considerations flow from special abilities and not the reverse. When this situation is continued a true aristocracy results. When it does not the aristocracy is an artificial affair, that is to say, one maintained only by artifacts.

Thus it comes about that there is one morality for heroic men and another for demotic men within the confines of the same society. We shall have more to say about this presently. The good life can be lived by many and that is indeed the goal, but the high life only by the few, and that is the goal for them. The high life of talented individuals can be defined as the life of extended obligations and privileges from the viewpoint of the society.

From the point of view of the good of humanity there are also bad aspects of human societies. I have said already that they are the aspects which operate against the logical requirements of consistency.

The first of these is the natural aggression which is to be found in many instances at the borders where it tends to erode the boundaries and so affect the consistency through its limits. The fear of strangeness is equalled only by the distrust of strangers. Societies make common cause but not so often nor so readily as they are prepared for mutual hostility and even armed conflict. Congruences and collisions are the pattern, and they alternate with almost reliable frequency. The unknown is always read by the adventurous as a challenge and only by the ignorant as a threat, but heroic man is adventurous man and demotic man is threatened man, and there are more demotic men by far than heroic men. Thus, in the hands of heroic men who must always answer to a large extent in their operation of society to the demands of demotic man, the society becomes an instrument for the repulsion of those beyond its borders, and in this way its consistency is put to the severest tests. When societies meet, differences lead to conflict, and on both sides consistency is challenged. No matter which way the outcome, both societies will be altered as a result.

The second of the bad aspects which operate against the logical requirement of consistency is the tendency of every society to equate its interests with humanity and so to stretch its inclusiveness past its capacities. The tendency to cultural absolutism in which the members of a society are regarded as equivalent to humanity and all other humans held to be barbarian and therefore not quite human puts the society in the position of demanding too much of itself. A system so strained may mean a consistency broken; contradictions and conflicts begin to appear, and the fabric of the whole structure may be destroyed.

(d) Isolated Moral Communities

By "isolated moral communities" I mean primarily those societies which have been separated geographically from the rest of humanity. It often happens that isolated moral communities do not know of their limitations. The rest of humanity simply does not exist for them, and they think of themselves as "the people". We are concerned here of course with the possible value to the human species of such communities. Some cultures in the middle of Africa until the nineteenth century had existed in complete isolation, as had many island communities of the South Pacific. But this was equally true of larger groups, of the original inhabitants of Australia and New Guinea, for instance. Many American Indian tribes knew of the existence of other Indian tribes but not of the existence of a large world of humanity outside the world of Indian tribes.

But what I have been asserting of geographically isolated primitive communities is also true, though to a somewhat lesser degree, of the great civilizations with respect to their subcultures. There is a sense in which every society imposes natural boundaries upon itself which make it indifferent to what goes on beyond it. France and England are only some thirty miles apart, and although it is possible to find in their capital cities strong evidences of an interaction between the two cultures, this is not so in the remainder of the two countries. After many centuries of neighborliness, the sexual practices and the culinary arts of Wolverhampton and St. Etienne diverge so sharply that they could as well be millions of miles and hundreds of years apart.

The phenomenon of isolated moral communities provides humanity with certain advantages and certain disadvantages. Let us have a quick glance at each.

The advantages are those to be derived from cultivating small fields intensively. Isolated moral communities may be compared with isolated breeding communities where new genetic developments can occur. In isolated moral communities fresh experiments in communal living, under laws which have not been enacted and customs and traditions which have not been followed anywhere else can be tried. In this way lies human progress. The laws, the customs and traditions, of the Andaman or the Trobriand Islanders led to no large scale imitation on the part of other peoples, but the same kind of isolated moral community was tried in ancient Israel and in ancient Greece and, with respect to some features even though not with respect to all, they have been imitated in many communities ever since.

The chief advantage, then, of the isolated moral communities is to contribute to the broad world of the human species that richness of difference which might otherwise be lost in a uniformity of culture. Morality, of course, has to do with a certain range of values, and values are not exclusive affairs. More than one kind of dance is possible and more than one kind of morality is also. While the Australian bushman envies us our freedom from the elaborate ritual behavior which is imposed on him in the presence of his mother-in-law, we envy the four wives and innumerable concubines which are permitted to the devout Arab followers of Mohammad. The color and texture which makes life worth while is not provided by a monotonous repetition of the same pattern but by a variety of patterns, and this is no less true of morality than it is of any other set of values. Men travel in order to find out how other people live, and there is a refreshment to the experience whenever it consists in an encounter with novelty.

The disadvantages of isolated moral communities are those which arise from the very fact of smallness. Small communities when they are self-sufficient tend to be hostile to neighboring peoples, thus denying that affinity of all members of the human species whatever their societies and cultures and in this way cancelling many of the possibilities for the sharing of values which is such an intense source of enjoyment for those whose width of experience as well as of empathy makes it possible. Small communities tend to be more tightly organized and therefore rigid. Change does not take place readily for the reason that there is usually little freedom. Moral prescriptions are rigidly laid down, and there is as a consequence little latitude for exceptional individuals to develop the kind of innovations which might spell progress for the society. The moral rules in an isolated community are apt to be more restrictive than permissive, more prohibitive than facilitative.

The solution might be a world civilization, having the advantage of wide communication and interfertilization made possible by a universal set of moral rules, with the additional advantage of the toleration of difference operating at the local level. In other words, there would be a kind of flexibility made possible by the absence of uniformity at one level together with the kind of organization made possible only by the presence of uniformity at another.

Finally, it must be noted that we have been discussing the ethics of the human species as though that species were confined to the surface of the earth. There is always the possibility that the human species as it is on the earth itself constitutes an isolated moral community, cut off as it is from other such communities on other planets. We do not know that the life, which there must almost certainly be on millions of other planets, does not resemble the life on our own to the extent that there are human beings more or less like ourselves and precisely at the same stage of evolutionary development, but we must acknowledge that this possibility exists; in which case when we speak of an ethics of the human species, meaning a universal species, we are doing no such thing but instead confining ourselves to a globally isolated moral community.

CHAPTER II

CHARACTERISTICS OF THE HUMAN SPECIES

(a) Species Type Responsibility and Confrontation

If humanity can be justified as an isolate in terms of its own organic history the rest is easy. For biologists do admit and even insist that it is an authentic species. *Homo sapiens* has progeny which are fertile and breed true. Moreover, the whole of humanity is a single species.

Every species has its own characteristics. And so as we should expect from the members of the species *Homo sapiens* there is a species-responsible behavior. This is the focal point perhaps on which the entire argument of this book rests, and so it is hoped that the fastenings are secure. The species is an organism in virtue of its similarity to other organisms, its possession or organic characteristics, such as self-repair, growth and reproduction, in a word its similarities; and it is set apart from other organisms in virtue of its peculiarities as a type of organism. What then are the peculiarities of the human type? The answers to this question have been many and varied, ever since Aristotle suggested that man is a rational animal. My own answer will be given in terms of a cosmic principle which was enunciated in Part II, Chapter 2, Section (b). There I spoke of type responsibility. Here I shall add a characteristic which I think it is possible to find in man alone. This consists in his *recognition* of his type responsibility.

Man in virtue of his consciousness finds himself upon various occasions stimulated by confrontation with examples of the entire furniture of the cosmos (including of course the conception of the cosmos itself). He is so to speak confronted by the cosmos, and by various types of material objects, from the physical through the chemical and the biological to the psychological and the cultural. To each he responds with a characteristic behavior. I shall have something to say about the nature and the consequences of the confrontation in each case in the course of this book. But I shall be especially interested in one particular kind of confrontation, the confrontation of man with the entire human species.

We shall see in the next chapter how universals are defined as the representation of (mainly) absent material things. Here we are able to observe the same phenomenon confined to the human. The universal character of confrontation for the human species mainly implies the representation of absent members. When the individual confronts his fellow members in a common humanity he generally encounters concretely only those of his own society. These are the encounters he has from day to day. But the greater part of humanity is absent, either in space or in time (or both). Those who are absent merely in space may count among his contemporaries yet live elsewhere on the earth. (We will omit here the very genuine possibility that the greater part of his human contemporaries may be on other planets in this or other galaxies.) Those who are not his contemporaries are absent in time; either they lived before he was born in any of the many preceding millennia or they will live after he has died.

It will be recalled here that according to the principle of type responsibility "all individuals are attracted to all other individuals in virtue of a common dependence upon type responsibility" and that according to confrontation theory "conduct toward another" took place "in consideration of all others." Our emphasis now shifts somewhat in view of the fact that the dependence of the individual here deepens and is stipulated for existence rather than attraction or consideration.

At the level of the whole of humanity the principle of type responsibility is in the form of a theorem, which reads somewhat as follows.

An individual exists among other individuals in virtue of those of his fellows who are not present and for whom through the species he is responsible.

"Not present" here could mean absent in time as well as in space, and in the majority of instances of course will mean the former. In this particular relationship man relies upon his type responsibility. It is with the common humanity of all men that the governance of type responsibility is to be found. My theory takes the global generalization seriously. It means that no individual however individual is merely an individual. Each individual is also a member of a type, and as a member he enjoys the privileges but bears the responsibilities. He lives, in other words, under the obligations of type responsibility. In this way humanity interposes itself between the individual and his society. The individual does not act entirely for himself because he is not an absolute individual. He is a member of a species, an example of a type. And so he acts partly as a result of his type responsibility. Humanity is a factor in every one of his social contacts and influences all of his social behavior. The effect of large aggregates of human individuals seems to be longer life for the individual. Consider for example the extended longevity of the individual in the great western civilization. The spectacle of India and China proves that such aggregates are not a sufficient cause of longevity though they may still be a necessary one. Science does not come out of isolated agricultural communities. The reinforcement given to the individual by surrounding him with members of his own species is certainly evidence for the principle of type responsibility at the species level, as stated above.

We have spoken of type-responsibility for the short-range self as involving society. For the long-range self, as we shall presently note, it will involve the cosmos. Here for the intermediate-range self it involves humanity. Thus with the ethics of the human species we find for the first time humanity playing a double role. It is the entity confronted by the individual and also the entity conditioning the confrontation. Humanity as a whole has to be taken into consideration when the individual confronts humanity as a whole. Thus every such encounter is fully human, and no other encounter is entirely so.

In the ethics of humanity the external relations of individuals are to be regarded chiefly (though by no means exclusively) as connecting the individual with other individuals. We shall discuss the external relations with types lower than his own in the scale of the integrative levels in this part, and we shall discuss the external relations of individuals with the cosmos when we talk about religion. Here, however, I might just add this by way of contrast. Anything lower than a living organism is incapable of acting against its type, but organisms have the choice. A sow who eats her young is violating the principle of type responsibility, violating it, that is to say, *in principle*; for in this case there is no confrontation. For only those organisms can be held responsible for the consequences attendant upon the making of a choice who have the choice. We are entitled to speak then of physical interaction, of animal encounter, and of human confrontation, understanding with the latter term the full development of type responsibility.

Type responsibility can best be understood as a kind of intervening variable interposed between any two members of the same species. The confrontation of any human individual by any other imposes a set of obligations as well as privileges upon the confronted individual. The privileges are those of mutual assistance, but the obligations are much larger; and this difference in degree lends to the human species its axiological superiority. The obligations can be understood only in terms of the theory of confrontation as it exists at this level.

Confrontation theory at the level of the ethics of humanity can be formulated somewhat as follows.

Conduct toward a society, in consideration of other societies.

The posture of individual man confronted by his species involves as the final step in organization the relation between societies. In having this concern the individual represents in himself the good of his entire species, and as he works toward an international social organization he works toward the good of his species. We must be careful to say now that we are talking only about the human species on the surface of the earth, since very possibly the species exists elsewhere, though for the present inaccessible from the earth.

Everything in existence looks upward for its end and downward for its means, upward for its purpose and downward for its mechanism. Confrontation here at the level of humanity means that when an individual deals with his society, he does so in view of the fact that his society is related to other societies. Those individuals especially who have promoted cooperation in international relations, such as the League of Nations after world war I and the United Nations after world war II, and sought the establishment of international law, but also those individuals who have sought to promote competition, up to and including armed conflict with those societies which stood across the efforts to organize humanity, have been acting in view of confrontation at the level of the human species and in some relevance to it.

(b) Demotic and Heroic Man

It will be recalled from the last part that order is good and disorder bad, and that such a distinction is assumed by the necessity commonly felt for maintaining a social order. Now social order is, as we have seen, supported by congruence and damaged by collision. Supported by treaties, for example, and damaged by wars. Let us next see how this works out for the individual faced with his moral obligations to the human species.

Employing as usual the distinction between demotic and heroic man, first introduced in the discussion of the ethics of the individual, it will be seen that the demotic morality of humanity includes both the right of every individual to be counted as human and his duty to behave like a man. This is not usually a matter of debate; everyone would insist upon the regimen of demotic man who counts all humans as men (though of course not everyone does).

The many unexceptional individuals who make up the bulk of the human population are collectively "demotic man." Everyone speaks for him and he does not speak for himself. He is in his quantity the matrix of everything which is both good and bad about the human species. Individuals do not count in this connection, but their numbers do. They are represented in every assembly, the basis of sovereignty. Subdivided by their majority trades, so that we come to speak of "the farm bloc" or "the voting bloc" or "the city bloc", they have values in the aggregate that they do not have separately, the clearest instance perhaps of a whole which is more than the sum of its parts. Yet the whole derives its properties from the individuals which are its parts. And we speak of this whole not collectively but in characteristic fashion, representatively: demotic man, the individual who is typical of the precinct (as we would now call the demes). One demotic man is like another; and this authorizes us to speak of him typically and to choose the type itself as a representative, in this case considered as an individual. For while it is the mass that matters, each individual is so like another individual that none differs appreciably from the type to which he belongs.

The morality of demotic man consists in conforming well to the demands of his society. Reaching upward toward humanity will be something which by definition he does poorly. He can in fact do so only by identifying his society with the ideal and seeking to impose it upon others as the master society. He understands the spread to humanity only in terms of master and slave. The leaders who belong to demotic man are slave leaders with the slave morality, dictators like Mussolini or his more powerful imitator, Hitler. In seeking the good beyond their reach they succeed in achieving only evil for themselves and their followers. It is not good to live beyond one's moral income, and no good comes of endeavoring to do so. The morality of demotic man is achieved when he succeeds in being a model citizen.

Many things distinguish heroic man from demotic man. Perhaps chiefly however it is this; that while each demotic man is like every other, each heroic man is *sui generis*. Achievements may be classified; but nothing significant is gained for knowledge in this way, since every achievement is distinguished from every other precisely in the respect that counts.

However, abilities are not evenly distributed among men, and obligation has therefore to be measured in terms of ability: a man can only do what he can. Thus one with great ability has no right to die until he has gained some victory for the human species; this is the duty of heroic man. It is the right of every hero to claim distinction and the duty of every hero to advance humanity. In his originality a man stands closer to humanity than he does to society since what he gains he gains for the whole human species. To this end the hero must rely upon his own strength. In his original works, whether they be of thought (as in inductive discoveries), of feeling (as in works of art), or of action (as in political or religious deeds) a man shows his inner essence, divested of his heredity and of his society. He stands alone, and in this stance he is one with all of humanity. His society often recognizes this superior affiliation and punishes him for it.

Thus he does not enjoy the affiliation without cost. The posture of a heroic man is taken toward humanity from within a particular society. When a man goes against his society to benefit humanity (as is so often necessary) he is living within the code of the human species, a code unwritten and often unacknowledged but operative and powerful none the less. The originality of the individual, given enough such individuals (who are always in any case a tiny minority of any population) contributes to the completeness of humanity. Societies were after all constructed by the inventiveness as well as the participation of individuals, and if humanity is to be richer than societies it must be because original individuals continue to forge ahead. Originative individuals make possible that richness of difference without which a sufficient number of structures and values could never be actualized and the dimension of completeness never fulfilled. The differences between societies provide the richness, but opposition is more likely than harmony under such circumstances. Collision is almost provided for when congruence is excluded.

In an hypothetical world society in which there was complete organization and harmony but in which the values were uniformly the same over the whole earth, the requirement of consistency would be met but not that of completeness. Thus there are limits to the extent to which society can subjugate the individual, when humanity requires individuality for completeness. The entire man is one who stands for himself in society but partly independent of it thanks to the support of the human species which is represented in him and made possible only by him.

It is the dilemma of heroic man that we see so clearly the divisions between the moral integrative levels and the conflicts as well as the congruences which so often are called out in particular instances. There are moral levels below the social, as we have already noted: the individual's moral obligations to his own person, for instance; and there are moral levels above the human, as we shall note in the next part: the individual's moral obligations to the cosmic universe. Here however the possibly conflicting obligations of the hero to his own society and beyond it to humanity are dramatically portrayed.

Let us consider an example. Perhaps friendship will serve us best. Friendships can be based on social considerations or on the human species. Two men may be friends because they have the furtherance of a particular social institution in common; they may both be musicians or postal clerks and so feel the bond which exists between them through society. In a far grander sense, two men may be friends because they feel a common humanity. What they have in common may be less social but far deeper, and may have a response to the awareness of a similarity of being in common. This is friendship at its most meaningful, even though either degree of friendship is good because friendship is good. The unrecognized or even persecuted genius is a familiar figure, if never among contemporaries then at least always in social history.'

Every act is the effect of a particular on a particular. Now it is necessary in this connection to recall the constituents of a particular. They are both particular and universal; particular insofar as any material thing is unique, and universal insofar as the parts which belong to the material thing and the class to which the material thing belongs are abstract. Now the strength of the morality of an act is determined by the extent to which its universal constituents are made central. Does a man act for himself as a particular or for himself as a member of society or for himself as the member of a species or for himself as a cosmic entity? It is sometimes possible to see the symbolism in the act even though every act is of course incurably particular, for the symbolism carries the generality and hence the significance.

What a man is responsive to depends upon his moral equipment as a man. How far is he capable of feeling, how subtle are his sensory receptors? Thus while type responsibility involves responsibility, it also involves generalization. For the responsibility extends from the individual through the type to all human individuals living, dead or unborn. It has been recognized since Kant that any valid moral principle must be generalizable but not what the principle of generalization itself is. Type responsibility is a universal moral law not as posited *ab initio* through the postulation of some particular moral principle, such as the categorical imperative, but because of the nature of the similarity of members of the same type. Not to be the only living representative of a given type means to have the help of others in sharing the burden, but to be a living representative among what is always a minority of all the members of a given type means to bear a proportional part of the burden of representing the absent members. Thus the universal moral law is not, as Kant says, universal because we will it, but we will it because it is universal. Kant's contribution, however, has been considerable. We owe to him the idea that happenings are conditioned; but how they are conditioned and by what is another matter, and even that they are conditioned in the way that he said they were is not sure.

CHAPTER III

THE MORALITY OF THE HUMAN SPECIES

(a) Two Limited Species Principles

But beyond social morality there is another morality which I have here named the morality of the human species, to which the individual is answerable in two ways: through himself as human and through his society. I have discussed the first way as divided into demotic and heroic morality. For the second way it will be necessary to go not beneath society to the essential nature of the individual but beyond society to a trans-cultural morality. Do any general principles of human morality exist? I think so, and I shall endeavor by way of illustration to point to two such principles.

According to the first of these principles, every society is stabilized and established on the basis of some limited moral code which its members regard as authorized. The authorization may be supposed finite, as for instance when the founding fathers of the state authorize it by writing a charter which is formally adopted by representatives of the people; or it may be supposed infinite, as for instance when a divine authority authorizes it by handing it in writing to a religious representative of the people; in the former case, the Constitution of the United States, and in the latter case the Ten Commandments handed to Moses on Mount Horeb.

According to the second of the two principles of human morality, except under very special circumstances specifically to be designated, no member of an in-group shall be hurt and no member of an out-group shall be helped. The special circumstances are when hurting a member of the in-group helps the group or when helping a member of the out-group helps the in-group. It is not socially tolerated in any society that a man injure his neighbor, and it is not approved that a foreigner be treated as though he were a member of the in-group.

From the first principle it is clear that the members of every society tend to identify their own moral code with the one possible morality. They regard it as part of the nature of things, they consider it the only fit and proper morality for any society and they are sure it is authorized by God or the gods. In short, they themselves identify their own morality with a trans-cultural morality. But at the same time, as the second principle illustrates, they also use the first principle to identify themselves with the morally-superior people. There is no evil involved in an immoral act toward a foreigner, just as there is no good involved in an injury toward a fellow-citizen. But the two principles appear quite differently from the perspective of the ethics of the human species.

We have noted that the first principle leads individuals to identify the moral code of the society to which they belong with the absolute and irrefrangible truth concerning human relations. But this militates against bonds which are nevertheless humanity-wide. The second principle leads to open conflicts between societies who regard each other as beyond the pale. Both principles therefore act against the best of the human interests which cannot leave any humans out of the account and cannot morally set any human against any other human in the use of force destructively.

If we can take a deep look into the distant past, we find discouraging facts. The two most ancient institutions in human history are cannibalism and astrology. The eating of human enemies, and the divining of the future by reading an analogy between the markings on the livers of animals and the shape of stellar constellations, have perhaps enjoyed more widespread practices than any other institutions that could be named. From the perspective of the ethics of the species the first is immoral; and from the scientific perspective the second is not only grossly misleading but, if falsehood is immoral, then also immoral because false.

(b) Beyond the Two Principles

In the long run the ethics of the human species cannot stop with the limitations of finite societies. Such societies are needed, and they are good, but in the end the good is limited if it is not subordinated to the other needs of the human species. These latter needs call for a more inclusive conception of humanity. It is not possible even to a society to survive merely on the basis of its local code. The local code is a necessary ingredient, an indispensable element in the day to day working of its institutions; but if the society is to prosper it must be open-ended, and this means making available horizons beyond the closures which are inherent in the codified laws.

As a single human society—the western—approaches in extent the

global society, the question of the ethics of humanity as a whole becomes more exigent. For instance it can no longer be said that what
furthers the continuance of life is good, as Herbert Spencer did. While
what is true of a limited neighborhood is true throughout the whole of
space, it is also true that the productivity of the earth and the human
capacities for organizing distribution—always dependent upon political organization—are limited. There may be too many people now,
from this point of view. Yet the more humans establish their own
artificial environment the more they have in common, for there are
many natural environments but there tends to be only one artificial
environment. Thus an international morality appears inevitable. The
fact that man seems on the brink of discovering how to control himself
through genetics does not detract from his moral responsibility but to
the contrary makes it more crucial. What about the issues of biological
evolution? Is it the duty of humanity to further the development from
its own species of a higher species? The extrapolation of the change
from ape to man would indicate a further change from man to moral
superman.

But more of this later. In the meanwhile one has only to remember
the origins of societies and predict the benefits of the global society of
the future in order to count all persons living and dead as well as not
yet born as members of it and so to include in it the entire species, at
least so far as that species is known to earth-bound creatures. It is
possible that if the progress of the spread of any single society be
carried far enough, the social and the human may merge and become
one, and social ethics grow into human ethics. There are many grounds
for this, especially the deeply common humanity of the members of
the species *Homo sapiens*.

Humanity in reference to individuals confirms generality. True and
false means having or lacking correspondence with something in any
and every society. Does not the basic similarity of all men and the
incurably general nature of all language tell us something about the
limits of morality? They lie far from the center at which we find social
morality, and they depend upon the conception of humanity as an
abstraction having exactly as much reality—no more but also no less—
then its individual and interacting concrete members.

Morality exists for the human species through its total commitment
to the universal. Individuals, social groups, artifacts, institutions, societies, all lose their particularity and merge into the general. Individual men are replaced by, and subordinated to, Man. Individuals

are merely the representatives of absent men, the living surrogates of
the class. Every man is a member of the class, Man. For the class
covers more than living men, it covers all those who have lived and
died and all those who have not yet been born. Indeed it covers more
still: all those who could be born but will not, the evanescent and the
possible as well as the concrete and the admissible.

What human individuals have in common, then, is their sheer
humanity. Not the way in which they live nor the customs they follow,
not the beliefs that they hold and not the pleasures they prefer to feel
—all these are as nothing when measured against the weight of the
basic facts of their existence: that they are born in pain, grow and
develop, decline and die, against a background of intermittent pain.
Except for the extreme rational dogmatist (who certainly is prevalent)
what people have in common counts for more than their differences.
In the end it is man who matters most to men. There is some allevi-
ation of pain in the recognition of a common brotherhood of suffering.
It is pain, and the final pain of death, that makes the whole world kin.

The thoughts, the feelings and the actions of the individual must be
predicated on the fact of a common humanity to which he belongs
insofar as he exists at all, from which so many of his pleasures are
derived, which can be itself the source of so much of his pain, and with
which such adjustments as he is capable of making will best serve his
interests and reward his efforts.

The good for humanity is what is needed by humanity, that is to
say, needed from the environment in order that mankind may survive.
A mild climate with a temperature range averaging somewhere between 50° and 75° F., an atmosphere containing the right amounts of
oxygen and nitrogen, a soil suitable for the support of living organisms,
a self-sustaining cycle of fauna and flora. These are in human terms
the needed goods. Humanity confronts its environment, physical,
chemical and biological, with the good as it appears to humanity at
the interface where mankind meets the non-human. In this way the
two segments of nature show a natural cleavage. Humanity is a small
segment of a large and all-encompassing natural world in which all
segments are bonded with structures developing their necessarily
emergent qualities. We shall see that nature appears to mankind in all
its harmonic integrity, through the capacity for feeling.

There is more of course to this confrontation, but we are concerned
merely with the axiological properties, in an effort to describe the
ethical. The relatively confining enclosure of man within the thin skin

of earth makes it imperative that ethics be understood largely in terms of the nearby environment. The far away environment affects chiefly those features of the nearby environment which provide the human goods. There are far-away layers of goods, with the earth at the center; for the earth needs the solar system, the solar system needs the galaxy, and in all likelihood the galaxy needs what the astronomers currently call the "local group" of galaxies. But the earth with its atmosphere and sunlight constitutes an available environment, an arbitrary isolate for the purpose of ethical consideration; for it is within this portion of the total environment that mankind finds its good.

Thus we are justified in considering as the good for mankind the qualities of the available environment. This is the world of mankind's external relations, the organization to which man is bonded. What is good in the environment from the position of mankind is what is conducive to prolonged human existence, and what is bad is what is obstructive of prolonged human existence. A common humanity is contained for individual man first and foremost in the fact that the confrontation with the available environment is the same for all men. Each man encounters such qualities at the interface, and knows in the external world of humanity a common source of help and harm. The good is what works for species survival, the bad what works against it.

CHAPTER IV

MORAL ENCOUNTERS WITH NEAR-BY SPECIES

(a) To Eat or be Eaten

Each type of organism is pyramided over lower types in an eating hierarchy, the more complex ingesting the less complex. Food is an intimate form of dependence; the freedom gained by the higher organism with its greater range of capacity is obtained only at the expense of the sacrifice of the lower. What is prey at a given level of complexity from above is predator at the same level from below. With living organisms the good begins to be exclusively an asymmetrical quality of external relations, unless it can be claimed that it is as good for the wildebeest to be eaten by the lion as it is for the lion to eat the wildebeest (and this has in fact been claimed by those who assert that were it not for the hunger of the lion there would be nothing to keep the number of wildebeests down and the consequent overbreeding would insure that most of them would starve). When a wildebeest is eaten by a lion that wildebeest has served the lion by its death, but what did it serve with its life? So complicated an organism could not have had the sole purpose of being destroyed.

It is difficult not to think of Nietzsche in this connection, and of his conception of life as a nutritive process united under the will to power. He tended to see the process in terms of rights rather than duties, so that one has only to change the signs in order to produce a moral perspective from the same data. In return for existence, an organism incurs duties.

All living organisms have a common bond in virtue of the possession of the property of life. There is a deep inner connection between all vital beings. Thus for any given species there is a moral obligation which it owes to all other species. The recognition and fulfillment of such an obligation is what I call species-responsible behavior.

Thus far, the situation would seem simple, yet it is not. For among the higher species which live as parasites on the lower is man. It would not be possible at the present time for man to live without eating members of lower species of organisms, though the day may come when food can be synthetically constructed from inert materials. Man in fact eats the individuals of many of the lower species; he preys on vegetables but also on other animals. He could not exist unless he did. Without sufficient aggression he could not kill and eat other animals, which is an indispensable condition of his own survival. But what about his moral obligations to those same animals in terms of the bond which is common to all organisms? What I call "species evil" is the evil inherent in the necessity of the human species to live as a parasite on all other organic species which serve it for food. More generally, species evil is the result of the inability of the species to survive without harm to other species. The closer to its own species another species is, the greater the obligation to it of individual members, it would seem. This fact is recognized in the care exercised on pets. Cats and dogs usually but pet sheep and goats, chickens and other farm animals, have been at times the recipients of great personal affection.

The subjugation of a subordinate species inevitably generates a certain amount of bad behavior. The morally bad is inherent in the eating hierarchy for the eaten as certainly as the morally good is inherent in food for the hungry; it was what was needed. Man needs beef to eat. Yet those who have been to a slaughterhouse are hardly in a position to argue from the point of view of cattle that man is what is needed. Animal husbandry has its unethical as well as its ethical side. The worst is that such conventional aggression tends to spill over into man's behavior toward his own species.

Professor Whitehead has observed that "life is robbery."[1] I would go much further and say that it involves murder. The life of one species is made possible by the murder and subsequent consumption of the members of another. Diet defeats all moral theory. If there indeed is a deep inner connection between all vital beings then the eating of beef is a kind of cannibalism, and the fact that we have prescribed manners for cooking, serving and eating steaks only means ritual cannibalism.

Not all organisms are eaten because not all can be. Some vegetables are poisonous unless properly cooked, while others are poisonous under all circumstances. Tapioca is an instance of the former, certain varieties of mushrooms of the latter. An important ethical question might be raised here. Of all the classes or organisms existing on the earth some lend themselves to supporting the human species while others do not.

[1] *Process and Reality*, Part II, Chapter III, Section S.

Why is the hierarchy so constructed that we can live pyramided over some species while we must keep our distance from others? Evidently there are definable limits to species support in terms of the generalization of the consumption principle.

We resent greatly our own parasites and seek by all means to destroy them, although some—varieties of intestinal bacteria, for instance—are necessary to our well-being and it may be to our very existence. Is it because they are lower in the evolutionary series than we? Would we welcome as good for the cosmos being eaten by the members of a higher species? Thus we are not good members of the cosmos, able and willing to take our places in the hierarchy and to be sacrificed as we ourselves sacrifice lower orders. At the present time we know of no higher organic species. And this gives us leave to behave immorally; worse still: to refuse to recognize such behavior as immoral, except in some connections. There are religions and religious leaders who take the crime of eating related organisms into the account. But their counsels have not generally prevailed. As indeed how could they, if the human species is to survive?

Upon the solution to this puzzle perhaps all of ethics depends. The existence of morality is not necessarily dependent upon the validity of some system of which men of good will might approve. A morality is simply a system of conduct, and the most repulsive and seemingly contemptible of moralities must yet be classified as moralities. Thus a thieves' compact or a murder ring is a morality even though in a wider context of judgments centered on what is good for the whole human species such arrangements must be condemned and if possible prevented. What we are talking about in the morality of the human species is what is good for it. Now what is good for the whole of it may be bad for part of it (such as a belligerent nation which wishes to enslave all the members of other nations), thus compelling us to distinguish between humanity considered as a class and individuals and societies considered as the members of subclasses. For the individual the good is clear. The purpose of life is to continue living; but this is true for the class, not so always for the individual. The individual's own end may be reached when he sacrifices his life to gain something for humanity. In this effort every individual fails directly but may partly succeed indirectly. Death marks the direct failure. Children and material culture indicate partial indirect success.

So much for the individual, but now what about the species? Here we encounter the problem presented by what the species must appropriate from its immediate environment in order to survive. It must have organic food. Thus animals are hunted and slain, and often exterminated in the process. Those which are good for man to eat may suffer an even worse fate. They may be bred in order to be eaten. Many organisms, from oysters to cattle, are maintained for this purpose. Such an existence would be acceptable if all morality were to consist in the obligation of man to himself. But it does not. Morality does not end even with man's obligations to near-by species, but continues on and does not stop until it includes everything in existence. For all animals live on plants and all plants live on inert materials. Everything in existence must be more or less what it is if man is to be what he is. The dependence is hierarchical and cuts right through the entire series of moral integrative levels. Thus the moral problems of man may be crucial when man confronts man but they exist in all of his confrontations, including those with far-away species. We shall examine some of the latter in the next part of this book.

In the meanwhile, there is the immediate moral problem of diet. From this point of view, eating far away in the hierarchy of organisms seems better than eating close by. Many moralists have felt this urgency and have sought to exist on grain, fruit and nuts. But vegetarians have not been notably successful. Meat is a condensed and highly effective food, besides, a certain amount of protein is essential. We are accustomed to it, by which we mean that it has become so traditional that we regard it as right as well as good. But is it right? We have noted the universal history of cannibalism, but we have come to despise it, at least under ordinary circumstances. The same man who is revolted at the mere thought of cannibalism will call for his beef rare or even uncooked, in "steak tartar." (I would not be surprised to learn that the Tartars call it "steak european.")

Human ethics is a subspecies of ethics, the external qualities of the individual human which come into their effects when individuals stand in some relation. We must answer for what we have done and continue to do to brother sheep and sister cow. "Good" or "bad" so far as the human species is concerned means having or lacking correspondence with something of value in every society. To the species of higher animals on whom we subsist we are guilty of immorality.

(b) The Incompleteness of Human Goods

For the third and last time in this part of the book we encounter two apparently conflicting propositions, and they are similar to those we encountered at the end of the last two parts. For there is an authentic level of ethics at which humanity is autonomous. And yet humanity is not an absolutely valid ethical isolate.

Below the species level lies the social; every society enjoys a certain autonomy. The autonomy of society is felt by the species in connection with those nationalistic claims which society possesses over against the ground which it holds in common with other societies. It is manifest in the obstacles it places in the way of exceptional individuals who reach toward a common humanity by contravening the laws of a more limited society. The species level lies above the social level but is not entirely independent of it.

Above the species level lies the cosmic level. Humanity is an organization within the greater organization of the cosmos, with privileges from it but also with obligations to it which argue against the absolute autonomy of humanity. The workability of an organization of the human species implies, as we have noted, an ethical ideal, and thus points to a condition of incompleteness in any local and immediate sense. In a word, no society is able to become tantamount to humanity, but humanity does consider itself tantamount to the significant part of the cosmos if not to the whole of it.

The higher the level toward which the individual aims the more he is compelled to neglect the legitimate claims of the lower levels. There is a sense in which noble aspirations have their immoral side. The conflict of goods so developed has been noted time and again. It is often impossible for the individual to do justice to himself, his society, the human species, and the universe of being, all at one and the same time. But if he seek to do so at different times, only one end can be sought, only one goal pursued, only one level served. Thus the bad is a necessary concomitant of the good in a finite domain, and evil an accompaniment of every good served, just in proportion to the degree of neglect. Given the richness of the ethical integrative series, the intensity of devotion is a measure of neglect. The good cannot be allowed to be served ultimately below ultimate goals.

The two levels by which the level of humanity is surrounded in some ways join hands across it. The society has connections with the cosmos in ways which transcend its participation in humanity. What is called a moral man in this connection is one whose actions look toward service to the whole of being—via religious morality. But this, paradoxically, tends to identify morality with the approved or established morality of a church. For there are many societies but there is only one human species, only one humanity; and when the individual recognizes his own humanity he does so against the being of other species. Thus he is caught by absolutes posing as relatives.

The autonomy of the species level is genuine and authentic, however, and there are rules against skipping levels. The hovering existence of the ethics of the cosmos is sufficient to remind the individual that while he is for all immediate purposes part of humanity and obligated to work for it because of the goods which he derives from it, he can also work through it toward the next integrative level. The individual, then, not only derives benefits from humanity of a social and human nature but he also aspires beyond it toward the ethics of the cosmos. Humanity for the individual is not only a goal and therefore the site of his prospective goal achievements, it is also a ladder whereby he is able to climb higher than his own petty, short-range self and aim above him in the ethical integrative series toward humanity and beyond.

One of the ways in which it is possible to rise in the ethical integrative series has little to do with fixed species. If any evidence were needed of the incompleteness of human goods *qua* human species it is the Darwinian evolutionary development of one species from another, the higher from the lower. The human species is not an absolute isolate because no species is. What greater participation in the universe of being can the human individual hope for more than that his species will develop into a higher species whose individual members will enjoy a greater participation in being? Not only "through hope toward the stars" but also—and more likely—through a determined and concerted effort—toward the galaxies. Ape may have become man through a series of fortuitous events but it was only after he took thought that the development became rapid.

We conclude then from the evidence that we are entitled to speak both of the ethics of humanity and of the incompleteness of human goods. How is this conflict to be resolved? Again, before that question can be answered we shall have to enter upon an examination of the entire commitment of the individual as well as upon the ethical nature of the world in which he is involved. He is involved with more than society, with more than his own species, for that matter, and with nothing less than the entire universe. And the next level after the human is the level of the cosmos. With the level of humanity we began to look at the problem of the individual as he examines his being apart from the specifically human, in an effort to gain insights into what it means to be a cosmic entity.

PART V

THE ETHICS OF THE COSMOS

CHAPTER I

THE COSMIC PERSPECTIVE

(a) Man Confronted by the World

My topic throughout this book has been the good for individual man. I began by considering just that, as though the individual were only a whole containing parts and not himself a part of any larger whole, or as though he were part of a larger whole which had to be considered just in connection with the perspective taken from that particular part. A certain amount of insight was gained in that way but the picture could not be completed because there are moral considerations which remain to be defined in terms of a larger context. For man is not independent but exists in virtue of his ability to adapt to his environment. Thus it became necessary to consider the morality of the human species, and now we shall have to include in our considerations the relations between the human species and other species.

There are severe limitations to human ethics. The world is wider than society—very much wider—and since society exists in virtue of a dependence upon a continual interchange between the human and the non-human environment, the welfare of the environment must be taken into consideration in morality. It was understood to some extent in the previous part that the human species is involved with other organic species, but here we shall have to include relations beyond organisms, for man exists not only in a world of organisms but also in one of physical and chemical elements: the earth, the solar system, the galaxy and indeed the entire contents of the cosmic universe. There are moral considerations which follow man in all of his involvements.

Man is confronted not only by other members of his own species but also by those of many other species which are to be found in the cosmos. Before entering on a discussion of cosmic ethics, it might be well to have a clear understanding of what is meant by the cosmos. By the cosmos here, then, is meant the actual or astronomical universe. Another and more precise definition would be: all material orders;

that is to say, all species of physical entities. For all existing things, the cosmos is the ground state.

Cosmic ethics has two broad subdivisions. There is the posture of man—individual man—confronted by the world, and there is the posture of anything in the world confronted by everything else in the world. Obviously the former is a special case of the latter, more interesting to man because it applies to man. But our thesis here is that the posture of man requires for its complete explanation everything in the world. Self-interest leads inevitably to an interest in nature. An individual who is really concerned about himself would want above all to know where he fits into that wider scheme of things out of which he emerged and into which he must disappear.

In philosophy we have fallen into a tendency to adhere to the division between persons and things because our chief concern is for persons. But that persons in the cosmic sense are superior things does not alter the fact that they are material things. That material things attract each other is also the reason why persons move toward the earth when they are deprived of support above it. Thus while stones cannot think, persons do fall. We need to know the laws of all things, of which persons constitute a subclass, before we can afford to attend to those laws which apply only to persons. We have, then, to make the two separate points and we must be careful not to confuse them. There is an ethics of man in relation to the cosmos. Man is a material thing, a part of nature and related to the rest of nature. The determination of just what those relations are is the task of ethics. But there is also a cosmic ethics, which man shares but in which he is not specially featured because he is an authentic part of the cosmos but actually a very small part. Cosmic ethics will have to be described first without reference to man.

This much seems certain, then, that human ethics is a special case of a wider area of non-human ethics, and requires that the non-human ethics also be defined and explained. I call that wider field of ethics when it is the most inclusive, "cosmic ethics." The cosmos extends beyond the characteristically human in two dimensions: the world of the very small (the microcosm): the world of elementary physical particles, of nuclear and atomic constituents, and also of molecules and microorganisms, for example; and the world of the very large (the macrocosm): the world of earth, of the solar system, the galaxy, and the meta-galaxy. Between these in size and extension lies the world of the medium sized (the mesocosm): the world of animal-sized objects, of people and furniture and trees. The mesocosm is available to ordinary human experience. It is roughly speaking what can be seen with the unaided eye, while the macrocosm needs a telescope and the microcosm a microscope. The cosmos of course includes all three divisions. Vast forces together with their qualities are at work in all three divisions, though they are not always equally or easily detectable. What is the quality of those short-range but very powerful forces which hold together the constituents of the atom? Yet where there is a quality, on our definition can there fail to be an ethics? We are dealing for the most part with a tiny world, a world of the human, but we can learn about it by learning about what is true of the whole of which the human is a part. For what is true of human ethics does not necessarily hold for the cosmos, while what is true of cosmic ethics must hold for anything in the cosmos, including the human.

In a tight and narrow band around the surface of the earth and extending a very little way above and below it there is wound an organization of living and non-living systems complex in structure and intimately related in a series of dependencies, all somewhat interlaced by means of a succession of both necessary and accidental occurrences. The occurrences are the expressions of the needs of the separate systems, particularly the living systems, more or less imperfectly driven to appropriate action in an effort to obtain need-reductions.

Life is matter shaped in terms of a maximum complexity of forms together with the qualities which emerge from those forms, such as self-direction and replication. Life, in short, is a higher form of matter, working through lower forms to accomplish its higher aims, to build within the animal organism of man himself those thoughts and outside him those artificial material constructions by means of which he hopes to transcend. The two sets of limitations on his conditions, both those limitations which lie within himself and those contained in his environment.

(b) Cosmic Ethics

Organic ethics as we know it is deeply committed to terrestrial ethics. The surface of the earth supports various layers of organizations of compound chemical substances, living organisms and material artifacts. These exist in various degrees of order (with various overlappings and intersecting orders) and of disorder, that is to say, of law obeyed but limited by chance disobedience. As with human social ethics the elements of this assortment are bound together qualitatively through bonds, each with the members of its own type, and each type with other types in a hierarchy of types which we may now describe as integrative level components.

There are of course local peculiarities, and for most of this book we have been gazing at some of these intensely. We singled out for special consideration a particular type of organism: the human. But now we must move outward and take into our perspective all types, and for this purpose especially those which are large either in size or in membership or both. The cosmos is a meta-galactic system, an organization of galaxies. And a galaxy is an organization of suns and planets, of dust and gas. Planets are rare and exceptional objects but so far as our limited knowledge goes they and only they furnish the conditions for the development of life. Taken in terms of a widespread chemistry of matter, living organisms are carbon rarities in a hydrogen universe.

We have not left our topic of individual ethics, then, if we widen it to the consideration of cosmic ethics. According to Plutarch it was a general principle of Chrysippus to begin all ethical inquiries with a consideration of the order and arrangement of the universe.[1] We have only planned to place individual ethics in its natural moral setting. But for this purpose we shall be obliged to talk for a while in cosmic rather than in human terms, involving moral encounters with far-away rather than with near-by species. No species lasts forever. Some species die out, others suffer evolutionary changes. And, perhaps more importantly, planets pass away as well as come into existence. The earth is currently estimated to be some 4.6 billion years old and has probably only an equal amount of time left. But there is a strong likelihood of life on many other planets in this and other galaxies, and presumably also other species take up the tasks and privileges of existence. But there is no prolonged continuity in any one place.

A brief recapitulation at this point may be helpful. By "cosmos" I understand the actual universe, by "ethics" of course the theory of the good. I will not speak of the good of the possible universe, since perfection is not the only possibility. The imperfect, or partly bad, is also possible, since it exists; and we must be prepared to account for the ontological status of future evil. I call "good" that object which does more good than harm, and "bad," that object which does more harm than good. There is also (gazing into the never-never land of hazardous prospects) the speculative ethics of Leibniz' "possible worlds," but I

---

[1] Plut. *De Stoic. Repugn.*, c. 9 (1035 a I–f 22). Quoted in Copleston, *History of Philosophy*, I, p. 395.

mention them only to show the obligation of the productive philosopher to keep speculation open. The discovery of anti-matter has stimulated such speculations once again.

For the theory is already sufficiently expanded. "Cosmic" in moral terms is a pretentious word. Perhaps I should say "global" rather than "cosmic." Our experience has been for the most part confined to this planet. I say "cosmic" then rather than "global" because I feel it is safe to assume the truth of Milne's cosmological principle[1] as perfected by Bondi and Gold,[2] that the perspective on the universe is substantially the same from anywhere, so that it is impossible to tell where one is—or when: for it is equally impossible to tell cosmic time. "Global" on this principle should be a fair sample of "cosmic." But it is true that the cosmological principle has never been established on evidence.

[1] E. A. Milne, *Relativity, Gravitation, and World-Structure* (Oxford 1953, University Press).
[2] H. Bondi and T. Gold, *Monthly Notices R.A.S.*, 108 (1948), 252.

THE COSMIC GOOD

(a) Matter as Good

Earlier, in Part II, chapter I, I defined the good as what is needed. When the need is felt, it becomes evident that the good is a quality. We are now ready to present the nature of the good more abstractly and more generally (and hence more cosmically) than we have been employing the term in connection with human ethics.

I define the good as the bond between whole material things. This time I use the term "bond" rather than "relation" in order to bring out the aspect of quality. For the good is above all a quality. I define quality as that which is ultimately simple. I mean here the quality of wholes, and by the definition of quality qualities are not composed of other qualities. But another aspect of qualities is disclosed when they are considered in connection with parts of material things.

I have defined quality. It now remains for me to define value. Values are qualities high in the integrative series. We speak of color as a quality and of love as a value.

Qualities (and values) are bonds between dissimilars: bonds between disparate wholes (the good), and bonds between disparate parts of the same whole (the beautiful). Qualities and values were described by Bacon as natural elections, a term adopted by Laird and changed by Whitehead, following McTaggart, to "prehensions."[1] For both of these latter philosophers, they constitute the fabric of the world.

Next I need to introduce relations in this connection. Relations are bonds between similars. Both wholes and parts are members of their respective classes and are bonded together in this way; wholes to similar wholes through their class membership, and parts to similar parts.

The good, then, is a quality. Now all qualities are connections. Relations are merely the forms of the connections. The qualities are

---

[1] A. N. Whitehead, *Science and the Modern World*, chapters III and IV; John Laird, *The Idea of Value*, chapter III.

the connections themselves, apprehended, as it were, in the middle, or at one end awaiting the other. Qualities are the stuff of existence, the essence of substance. All else—the relations and their logic—only shows where the qualities are. The way in which everything in the world is bonded together with everything else is its ethical aspect. Thus when we speak of the good we are not confined to human values but to the importance of anything to anything else. The good and the beautiful are not adjuncts to being but indispensable parts of it. What are material things without their bonds, except the irrational ground of individual reaction? But this is also the meaning of substance. Being, substance, value, these are different ways of talking about the same material entities as the necessity to do so presents itself from different perspectives.

The values of the good and the beautiful are substantives (as compared with relations, which are regulative); indeed the values are the *only* substantives: bonds seen from their qualitative side. (Seen from the quantitative and structural side they are the wholes and parts themselves bound together in this way. Consider for example bonds at various integrative levels: nuclear forces at the physical, valence at the chemical, life at the biological, awareness at the psychological, and the ethos at the cultural.) The good is constitutive rather than regulative, a bond which is constitutive of what it binds. (It should be remarked parenthetically that here we are undertaking to present little more than an attempt to analyze the ethos and to present it in its natural setting.)

Qualities are further subdivided into the intrinsic and extrinsic aspects. My understanding of intrinsic good is as old as Euclid of Megara who seems to have identified good with being.[1] It is the same bond regarded from divergent aspects. The intrinsic good is the good as felt; the extrinsic good is the good as useful; what we called earlier Mill's good. Intrinsic good is static and passive good. Extrinsic good is dynamic and active good. But in both cases it is the same good.

The very nature of a quality is to be intrinsic. And, intrinsically, the same qualities are always equal, whatever their dimensions. In the *New York Times*[2] there was an advertisement of Tiffany and Co. for two diamond rings, one priced at $154 and the other at $129,800. "Would you guess," Tiffany asked, "that these two rings are equal in value? They are because they are Tiffany diamonds and are *equal in*

[1] Diog. Laert. I, II, 106.
[2] May 7, 1964, p. 3. Italics mine.

quality. The price of the one is higher only because it is larger."

We noted early in the second part of this book that the intrinsic good is the good as understood by G. E. Moore, and the good as an ultimate real in its own right, as that which would be good if it stood entirely alone. Unlike Moore, however, I assume that quality has the character of a genus. The good is the genus and the various goods are its species. He is right in denying that there is any point in preferring one special good over another, when all special goods are equally good; but he is wrong for this reason in supposing that the good is extra-special in the sense of being non-natural when it is extra-special only in the sense that it is a genus; for a class is no less and no more natural than its natural members.

A bond is a connection; it has both a qualitative and a quantitative or structural side. The bond is symmetrical. The quality relates equally two things having a bond; it equally affects both. Thus in terms of the good everything is dependent, for every whole must have some other whole to which it is bonded.

The good, then, is a world-quality since it holds between any two material things. And since matter and energy are interconvertible, it holds between any two things which either can affect other things or can be affected by them. Every entity and every process is naturally good, and every entity and process being naturally good is also morally good. No power, then no good, because power is required to effect the good. Although power is power for good or bad, power for good or bad includes power for good, since power is needed for the good. Thus power as such must be accounted at least partly good. The only point is that some entities and processes contain more good than others; some for instance are symmetrically good while others are asymmetrically good. The good is a way of talking about the effect of a thing. And the thing is always at the very least material (for a man whose body has the material properties must also be said to be at least material even though the complexity of form of such higher organisms obscures this fact). Thus the good is the quality of a material thing considered as a whole for other things. And the good is what is needed by another thing in order to become or remain itself. It applies at all levels of existence and is not confined to human individuals and their wants.

It follows that it is better to be than not to be, and since being is a mere possibility (though a genuine one), it is also, and more definitely, better to exist than not to exist. And to be something in the most basic sense is to be something material; for without matter nothing can be and therefore nothing can be good. Thus a minimal amount of matter is a minimal good, for without it nothing can be but on it all manner of good things can be constructed. Existence is a subdivision of being, but so important that in this case the tail wags the dog. What exists has being; and even though not all of being exists, what does exist has an insistence which is peculiar to it: the qualities as well as the logic of being. It follows never the less that if it is better to be than not to be, it is also better to exist than not to exist, then it follows that the primary meaning of the word, good, is helping to exist, improving. "X is good for Y" means that in some way or other Y is improved by X. Thus to be useful to aid through a skill, to provide social facilitation, to give pleasure, to justify, to further the species, to help the individual, to express something emotively or linguistically, all are kinds of improvement. The good consists then in the margin of construction over destruction, of building over destroying, of benefiting over injuring.

From the two premises, namely, that the good is the bond between material things, and that it is better to exist than not to exist, it follows that the good may be regarded as the preserving relations between material things. The conventional units of whole material things may be anything on the scale of the integrating levels in nature, from a proton to a galaxy, and include (among other things) persons, social groups, institutions, societies, cultures, and indeed the whole of the cosmic universe.

Gravitational attraction provides us with our most graphic example. Gravitation is an example of the good at the level of the purely physical. It is presumably cosmos-wide. Every material particle "needs" every other particle and they are drawn together directly as the square of their masses and inversely as the square of the distance between them. Each is attracted to the center of the other. What is needed is from this perspective exhibiting the quality of its external relations.

If ethics is the theory of the good and the good is the attraction between wholes, then gravitation is morality at the physical level. All physical forces may be moral forces: masses rushing together so fast they damage each other or even destroy each other: a surfeit so to speak of material needs. Value at the lower of the integrative levels is a manifestation of quality and hence of the good.

(b) Good and Beautiful Quality

Considered from the side of any single material thing we have noted that the good is the quality of its external relations. Every material thing reaches out to every other with which it has a bond, and so the good is the qualitative correlate of the property of completeness. Insofar as the material thing is a whole and has parts, the bond between the parts is the beautiful and has the qualitative correlate of the property of consistency.

I call external qualities those qualities which prevail between wholes. I call internal qualities those qualities which prevail between parts (and also between parts and whole). Thus ethics is the theory of external qualities and esthetics the theory of internal qualities. Goodness and beauty are the qualities manifested by the two directions in the whole-part series of integrative levels. They are convertible. The good seen from one direction is the beautiful seen from another. That is why we are entitled to say that there is only one world-quality, and why it is permissible to assert that it is good that things should be beautiful but not necessarily beautiful that things should be good (the beautiful is higher in the series and more inclusive). If this is true, as I have elsewhere maintained,[1] then to do justice to the topic of cosmic ethics it would be necessary to insert here a treatise on the philosophy of qualities as being essentially a moral topic. It would not be of interest to those who wish to confine morality to the human variety.

Thus insofar as the conditions I have been describing are those of everything in the cosmos, it can be conceived that the world-quality appears in two guises: as goodness, the quality between wholes, and as beauty, the quality between parts. Both are internal to the cosmos, but beauty is more intense and goodness more pervasive. Goodness is external and beauty internal. When we call some things good and others beautiful, we do so because we are regarding them from a particular perspective under which these features are prominent. But there are some things generically good and some generically beautiful because these features remain prominent from many perspectives. That every good thing must have its beautiful (or ugly) side is as true, however, as that every beautiful thing must have its good (or bad) side.

Does it not come to this, then, that every quality is both a good and beautiful? It follows from the definitions of part-whole bonds in terms of the qualities of internal and external relations that the good and the beautiful are the genuine substances of the universe. The good consists

[1] "On Quality," in *Foundations of Empiricism* (The Hague 1962, Nijhoff), pp. 76–86.

in world-connections and the beautiful in how these connections are organized. The world cannot be completely good[1] but it can be completely beautiful. If it were to be completely good then it would have to be good for something beyond the world which needed the world as it is, but this lies beyond our knowledge; whereas we can know that it is completely beautiful because its total beauty is internal to it and therefore can be apprehended by a part of it.

Kant, as we have noted, was impressed by the starry heavens above and the moral law within[2] but he failed to see that there was any connection between them except such as could be derived from the consciousness of his own existence and the unknowability of the thing-in-itself. He could find a connection only by assuming that the moral law was independent of all animality even though he knew himself as an animal to be dependent on the planet earth. He was blinded by his utter subjectivity to the connections between man and the cosmos in the very terms he explicitly rejected, the continuity of material being with its multiplicity of forms.

It follows from the above that the cosmos itself considered as a whole cannot be completely beautiful. Assuming that the cosmos is unlimited then there is no whole outside it with which it can have a bond; there is nothing for it to need. This fits the description of the relation from which the quality called beauty emerges. Also, is the holy not another name for the greatest beauty, that whole which contains all things as parts and with which no other can stand outside it in bonded relation to it? The cosmos considered in this way is the *Deux sive natura* of Spinoza; there is nothing it needs. Yet the issue on this score between ethics and esthetics as to which is supreme will never be settled until we can discover whether the universe is open or closed.

(c) Particular Goods

All things are good intrinsically, some extrinsically. All that is is good in itself though not necessarily in its effects. That is to say, everything that has being except the cosmos as a whole needs and is needed by something outside itself. About the cosmos as a whole we do not know. This has become the province of religion, which often claims supernatural insight into the cause of the cosmos and its relation to a creator. But about lesser goods we are entitled to know something, at least. What is good is what is needed by anything, any entity or process.

[1] *Ontology*, IV, 1, A, iii.
[2] *Critique of Practical Reason*. Concl.

Thus a hydrogen ion is a hydrogen atom in an excited state because it is "in need of" an electron.

If the good is completeness, then every event is a moral event. How things behave, then, follows from what they are. Material things are not compelled by law to behave in accordance with law. Law is simply the way in which it is the nature of material things to behave. The natural order is the order of natural law. A particular good is accidental for a material thing possessing it, but that the thing must have some particular good is necessary. There are no material things without qualities but there is no particular quality that anything *must* have.

It has long been the custom to distinguish between the natural order and the moral order. They were present and their presence noted by two Greek gods, Dike and Themis, long before the fifth century B.C. when the philosophers distinguished between *physis* and *nomos*.[1] It is a distinction which is carried today by the terms empirical and normative. But it cannot be sustained in the presentation of cosmic ethics which is here being developed. Here the two are one and the same, and the distinction is abandoned except as it illuminates aspects. Thus in the cosmos the good is directed toward the organization which consists in a single all-embracing world-order.

Material things may be considered from their relational or from their qualitative side. On the relational side we are dealing with commensurable structures and quantities. On the qualitative side we are dealing with qualities. Many of the qualities of the more complex structures have not yet been measured. Structural properties are extensively discrete, qualitative properties intensively continuous. The continuity may be inherently incommensurable. Qualities may be defined both as that which is ultimately simple when considered as a whole and as that which when analyzed into its parts reveals infinity of quantities lying very close together. In philosophy we follow mathematics as close as we can with our irrefrangible baggage of qualities. The chief concern in ethics is with qualities: the good is a quality. This may mean that we may someday be able to measure the good. But not now, not yet.

---

[1] Jane Ellen Harrison, *Themis* (Cambridge 1927, University Press), Ch. XI.

CHAPTER III

TRUTH AND VALUE

Ethics, esthetics and logic are not addenda to philosophy but descriptions of the contents of reality, inventories of the properties of the matter and energy of the cosmos. The world is *composed* of the values of the good and the beautiful hung upon the structure of the true. Matter has truth and value because it occupies space and time. If we knew the totality of truths about any material thing, we could deduce from this its value. Understood in this way, truth is a function of space and value a function of time.

(a) Truth a Function of Space

The things to which a statement refers and whose existence in the condition which is called for by the statement make the statement true, it is assumed could exist throughout the whole of space. To say that truth is a function of space is to speak in a very general way. It will not hold unless it is legitimate to assume the truth of the cosmological principle, which suggests that there is a uniformity of spatial occupancy throughout the cosmos. But we have access only to limited portions of space in our immediate neighborhood. The existence of general knowledge relies upon the undemonstrated principle that what is true of a limited neighborhood is true throughout the whole of space, and such a principle may or may not be sound.

If "true" means "occupying space," then a true statement must be a general one for which no exception can be found in any extended situation. Extension itself must be considered as not limited to "extended now." It might be more illustrative to say that a universal proposition sweeps out a particular path in space. Thus "All men are mortal" means that "All members of the species *Homo sapiens* who ever have, who do, or who ever will, occupy space will die." Past and future extensions are also extensions. There are always more absent than present material things in any given class, and the class itself includes them equally. Truth is a function of space only if it means that for every true proposition there is a correspondence with all relevant situations throughout the cosmic universe. If it is true that $2 + 2 = 4$ there can be no exception of any remote planet or within any solar system in a distant galaxy. Abstract truth, the truths of logic and mathematics, refer to *all* of space. We insure this by deriving truths from axioms. But the same must hold for the truth of a particular proposition. "Abraham Lincoln was assassinated" means that for every Abraham Lincoln in the universe this was the manner of his death, no less true just in case there should only have been one and that one have died in this way. "Lyndon B. Johnson is President of the United States" means for every Lyndon B. Johnson and for every United States in the universe this is true, and no less so just in case there is only one. Falsity is a function of space in the same way, for it means illogical reference to spatial occupancy.

A sharp distinction must be drawn here between knowing what truth is and knowing what is true. Our position in the cosmos is somewhat limited; we are confined to the surface of a single planet in a single solar system which is eccentrically situated in a single galaxy. Now, truth is of two sorts: truth by correspondence and truth by coherence, factual and logical truth respectively. Obviously, the verification or falsification of statements referring to fact must be limited to just those which lie within the range of our experience (including in this category the experience which is obtained by means of instruments).

If we are to make up our logical and mathematical systems out of applied logic and mathematics, then the completeness of factual truth and the consistency of logical truth are somewhat incompatible. For the actual world of matter and energy is irreducible to logic and mathematics because it is not entirely answerable to law. There is always a surd element, an irrational component of chance or of disorder, which lies at the very basis of substance. Thus in any formal system purporting to account for fact we can get completeness only at the expense of consistency and consistency only at the expense of completeness. Our knowledge can be complete or it can be consistent but not both.

(b) Value a Function of Time

In showing that truth is a function of space, I argued that the extension involved was one which included extension in the past and future as well as in the present. It is clear now that in so doing I introduced time and value, although inadvertently and surreptitiously. For by bringing in the time categories I raised the question of survival in time, and value is a function of such survival.

Whatever exists in space must exist in time also. However brief the time it must be of some duration; to exist is to endure. For a material thing to exercise its effects, or to be affected, it must endure. Thus endurance is a condition of value. But to regard endurance as a condition of value does not make of the length of endurance a measure of value; a rock lasts longer than a man. There is no doubt some evidence to support the contention that the higher and more complex an entity the shorter its existence, but against this is the fact of the brief span of existence of some of the elementary physical particles.

To say that value is a function of time is to speak of the value of endurance in time. For anything to have value it must exist, and the longer it exists the longer it has value. Time on the whole is a reliable evaluator, but it is not absolute and instead employs statistical trends. To make an exact correlation, however, between amount of value and length of time of endurance is impossible. It often happens that some things which are entitled to exist the longer because of their greater amount of value do not do so because of extraneous events and influences. "The good die young" it is said, and the beautiful may also. As we shall shortly see, however, value and time tend to approach each other in extent only when many similar items are involved.

(c) Evil and Ugliness

The picture I have been endeavoring to paint thus far is one of cosmic order. The good as defined and explained assumes order. But the fact is that order is not complete throughout the cosmos, which is composed partly of order and partly of disorder. Disorder may be defined as the extent to which the elements of a given order are distributed outside that order among the elements of other orders. Order, then, is the similarity among differences, and disorder is equivalent to the difference among similarities.

If the good is the effect of order, then the bad is the effect of disorder. Disorder is not confined to logical elements or to terrestrial conditions. The astronomers have at least one photograph which they interpret as colliding galaxies and another of the "Crab" nebula which seems to have been a supernova which exploded in the year 1054. Now the cosmological principle makes the appearance of any completely unique body or the occurrence of any absolutely unique event impossible.

Uniformity is based on the cosmological principle, and the cosmos is characterized by order and disorder. Thus if there are instances of types of disorder, then there must be many other instances of the same types of disorder. The fact that they are *types* points to a certain degree of order and so the two generally are to be found together. Thus we speak of cosmic good and cosmic bad insofar as there is cosmic order and cosmic disorder.

I have defined cosmic goodness as the attraction between wholes, and cosmic beauty as the attraction between parts. This may become clearer if we place cosmic evil and ugliness on this scale. Evil then becomes the repulsion between wholes, and ugliness the repulsion between parts. Cosmic evil is that which tends to divide material things just as cosmic good is that which tends to unite them. Cosmic evil then calls attention to the limitations of finite being, that it is not infinite. Evil is the substitution of the lesser good for the greater, of the part for the whole, or the denial of the bond. In terms of material things, the good is constructive and the evil (or bad) destructive. Thus the good is whatever assists an organization and the bad whatever damages it. The bad is the quality of incompleteness, the ugly the quality of inconsistency.

Every material thing has a right to its own existence regardless of how this affects the existence of other things. To protect its existence it needs to fend off other things which by their very proximity might impinge upon its integrity. Thus intolerance of opposition is a characteristic of material things, and imposes defects which in the end tend to be fatal. But the collective result is a struggle for existence similar to the struggle for living space engaged in by plants in a tropical jungle. Not everything that could exist does exist, for there is not enough space. Occupancy always implies exclusion. Cosmic evil, then, is the result of the limitations inherent in anything actual. Roughly speaking, this is the same principle that Leibniz called "metaphysical evil." Cosmic evil is the result of the inability of any material thing to act without disturbing its environment.

Since the right involves action appropriate to the good, cosmic right calls for the proper distribution of cosmic goods. The right implies an obligation to act in accordance with the good. In order to know what is good it is necessary to know first what is right and what is true. The grand scale of the action appropriate to the good is evident in cosmic right through the cosmic universe conceived as moving in the direction of integration. But just as evolution is an exception in a cosmic universe of entropy, so ethics is an exception in the cosmic domain of species aggression: it swims upstream and makes slow way against the current.

I have tried to establish the existence of cosmic right, that is all I can hope to do here. For a full discussion of cosmic right would require the possession of all sorts of information which is not now available to us. The restoration of the good suggests an implosive universe in which all material bodies would be rushing toward each other instead of (as at present) away. The cosmic right suggests the conditions which prevailed before the "big bang," if there was one, which sent the stars and planets, the galaxies and interstellar dust and gases, separating at tremendous speeds. For the ultimate outcome of the good is not proper relations but unity. In a finite world where everything is, so to speak, divided, A and B can be "good" for each other only so long as they are within reach yet not united into one entity. But the universe never stands still, and such an arrangement, as for instance the orbits of the planets around the sun—and that of the earth in particular—can never be anything more than temporary.

The phenomenon in the cosmic universe whereby we judge cosmic good and bad is the degree of congruence and collision to be observed. The order exceeds the disorder, as we should expect of any functioning system. But there is disorder and so there is the morally bad. We tend to think of "good" in terms of approval and of "bad" in terms of disapproval. Perhaps this is right; perhaps we ought to. But not always. For it is certainly from our own limited perspective that we do so. To think in these terms is to make no sense of cosmic ethics. But then approval and disapproval in a much more limited context often has made no sense, either. They are usually based on the values of a particular species and then make the evaluation of some species in what is, for that other species at least, unwarranted terms.

Evil is not confined to the human species but is inherent in the nature of existence. An innocent young child who dies a painful death from a bacterial infection, or from an injury sustained when struck by a falling tree, is the victim of a collision between species, and no less one for not having been intentional. Anything can suffer destruction and in so doing allow for the quality of destruction, which is evil.

CHAPTER IV

COSMIC TYPE RESPONSIBILITY

I define the cosmos as all material objects and energies in space and time, all particles and all events. And I use the term "cosmos," "cosmic universe" or "universe" interchangeably. The cosmic universe is not a simple affair except insofar as it may be said to constitute a whole; (and whether it is a whole and whether as a whole it is finite or infinite, we do not at present know). It will not be necessary here to decide whether the universe is a whole except for the purposes of regarding its contents as constituting an interrelated network in which all of the particles are involved in activity-reactivity systems at various energy-levels. By asserting that the universe is a whole we are committed to nothing more than the assertion of the unity of its contents. But if it is a whole then it is unique, there being only one such material thing of which this is true.

All other material things are members of types. In any case the universe is integrated and contains many complex levels of analysis. The analytical or integrative levels, it will be recalled from the first part of this book, are roughly: the physical, the chemical, the biological, the psychological and the cultural. Each of these levels, we noted there, contains a number of sublevels. Here it will be necessary to remember only that at each level there are characteristic types of material things, with their classes, their degrees of organization and their emergent qualities.

Every material thing, whether a galaxy, a star or planet, or a living organism, belongs to a type in virtue of its similarities to many other such things. Membership in a type entails mechanical participation. Every member of a given type responds after the manner of its type. Bonds exist between any two material things in the universe, but the bonds are stronger when they are between the individual members of a given type. Bonding is not confined to contemporaries. In virtue of predominant similarities, any thing is bonded to all other things of the same type in the past and future as well as in the present: to all those which have existed and which will exist as much as to those which do exist. Ontological and epistemological absences must be accounted for in any cosmic ethics. The terribly limited contemporaneity of most ethical conceptions has a disastrous effect upon their very structure.

Such type responses make possible a mutual reinforcement which enables the members of a given type to endure, and the greater the number the longer the endurance. The largest aggregate of similar things tends to endure the longest. Consider those enormous aggregates called hydrogen clouds. Consider also those smaller aggregates of plasma called suns, or those even smaller (though still very large) aggregates of solids called planets. Thus we speak of a kind of type responsibility which any individual thing possesses in virtue of its membership in a given type. I should hastily add that no suggestion of conscious awareness is intended. Responsibility here means merely the commitment to a certain capacity for response and the likelihood of any member of a given type making the kind of response which is characteristic of that type.

But the point can be carried one step further and it is important to do so. For a member of a given type is responsible not only to all the other members of that type which exist at the same time but also to those members which did exist but do so no longer and to those which will exist but do not yet. The non-existent members of the same type belonging to the past and the future constitute by far the larger number, and so there is a responsibility to them which is even greater. The ultimate extension of species responsible behavior is responsibility to species other than organisms, and widest of all commitments. It may be formulated as follows.

An individual exists in virtue of those members of other species which do not and for which through his species he is therefore responsible.

This is the principle which I have called type responsibility. The universe at any instant contains a cross-section of its enormously extended contents through time. Whatever exists is a sample of all that did and all that will exist. The present samples are therefore representatives: symbols of what existence means in the round and on the whole. This is the true meaning of cosmic type responsibility. All types and species of beings converge to a past when their differences had not been developed. These differences are genuine—but so are the similarities; and in the struggle for existence the differences loom larger than the similarities and are the cause of mutual destructive efforts. And at the same time representing in existence those which are not in existence means responding as they did or will (or would).

Nothing is alone in the cosmos and nothing is independent. There are many kinds of dependence, but the first kind is the dependence of a member on other members of the same type. The long-range self makes demands that can be met only by a conceived identification with the whole of humanity. But the series of dependencies does not stop with the species. Thus each individual member of a given type carries the type with it, and in virtue of that type a certain responsibility. The individual member is through his species involved with the cosmos, and in this way is indicated what he can expect of the cosmos but also what he owes to it. When the individual acts, he does so in a sense as that part of the world which is an agent for the world, and therefore he is responsible—for this connection and to this extent—to the world.

CHAPTER V

COSMIC CONFRONTATION

We are now in a position to indicate some of the properties of every material thing or energy-bundle in the cosmic universe. We shall be concerned here of course only with those properties which concern value-interchanges. The ethical and the esthetic are merely special considerations of how the world is made. It is made of matter and energy and of the forms of entity and process which compose them. Ethics and esthetics are how their substance is organized. If the good is the bond between material things and, seen from the side of a single material thing, the quality of its external relations, then we are entitled to speak of the other material thing involved in the bond as the needed good. The material thing in need confronts that which it needs, and such a confrontation takes place at the interface, for the view must be the same from the other bonded thing. Moreover, there is a type responsibility involved in being a material thing at some one of the integrative levels where other (and usually many other) things of the same type are found. All material things have bonds of some degree of strength with all other things irrespective of the integrative level involved; but a special bonding is reserved for those material things which are members of the same type.

The good for the cosmos is what increases order without loss of completeness. The bad is what decreases order (or increases disorder). Intrinsic good in a material thing (other than organisms) is what is called "beauty." Extrinsic good is what is called "good." But the final word on the moral aspect of the actual universe is carried by what we may now call cosmic confrontation.

In the second chapter of the second Part of this book I spoke about confrontation and there defined it as "conduct toward another, in consideration of all others," meaning of course all other members of the same species of human individuals. Now the definition must be widened to include all other material things in the cosmic universe.

Cosmic confrontation is *conduct toward a species in consideration of other species*. Cosmic confrontation applies to all encounters between material things. There is cosmic confrontation at the boundary whenever two material things of different species encounter each other. Individual human confrontation becomes then merely a special case. Given that interactions between material things occur with great frequency, since all material things are continually on the move, it is true of cosmic encounters in the case of any one material thing that they are the rule rather than the exception. At the lowest material levels it is clear that the effects of such encounters are constitutive of the participants. Physicists speak of the strong interactions of nuclear constituents and of the weak interactions of atomic constituents.

For all encounters, human or other, there is a criterion of its moral effectiveness. We can ask, does a particular encounter increase order without loss of completeness? Then we know it was good. Does it increase disorder or increase order with loss of completeness? Then we know it was bad.

In cosmic confrontation the principle of ethical confrontation is of course expanded. In place of the conduct of the individual members of a given species toward other members of the same species, we have the conduct of any discrete thing toward all other discrete things. The principle of confrontation, which reads "conduct toward another, in consideration of all others" means in terms of the cosmos "the conduct of any material, in consideration of all other materials."

With cosmic confrontation we reach once again that level of generality which is somewhat denied to intermediate levels. But this is true of all series; the important places tend to be the base and the apex. For a member of any species, the base is the level to which he belongs. Thus for the human individual his own level is the base of the ethical integrative series, and the cosmic is the apex. Humanity rests upon the individual and his society, but the cosmos rises above the human species to embrace all species of existing beings. Thus cosmic confrontation is the most demanding because the most inclusive: nothing actual can be allowed to be excluded from its purview. And we are adding to our knowledge of the actual continually, so that the ethical obligation is kept widening and is not allowed to be closed.

The same conditions prevail throughout the cosmos. The same kinds of material entities are to be found everywhere in the meta-galactic system, and a galaxy is a fair sample. Through the experiments, observations and explorations of the space age, we are learning more and more not only about our cosmic privileges but also about our cosmic obligations. Those who have called attention to the dangers of pollution in the case of solar probes and landings are clearly mindful of these obligations. In addition to confrontations which are characteristic of the cosmos there are affronts, offenses which arise commonly to all cosmic occupants. For this last detail we have the advantage of conceptual tools which were established earlier in this work. I am thinking particularly of what in the second Part of this book I have named "excessive behavior." Here the notion can be applied and widened.

There is a sort of excessive behavior to which the very existence of anything commits it, for in terms of the given date and place at which that thing exists nothing else can. Some kind of usurpation is inevitable in the very nature of existence. To the extent to which anything exists, everything else in the cosmos has the task of adjusting to it. In the fourth part of this book I quoted Whitehead to the effect that life is robbery, but it is true also that existence is robbery. This is what Schopenhauer was talking about when he pointed out the moral significance possessed by the world. Existence as well as life is a crime, and one inevitably expiated only by damage, destruction and obliteration. Hence it is fair to say that in this sense justice reigns, and to adopt Hegel's famous statement that "the world itself is the world's court of judgment."

Earlier in this part[1] it was asserted that it is better to exist than not to exist. What exists is to that extent good, but the good obtained in this way (and all good must be) is had at a price. The price is the degree of excessive behavior contained in the very fact of existence itself.

---

[1] Chapter 2, Section A.

NORMATIVE COSMIC ETHICS

(a) The Cosmic "Ought"

What does "ought" mean in terms of material things below the level of organisms? Is a stone all that it ought to be? Is a galaxy? How deficient is unoccupied space? Are we anthropomorphizing when we charge an eclipsing binary system of stars with inadequacy? In a sense it is always possible that the findings in any study conducted by human beings is open to this charge. Since there is considerable evidence that the universe existed for a very long time before man appeared on the surface of the earth, any conception of the cosmos or any part of it except the human part which is conceived in anthropomorphic terms is defective. Yet the fact remains that some accounts are obviously more guilty of this than others. Unless the description is one of human beings themselves, any resemblance to human beings is suspicious and lends itself to the charge that we condition constrictively all that we know and thus render the effort to get beyond ourselves in our knowledge both hopeless and foolish. However, some studies seem more anthropomorphic than others.

It might just be possible, then, to continue our description of cosmic ethics by adding a normative section. In terms of the organization of matter, a galaxy can become more what it is. Self-realization though unconscious in such cases can still be genuine. And if it proceeds with incredible slowness it may be no less effective for that; a product of law and with a direction modified by chance encounters.

Ethics in being defined as the study of the good includes the study of how the good can be brought about, or in other words the study of the "ought." But this means ought-to-be as well as ought-to-do. The elements in the world which ought to be better show two aspects, being and doing. They are what they are and they do what they do; but it is possible to envisage how what they are could be improved and how they could do what they do better. Thus ethics is the study of what ought to exist and not merely of what ought to be done.

Men are more interested in doing than they are in being, because it seems to them that their only hope lies through activity. Thus their interest becomes narrowed to the issue of activity in terms of human problems. But it may be that the larger issue contains information and values which could be applied to the smaller, that there are cosmic considerations which could be brought to bear successfully upon human consideration. Man may not be necessary to the world but it is necessary to him. However, although he is a small part of the world he is an authentic ingredient and cannot legitimately be considered apart from it. For instance, if all material things are interrelated, and if the fate of any thing depends, as it seems to do, upon that of all others, then if all men are brothers, all animals are first cousins and all lower organisms second cousins and all material things cousins of more remote degree but cousins. Men, then, are cousins to material things.

In terms of human welfare because of relevancy nothing in the environment can be neglected. Completeness is an all-inclusive requirement. Cosmic ethics, then, is simply a way of saying that what brings things together is good and what sets them apart is bad. (Bringing things together in the wrong order, however, is a way of setting them apart.)

As we have noted, like all attempts to be complete as well as consistent, the marshalling of the evidence for the theory of cosmic ethics suffers from a lack of information, and suffers more perhaps because so little is known about the general conditions in a world where we are restricted to what can be learned from the surface of a single planet. But if cosmic ethics is to be a complete account it must include normative cosmic ethics as well as that empirical cosmic ethics which we have been endeavoring to sketch all too briefly.

(b) Objective Chance and the Normative

Chance considered as a world property provides the entering wedge for the normative. If there can be fortuitous deviation, then there can be a norm from which the deviation takes place, one provided by natural law from which it constitutes a departure. The great problem of ethics as I see it is this. Necessity applies without extenuating circumstances only to logic, whereas matter always involves such circumstances. Thus chance is as common as law. Everything that happens is actual, whether due to law or to chance, but it is also possible; because what is actual was possible else it could never have become actual, and whatever is possible is equally possible, there being no degrees admissible to possibility. But in a world in which everything that happens does so because it was possible how can some happenings be preferred to others? Presumably whatever happens was brought to that point by the nature of things and is to that extent at least preferred. But which is to be more preferred, the law, or the modifications of the law through chance? Even if we do not know the answer, in asking the question we have provided for the normative as natural. Thus because of the existence of objective chance the cosmos, too, can be talked about in terms of the normative as well as in terms of the empirical.

Every material organization has a cycle of existence; it comes into existence, it endures and it passes away. And it does so, moreover, according to its type. But there are always some individuals whose existence is defective judged from the type as a standard, and these are, so to speak, the pathological cases. The disparity with regard to structure and function between the norm of the type and the pathological deviation from the type permits us to say that from the point of view of the pathological the type is the normative.

What exists, exists while it exists, even though once it may not have existed and at some time will not exist. But through their exemplifications in particulars types of material things have the capacity to recur in existence, and this prevents us from declaring them confined to existence (as for instance the material things themselves are). Material things do evolve; they change, some varying so much that the old type disappears and a new one takes its place. But the types, at least as possibilities, continue. In their role as universals they represent absent as well as present things, things absent in space as well as in time. Thus the structure and function of a set of actual material things sets the type, and deviations from it are marked accordingly. The average of the structure and function of a set of similar material things establishes the norm. Standards are therefore relative and they may be transitory; but for all that they are no less standards.

(c) Cosmic Justice

If nature is normative in every one of its aspects, then there is such a thing as cosmic justice, and it would consist in the restoration of order to the extent to which there is disorder. Cosmic law would then be the natural laws discovered by the empirical sciences: the "laws" of physics, of chemistry, of biology, of psychology, of anthropology. The rights and duties of the entities in all such empirical fields are spelled out by the conditions in those fields. Thus whatever is done or could be done is a natural right, by which is meant, not inconsistent with physical, chemical, or biological laws. The laws of nature spell out the natural rights so that it is possible to predict the penalty for infraction. These are given, however. There are no legal enactments at any of the integrative levels except within the split segments of human society, but the conditions do point to obligations all the same. The physical, chemical, biological, psychological and anthropological levels of nature see to it that their "laws" are observed. The punishments for infringements are severe and impartial. Thus cosmic justice is done. For nature as a whole has its moral code. As Anaximander is said to have observed, "the source of coming-to-be for existing things is that into which destruction, too, happens 'according to necessity; for they pay penalty and retribution to each other for their injustice according to the assessment of Time.'"[1]

There is a lesson to be learned from the way in which material things behave toward one another. Since all things are constantly interacting, some things are shifted about in the world by other things in such a complex way that the calculations have not yet been made. For instance the interactions of three bodies in the solar system have not been accurately gauged, to say nothing of the pull of the rest of the galaxy, and of other galaxies, on them. The solution awaits the prior mathematical solution of the three-body problem.[2] But we do know this, that gravitational attraction, which is the bond between wholes at the physical level, tends to bring things together, but unless a counter-force held them apart there would be an excess of completeness. Over-reaching and self-exceeding here would be represented by the forces of gravitation alone, bodies coming together so fast that there would occur the movement to occupy the same space at the same time. Conflict and destruction would result. Instead, the lesson of the behavior of material things toward one another is given in the equilibrium which is maintained by the opposition between gravitation and angular momentum.

Considering again the integrative levels, the relation between the normative and the empirical becomes one involving merely a difference in directions. The empirical looks down the levels, the normative looks up. Normative considerations always involve wider contexts, but

---

[1] G. S. Kirk and J. E. Raven, *The Presocratic Philosophers* (Cambridge 1957, University Press), pp. 106–107.
[2] "Evolution as an Active Mathematical Theory," in *Science*, 145, 453–54 (1964).

there is no specifically empirical (as opposed to a specifically normative) subject-matter. We may recall from Chapter II, Section B above
that goodness and beauty are also directions in the series of wholes and
parts; goodness looking up and beauty down the same series. No
wonder, then, that goodness appears to be normative and that beauty
by contrast always appears empirical.

It may be also why the normative is so closely allied with ideals.
There are no good reasons for supposing that ideals have to be confined
to human affairs. The cosmic ideal involves the complete self-realization of entities and processes in nature. Those who are accustomed
to dealing with physical properties talk in this way; there is the "ideal
gas," the "perfectly radiating black body," the "absolute vacuum."
Thus men perceive however dimly that there are conditions in nature
which could be different from what they are; and not merely different,
but different with respect to the degree of perfection: more consistent
or more complete.

Lastly, the very prevalence of change might serve as a reminder
that the world is not as it ought to be. Things that are changing are
changing for the better or the worse, and what changes for better or
worse may be changing for the better. But there will be a reparation,
as Anaximander said, and you may depend upon it. For as he pointed
out things see to this for each other.

THE ETHICS OF MAN IN RELATION TO THE COSMOS

(a) Relations Mediated by the Ethical Integrative Series

The cosmos of course includes everything, the individual as well as his particular society and the whole of humanity, and also every species of entity and not just human beings. Thus when we address ourselves to the question of man's relation to the cosmos we may have several quite different things in mind. We might have in mind a direct relation to the cosmos as a whole without regard to the intermediate levels of the ethical integrative species or we might have in mind his relation to the cosmos through the various grades of obligation, first to himself, then to his society, next to his species, and finally to all species.

I will postpone discussion of the first point until the end of the last part of this book. Here it is necessary only to remind ourselves that an individual confronted with the spectacle of the cosmos gets back his own again because in this way he is brought face to face with himself as an individual. With regard to the second point there is something more to say. For the important fact in any case is the "finding" of nature, but we find that nature is structured and while consisting in a whole in the round nevertheless fractures with definite striations. For it is through the capacities of the individual *as* an individual that he is able to function as a member of society. Society is composed, in addition to those material things called artifacts which were man-fashioned, of able-bodied individuals. And it is through the social functions of the individual that he is able to exist as a member of his species. Humanity consists in a collection and inter-relation of man-fashioned societies, together with their artifacts and institutions. And it is through the human species that the individual plays his part in relation to other species and so participates in the cosmos. The cosmos has as its first level of analysis, then, the various species.

There are functions which hold throughout the ethical integrative series of which the individual must take note. For instance, the lower the ethical integrative level the more pervasive. Individual entities are the most basic elements and are present in every consideration. Thus the individual operates ethically against a broad background of cosmic ethics, a less broad one of the ethics of the species, and, declining in breadth still more, social ethics and lastly the ethics peculiar to the individual himself.

The levels of the ethical integrative series are not merely to be construed as stepping-stones, however. Their function is not only to lift the individual to a higher obligation and a more elaborate set of privileges, although they perform this service, too. For they exact their toll as just what they are, and each of them is *sui generis*. For the fact is that each level is a slice of existence and has its own autonomy. We need a principle to recognize this and it could be called the Principle of Level Indifference. It could be stated as follows.

The values of entities at any given level are indifferent to the values of entities at any other level.

The recognition by the individual that the need to preserve his own integrity and dignity exercises an importunateness which exceeds in that respect the greater importance of other levels. The point needs some random illustrations. The old adage that "self-preservation is the first law of nature," while not altogether true is by its very existence a limited instance. Again, stable societies from within disclose a kind of authority which locally at least seems equivalent to the absolute. There are no over-riding considerations that are strong enough to preempt it. Finally, in some connections the cosmic level owes nothing of its own to lesser and lower levels, and we shall need to take account of this statement in another section.

(b) Immediate Relations

The cosmic universe is a set of facts. Every fact consists partly in values. These statements are not incompatible, but in certain contexts they seem so. For instance, the cosmos is value-free in the sense that it seems to show no preference for any particular values over any other. Thus cosmic ethics does not interfere in any way with individual or social ethics. It is well known that "the rain falls on the just and the unjust." Heraclitus insisted that while men hold some things good and some things bad, God holds all things fair.

We have seen earlier that natural elections are the fabric of the world. Values are the natural elections of complex things, as for instance the higher organisms and particularly man. We assume that nature as such is indifferent to human preferences. But we know of influences which could be construed as evidence the other way. Since the human species emerged from a cosmic background, it should not be too surprising a fact that the human individual still responds to cosmic influences. His physiological organism is still linked to cosmic rhythms. Night and day, the lunar cycle, the seasons, all affect him.[1] His body follows a physiological pattern conditioned by changes in the interactions between earth, moon and sun. Hormonal activities, sleeping cycles and many other physiological processes are affected. Man, Professor Dubos concludes, responds to his total environment, not merely the one immediately surrounding him. It is possible that cosmic effects which alter his physiological patterns also have effects upon his life in ways which are more subtle. Does he have the same thoughts summer and winter? Is his outlook unchanged by geography? It would seem not; though the changes be difficult to trace, they are probably there. Certainly, societies are sensitive to physical surroundings, and differ with respect to the ways in which the physical challenges are met.

Finally, religion in so far as it promotes an ethics seeks to indentify that ethics with cosmic ethics, claiming direct and immediate knowledge and authorization for so doing. Most societies seem to have some kind of religion, some particular sort of religious beliefs and observances. These may certainly be interpreted as efforts to get in touch directly with forces in excess of those available to the near-by environment. Nature as a whole, a supreme god or a pantheon of gods, all represent the same end to inquiry: a power consisting of the whole world or of something beyond the world to which immediate appeal can be made. For religion is more a practical than a theoretical inquiry, and more a personal or social than a detached and objective interest. Confucianism and Buddhism are the exceptions; the former looking to authorization from an unlimited ancestral community, the latter seeking a solution in the nature of the human predicament itself. All others, it appears, claim divine connections.

---

[1] Rene Dubos, "Humanistic Biology," *American Scientist*, 53, 4–19, 1965.

BOOK THREE

THE MORAL SITUATION AND ITS OUTCOME

PART VI

IDEAL MORALITY

CHAPTER I

THE CHOICE OF IDEALS

In considering ethical ideals and moral practice, men have tended
to neglect a third area which necessarily interposes itself between
theory and practice, between the choice of ideals of conduct and the
actual conduct itself. Those who are dissatisfied with things-as-they-are
on the assumption that things-as-they-are are not identical with things-
as-they-ought-to-be are constrained to consider a third area, that of
strategy. Given an ideal and the knowledge of the special limitations
involved in all practice, the next thing to consider is how to get there,
so to speak, from here. Thus three ethical areas exist and must be
reckoned with: the actual, the ideal, and the strategy for getting from
the actual to the ideal. For an ideal, however abstract, functions as a
goal for strategy and so wears a practical aspect. In this chapter I will
propose a set of ideals, in the next chapter I will consider obstacles in
the way of their attainment, and in the last chapter I will work out
the proper moral strategy consequent upon the existence of both the
ideals and the obstacles.

(a) Rival Claimants for The Ideal

Ethics treats of the good; and the good, as we have noted, is a condition of being. Thus the domain covered by ethics extends far beyond
questions involving the moral import of human behavior. However
such questions must be considered, too. Thus one of the two chief
divisions of this work have been reserved for them, and accordingly
we are now ready to undertake their consideration. That the discussion will not be a simple one follows from the nature of the good
as it separates into the various levels of the ethical integrative series.

Every person and every thing has the same universe in common.
We have noted earlier, in fact, that everything interacts with everything else. Persons and things do not receive their ethical content from
acts but from bonds. The acts cement the bonds or constrain them
and so have an ethical relevance; but ethics is concerned with the

qualities and the values, which are bonds ranging from the lowest physical level (the qualities) to the highest cultural level (the values).

Every event is an encounter and every encounter takes place under a prescribed set of conditions. The conditions are static because unchanging, while the encounters are dynamic and changing. The conditions are persistent in the sense that they tend to recur, the encounters never occur again exactly in the same way. Thus another story above existence has been described to account for the conditions under which encounters take place and to set them a little apart from the encounters. The order of essences names the conditions, the order of existence (as heretofore) sets forth the encounters. Essences constitute the second story of the two-story world: existence is the lower story.

I recite the details of this situation here because I need it in order to make an important point about ethical ideals. The distinction is one between The Ideal and the knowledge of rival ideals. Rival ideals presumably are rival claimants for The Ideal. Now The Ideal, just in case there should be one, belongs to the set of conditions for encounters, and rival ideals are formulated in the heat generated by the encounters themselves.

The ethical integrative series for that matter belongs also among the sets of unchanging conditions. Consider, then, the plight of the poor harassed individual. He has obligations to entities at every one of the ethical integrative levels, individual, social, human and cosmic. These do not change, he does; they are fixed, he may shift. His problem is both to select an ideal and to work toward it. And he must play this out so to speak, in four keys.

What is the end at which all men ought to aim? It is not easy to know what our concrete ideals are or what they should be. The study of facts is observational, and concrete ideals are facts—facts of society; while the study of theory is more speculative, for there are probably as many ideals as there are men. Which ideal is the best, which ideal, it might be almost possible to say, is The Ideal?

Ideals are as various as differences in temperaments, in institutions and in societies can make them. There always are a number of rival ideals, ideals set forth from highly divergent points of view. We never think enough about the choice of ideals and how it is to be made, a problem as crucial as the problem involved in getting to the point where we are ready for a choice. Men by and large think otherwise; they suppose that it is difficult to attain to an ideal but not difficult to know which ideal because they think of ideals singly and only in accordance with their own formulations. It is in the choice of ideals and the attitudes toward them more than in any other way that a man shows his narrowness and provincialism. For each man dreams of a world arranged to accommodate all that he wishes to exist, and his wishes are usually flattering to his own ambitions and submissive to his needs.

The actual practice of morality is a mixture of the worst and the best, the establishment of a concrete ideal in terms of which the lesser good is, as often as not, substituted for the greater good. Ideals are perforce abstract and their consideration speculative, whereas conduct is concrete and its practice immediate. The business of setting up an ideal and then of working toward it through practice has been responsible for much confusion simply because the question of methodology has been neglected.

In much ethical speculation there has been an unfortunate confusion between theory and practice. The confusion arises perhaps for two reasons. The ideal has not been recognized as a debatable area, and the practice has not been understood as requiring its own theory. It is one thing to contemplate a preferential procedure and another thing to try to carry it out. To entertain an ideal means by definition to be a long way from it. We never regard our situation as in any way ideal; if we did we would make no effort to change it.

Consistency of behavior can only be had by adopting some regulative rules. The adoption may be a result of habit, it may follow the customs of a society, or it may be a matter of character; in any case it may or it may not be a logical element of which the individual is aware. Now human behavior is never altogether consistent. But then too—and more importantly—it is never altogether random. That it is not random presupposes a working goal toward which activity is on the whole directed, and such an arrangement may be called a concrete ideal.[1] Concrete ideals are of course ethical, whether or not they be recognized as such.

Ethical ideals are regarded with some scorn by men of the world, not entirely without reason. Most ethical treatises are composed with regard to stipulated ideals by uncompromising speculators who were very sure of their choices and therefore concerned only to compel others to behave in conformity with them. A certain amount of this attitude and procedure is unavoidable. But the term, morality, has a

[1] *Cf. Supra*, Part III, chapters 3 and 5.

bad name, acquired no doubt from having been too long in the possession of those who prefer keeping others in line to practicing virtue themselves. We need to rescue it from their exclusive use by proclaiming it a speculative field. Every intellectual inquiry defines an area of ignorance; without the existence of such ignorance and the belief in the existence of possible knowledge, why inquire?

There is no doubt a speculative field devoted to the search for the ideal of ideals. What kind of ideal ought the ideal to be? It is at once evident that ideals of any sort are inherently esthetic. They envisage harmony and perfection in a way which is admissible only to the beautiful. Excellence can be defined as the quality of perfection. The good looks up to the most complete (which then becomes also the most beautiful). Thus Plato was wrong when he placed at the apex of his hierarchy of forms the Form of The Good. It should have been the Form of The Beautiful. For the beautiful has a perfection envisaged as the harmony of the parts. Plato's ideal man in an ideal society, in the *Republic*, is a beautiful ideal, and this is in the end what ethics comes to be. It has to find its ideal of goodness in the beautiful, for the beautiful needs nothing beyond it to which it can be beautiful whereas the good does need something beyond it to which *it* can be good.

It is because the beautiful needs nothing beyond it to which it can be beautiful, beauty being the quality of internal relations, that it can characterize the goodness of The Whole, of the cosmic universe. The cosmos stands in its perfection of beauty without the external requirement of goodness, for if there were such a requirement it would be contradictory. The definition of the good requires external relations and the Whole understood as the cosmos is that which has no external relations.

The problems of ethics will never be solved until we have succeeded in discovering the proper ethical ideal. The ideal of ethics would presumably be set forth in terms of a perfect individual, a perfect society, a perfect humanity, a perfect universe. Ethical idealism is a speculative field. Whose ideal of the individual of society, of humanity, of the universe? Whose ideal, in short, is ideal? There are as many candidates as there are speculative ethical idealists, some with theories which differ sharply from others. On the basis of what criterion is there to be a choice between them? And how is the choice to be made?

The ethical ideal is predicated on the proper ordering of goods. Among all the things which are intrinsically and extrinsically good, some are better than others. But what scale is to be used in the ordering? Here we are both forced back upon an anterior metaphysics and compelled to contemplate the actual facts. For ethics as a theory is suspended somewhere between the more general theory of ontology and the data of concrete practice. Thus ethics is required to be at once consistent with a theory of being and compatible with practice. If the lines from ontology to practice are drawn rightly enough, they will pass cleanly through ethics and hold it in suspension. For we never apply an ontology directly to practice but always to a less general theory; but in such a case the result cannot be allowed to be inconsistent with the relevant facts.

As with most treatises on ethics in which metaphysics is not debated, an ontology is assumed.[1] Its outlines can be discerned by analyzing those elements which are implicit in the ethics itself. But the problems of ethics must also be met on their own grounds. Accordingly, our task is to find the channel which will lead us to the choice of the appropriate ideal.

Let us recall at this point that some ethics lies at the foundations of every society. There are ethical systems without societies (as in speculative ethics) but there are no societies without ethical systems. The morality which holds the society together and constitutes its affective element of consistency is ethical. With this reminder then we are ready to consider the third and last candidate among the three alternative human capacities for guidance to the choice among ideals.

We have been examining ethics from the individual through society and humanity to the cosmos. We started with the least inclusive and ended with the most inclusive. Now we shall build back up again, starting with the individual and ranging upward through the ethical integrative series, from society and humanity to the cosmos. The close study of the ethics of the individual discovers duties and obligations in terms of which life is made possible. Neither the devotion of the individual to himself, on the one hand, nor to the service of larger organizations, from society to the cosmos, on the other hand, can be wrong, though one alone is hardly enough.

There seems to most individuals and most societies to be a conflict between short and long range goals so that they choose one group and neglect the other. Religious cultures tend to neglect the needs of the body for immediate survival, such as food and shelter, for the sake of the larger considerations of ultimate survival. Material cultures tend to neglect the larger considerations of ultimate survival and attend only

[1] *Ontology* (Baltimore 1951, Johns Hopkins).

to the immediate needs of the body. Thus there arise two groups of moralities, each devoted to one phase of human existence to the exclusion of the other.

(b) The Four Grades of Obligation

That the choice either way amounts to an oversimplification of the human problem seems to have occurred to very few. We have been dealing throughout this book with four moralities, always on the assumption that each involved the others and that in the larger view there was only one morality having four distinguishable segments. But life is not so simple and human individuals so uniform that all can share a common pursuit of the good; not, that is, unless the good can be subdivided in such a way that the individual is offered a choice in terms of what he has the ability to pursue. Those who can see the farthest will reach the highest. He who has ears, let him hear, it has been said; but it has been said too that he also serves who only stands and waits.

For the individual there are four grades of obligation, four grades of "ought." He has obligations first of all to himself, to achieve if possible self-realization. He has obligations to his society, to obey its laws and if possible to improve them. He has obligations to the whole of the human species, to bring about its welfare and to insure its perpetuation. And finally he has obligations to the cosmos, to restore order by securing the proper hierarchy of all species of beings. Thus there are four levels of the good with which, as Peirce would have said, he must identify his interests. There is a graded responsibility on the part of the human individual to each of the ethical levels in turn. The range of the good life runs from happiness for the individual, through welfare for society, through the evolution from man to superman for the human species, to an absolute unity of total consistency and completeness for the universe of being.

If the aim of the individual is to exceed himself, and by means of aggression against his immediate environment to achieve short-range survival, and by means of identification with his far-away environment to achieve long-range survival, then what is the good for him? The answer can be formulated as the obligation to interpolate greater organizations at lower levels: society for the individual, the species for society, the cosmos for the species. Thus there are no simple single-level confrontations but always more is involved. The greater the individual the more his confrontations mean. The greatest individual would be presumably one who while omitting no lesser considerations and over-looking no lesser levels could still do nothing that was not done in full view of the cosmos.

For the moral obligations of the individual must *all* be met. They are internal to himself and external to his society, his species and the cosmos. This requires the proper ordering and appropriate activities conducted in series.

Thus the short-range goal of ethical endeavor is the construction of a perfectly good individual, the intermediate-range goals are those of a perfectly good society and a good humanity, and the long-range a perfectly good universe. The higher an entity or a process in the inte-grative levels the more it needs to maintain a constant state of inter-change with its environment. Life, as we have noted, is a nutritive process. In human terms, the more intelligent and sensitive—the more aware—an individual is, the greater the segment of the world to which his actions will be responses. The interchange with the environment of the individual may (in his conscious moral understanding) be limited to himself, or it may extend to his society, to all of humanity, or to the entire universe.

The end of the individual is the service to something, himself or something larger: his society, all humanity, or the cosmos. He must, if he can, construct something greater and better than himself, some-thing which can outlast him and benefit a larger organization in some way. It will be our next task to examine ideals in this order, beginning with the ideal for the individual, and running through the ideal for society, for humanity, and finally for the cosmos where the individual finds that he has come full circle and discloses again his own individual ends, finding in this way the ideal for the individual though much enriched and deepened in the process.

CHAPTER II

INDIVIDUAL IDEALS

(a) The Obligation to Widen Life

We have seen that the individual has a number of obligations: to himself, to his society, to humanity, to the cosmos. Thus in terms of a widening series of organizations he has both proximate and ultimate obligations. Here we shall want to discuss the proximate obligations, those which he has to himself.

It is necessary to begin the discussion of the individual ideal by pointing out that the aim of the individual at the level of the individual as an ideal must not be made subjectively. The meaning of entire man is to be spelled out not in terms of his own awareness of himself but of his functioning as an integral personality. The life of the healthy individual is not devoted to introspection. The aim of life is not absolute self-devotion. The self as such is a limiting case; in itself nothing, a point of orientation toward other things. Thus to aim at it is to aim at nothing. The ideal for the individual, then, is not himself as subject. For a well-integrated personality is not a mere point of reference. The individual involves a certain set of interrelations and interactions, of bonds, with his environment. It is these from the subjective end that we are considering. A well integrated personality is the ideal for the individual.

Importunateness is an internal demand for integration; importance is an external demand for the proper kind of activity. The individual is at one integrative level a whole containing parts, and he is responsible for the integrity of the whole. He must therefore provide for the parts, and this involves him in the effort to maintain equilibrium through a continuing search for need-reductions. It is at this level, curiously, that it becomes necessary to include among the ideal obligations of the individual those to himself as an authentic instance of the ultimate and irreducible worth of every human individual.

The stability and equilibrium of the individual as a functioning unit is a necessary prerequisite to the principle of confrontation. For "conduct toward another, in consideration of all others" would become an impossibility should the individual have to devote all of his energies to designing and executing the proper conduct of himself toward himself. Health is a liberating force. A healthy individual is one who does not have to think about himself or be concerned with his own welfare, for he is in a position to turn his concern outward toward others. The whole personality operates in the same way as any organ; a man with a healthy heart and liver is one who does not need to remember that he has a heart or liver. They become noticeable only under the strain of disorder, only when disease or weakness in structure produces illness. A healthy individual, then, is one who is prepared to throw all his energies into his conduct toward another.

We have noted already that the short-range ethical ideal is the perfectly good individual. We have now to be more specific. The perfectly good man is the one with the proper hierarchy of needs: how the individual's needs are to be met, generalized to a principle of society suitable for all of its members, and extended to other societies and their members, and from them to all of humanity. The ideal for the individual, in other words, is through himself to widen his own participation in being, to widen life. The obligation of individual life is to increase life and to extend it. The moral obligation to widen life means to extend the self as much as possible, to include as much as possible in experience, to know, to feel and to do as much as possible, and in this way to exist as completely as possible. How do the needs fit in with these goals?

The needs arose from the adaptation of the individual to his environment as a means of survival. Immediate survival is a product of the reduction of the primary needs, ultimate survival a product of the secondary needs. The reduction of the primary needs are stages on the way to the secondary. However much satisfaction there may be in dining, it is not the end of life for the individual, and to make it so is a form of pathological behavior. To have enough to eat means to be set free from that need in order to pursue another, the need for knowledge, say. Thus it is that the proper superordination and subordination of the needs becomes the ideal for the individual.

The moral element predominant in the individual is his conscience. The mechanism of the conscience is the retention schemata, divided into public and private elements. In the ideal individual the public and private segments of the retention schemata would not conflict but would be well integrated. No ideal can prevent an individual's experience from being to some extent private or the inferences he draws from it from being private inferences. However, in the perfectly balanced individual nothing would be inferred from the private schema that would in any way deter the operation of the public schema. In the ideal individual the conscience would be a guide rather than a restriction, and its mandates would not be felt as anxiety.

(b) Demotic and Heroic Morality

There is an earlier distinction which must be elaborated at this point between what I have called demotic morality on the one hand and heroic morality on the other. Broadly speaking, demotic morality is founded on those actions of the individual which are aimed at reducing his primary needs and which thus take himself as his end. Heroic morality is founded on his actions aimed at reducing his secondary needs and which thus take his society or, beyond it, humanity or the cosmos, as his end.

All men have exactly the same sets of needs; only, in demotic man the primary needs maintain an ascendency over the secondary, and in heroic man the secondary needs gain an ascendency over the primary. It should hardly be necessary to add that in any society the demotic individuals greatly outnumber the heroic. It is possible for the two moralities to conflict. Demotic man however he may employ the achievements of heroic morality is opposed to it. He accepts heroic achievements but he is opposed to the living heroes who are his contemporaries. The heroic morality is often conducted in the face of the opposition of demotic man. For what demotic man accepts of the heroic morality belongs to the past and has been established for so long that the circumstances surrounding its discovery and establishment have long been lost to sight. Yet demotic and heroic morality are always to be found living side by side in the same social milieu. Demotic man has his reinforcements ready and waiting for him in the similarities between himself and his neighbors. The individualism in the demotic individual is missing. Heroic man is a loner; he operates under the uncomfortable circumstances of glaring individual differences, differences which demark the individual hero not only from demotic man but equally from other heroes. He can find his support if he needs it in those heroic men of the past who most resemble him.

An illustrative contrast can be drawn between demotic and heroic individuals if we compare them in the matter of conscience. For demotic man the public part of the retention schemata dominates the private. Since he draws his sense of security from his fellow citizens in the society and especially from those of his institutional associates, he will tend to agree with them in their most basic beliefs, for such agreement is a condition of his security. He would not feel comfortable with any deviation which his private schema might present to him; and when it does so he either dismisses it or feels the consequent anguish. If he cannot control such tendencies and prevent them from getting out of hand he becomes pathological.

For heroic man the situation is somewhat different. He draws his security from a different society, from an ideal society, in fact, whose citizens may come from any date and place, from the past or the future. He thinks, feels and acts with the best that has been thought, felt and done by historical figures whose heroic nature has been recognized in literature. Consequently, when his private schema fails to validate the public schema he does not at all feel put out or insecure. In his view it is the public schema which has failed him and not he it. And so he is prepared to go his own way, safe with his conscience and indeed protected by it against the criticisms of his contemporaries. He is the leader, not the follower, and whether he is rewarded with honors and prizes in his lifetime or neglected or even punished might make him feel good or bad but will make no material difference to his convictions or his actions; he must do what he must do in virtue of the society of ideal individuals to which he belongs.

Thus in any given society, demotic man vastly outnumbers heroic man, a fact which every demotic man reads to his own advantage so that he thinks he is able to claim his own superiority to heroic man. But given humanity as the matrix of all societies throughout history, the relative proportion of the support for heroic man changes radically. For the demotic men of the present revere all of the heroic men of the past as well as some in the present. Historical heroic men (which all heroic men will become in time) thus have greater support than any other. And so the moral effect of heroic men, however they are received by their contemporaries and even when they are read as unimportant or even as evil, is tremendous.

In some quarters it is fashionable to value mere quantity over quality, or to associate all quality with heroic man and concede none to demotic man. This is an error. The values of heroic man are admittedly higher, but the higher values are not all of the values. Demotic man has his own qualities and they need not be inconsiderable. He is what he is: a human being in need of no apology, good because what-is is good. For human good is great good, and no less great as good because accompanied by great bad. Heroic man too often has the bad qualities to match his good ones. Demotic man counts no less because there are so many of him. The goal of the individual ought to be the service of society, and pleasure the satisfaction to be derived from such a service well performed. And this goal and its pleasure are certainly available to demotic man and indeed the treasured possession of many.

(c) What Should We Think, Feel and Do?

Of the three human faculties, thought, feeling and action, which one will furnish the best guide to the choice which must be made among ideals? Perhaps it would be wise to make up our minds first about the best approach to such a decision. The perfectly good individual is the one who has the best thoughts (verifiable inductions or correct reasoning from defensible axioms), the best feelings (those for the largest and most far-away objects), and the best actions (behavior consistent with the furtherance of the welfare of the largest organization). What should we (a) think, (b) feel, and (c) do? Next a word about each of these.

What should we think? Inquiry tends to increase knowledge; first that of the individual, and this may come from the social pool of things known; secondly, that from the unknown, which tends to increase the social pool of things known. Such increase of either kind is made possible by inquiry through verifiable inductions, guesses as to how things are which later prove to be correct; or through valid reasoning from defensible axioms, which leads to an increase in knowledge through the discovery of hitherto unknown relations or facts.

The first and most obvious guide, then, is thought. The best thoughts are those which are the most productive of true knowledge. Individual happiness lies in dedication to inquiry. That is why Plato and Aristotle, Spinoza and Hegel, have supposed that the highest form of life for man is the life of the intellect. It may be passive, as with contemplation, or active, as with discovery, but intellectual in any case. However, it is the active type that is emphasized here, the life of inquiry leading toward discovery. In general, passive inquiry belongs to demotic man, and active to the heroic variety. But in either case it is clear that ethics is related to knowledge. The deeper an individual's penetration of the external world, the wider his sense of moral obligation. At the narrower end of limited awareness he owes everything to himself, just as at the wider he owes everything to the cosmos. In between lie all those details which reason can sort out in its effort to prepare a conclusion which can lead to appropriate action. Since the Greeks it has been supposed that there is no faculty superior to reason. This is true; yet what has been overlooked is that reason cannot work without an empirical subject-matter when it is asked to make an empirical decision. Pure logic has no reference to the data of experience; indeed that is what is meant by the term. Applied logic, which is what we mean when we talk about the use of reason in experience, can only be applied if there is something to which logic can be applied. And to what is it being applied when we ask it to tell us which of the available candidates for ideals in ethics is the proper one? Thus reason alone, or reason first, is not the faculty which will be of the greatest help in choosing an ethical ideal.

True knowledge is gained only through arduous efforts at inquiry. Thus the end for man is inquiry. Happiness for man lies in dedication to inquiry, this is the prime individual goal. But it is not given to every man to be a productive investigator; only a few are ever self-selected by reason of their equipment for such a task. But the rest can imitate the virtue, and by their support and tolerance back up the few who inquire in a free spirit. Thus it is given to all to support inquiry through a solid conviction of the strategic value of tolerance. All doors must be kept open if it is possible that through one a way may be found to a significant human advance.

What should we feel? Ethics has always been thought of in terms of the effectors, the good considered in connection with good behavior; but there is also an ethics of the receptors: how should we be stimulated? What is it we want done to us so that ours will be the corresponding feelings? What is the moral excitation of the sense receptors? To some extent at least life for the individual is at his own disposal. He can so arrange things that certain anticipated feelings will be the result. He can buy perfume, plan to dine at a particular restaurant, go to a concert of music. The best feelings are those which are stimulated by the largest and farthest objects, or by symbols which represent them. Thus esthetic feelings outrank gustatory, although of course one may be necessary in order to provide for the other; a hungry man is not in the best condition to appreciate music. The idealist in ethics is an esthete, the nominalist a libertine and the realist a moderate. Virtue as I see it is not a middle path but a call for justice for the values, an arrangement whereby the least of worth can help in attaining the most.

The feelings have often led us astray. Intuition or insight has been at times an indispensable guide, and we might wish to check by it a choice made on some other grounds. But as the sole ground it will not prove sufficient, for it is not infallible and we have nothing to check it by. The most familiar form of feeling in this connection is religious faith. Every religion has of course its own moral structure; indeed it is to be doubted whether there is any such thing as a religion without a morality. Now, religions rely upon faith as a guide to religion and hence also to morality. Is faith then our answer?

It would seem not. For faith is a variety of emotional belief. Faith is belief without reason. But faith does not help us to choose among the faiths. There are many religions, each with its own morality and each susceptible to the appeal of faith. Faith is comforting, but the difficulty about the comfort of faith is that all faiths are comforting. Doubt is an uncomfortable state, belief is comforting. And the deep emotional kind of belief which takes place in religious faith is even more comforting, but any religious faith will do as well as any other. It is, then, no help to us in our problem. Religious prophets and indeed all religious leaders are only intuitive philosophers who depend either upon authority or upon intrinsic appeal of the rightness of their views to gain acceptance for them.

In helping us to feel, knowledge is an indispensable aid. It is one purpose of knowledge to deepen pleasure, and I make no distinction in this regard between the pleasures of the senses and the pleasures of the mind; for, in the cases both of sex and of that intense feeling of belonging to the universe that religions attempt to restore, it is true that knowledge increases enjoyment. However, the aim of life is not mere pleasure. If it were it could be supplied by any neurosurgeon by electrodes implanted in the amygdala. Instead it is objective achievement and the satisfaction following upon it: objectively, achievement; subjectively, the enjoyment of achievement. Thus we are led to the third aspect of the perfectly good individual, his best actions.

What should we do? What kind of moral ideal would lead to the perfect society if employed as the morality of that society, as its concrete ideal? This can be tested only in practice, on the assumption that its contradictory proposition or its opposite will fail to work also. The justification of faith in the good will have to be made on the basis of a pragmatic criterion, on the workability of the ideal in operation. Given an ideal as the best choice that can be made, and employing it as the concrete ideal of a society, internally what kind of society will it produce, and externally what kind of relations will it promote with other societies? Internally, will the behavior of individuals be a matter of "conduct toward another, in consideration of all others"? Externally, will the effect of the society toward confronted societies be on the basis of the consideration of all humanity?

I have already laid it down that the best actions are those which further the welfare of the largest organization. This is a matter of the development of the individual's behavior: the stages in his life cycle interpreted as increasing objectification of achievement, together with its attendant changes in his philosophy. Progress toward good behavior in human affairs has consisted chiefly in modifications of the material environment in conformity with the formulations of the appropriate ideals. It has not consisted in any advances in motivation. Indeed there has been no change in motivation throughout the million years during which man has been traced from his ape-like ancestors. He wishes to help and hurt his neighbors. The ideal is of course to help without hurting, and in this way to increase the achievement by increasing the consistency and eliminating the self-defeating ambivalence. Modifications of the immediate environment become increasingly efficient, but the retardation in motivation cuts across the attainment of the stipulated ideals.

A lifetime is not long enough for the correct behavior to result in the perfect achievement, but we must make it do. This inconvenient necessity can, however, be turned into a good. For if we have less time than we require, then we are compelled to conserve it and order it, to give it some shape. Thus the empirical field of the ethical is limited and a finite ethics rather than a transcendental and infinite one is appropriate, and indeed, if it is to be efficacious, assured. In short, mortality calls for a finite ethics.

The criterion by which the individual finds the answer to the question of what he should do under any and all circumstances means one which is sufficiently evidential to carry conviction. He wants, in other words, a general principle of conduct and a formula for guiding its application in those specific situations which might arise but which cannot necessarily always be foreseen. This is a matter of strategy, and so we shall postpone the discussion of it to a later part of this book. Meanwhile it might be advisable to observe that just as in the case of feeling knowledge was an aid, so in the case of action both knowledge and feeling are helpful.

The ideal of ethics for man is of course perfectly good behavior. In ideal behavior it is the entire man who is involved. For the individual the ideal is one of the entire man. And for entire man the ideal is an imperative of productivity.

He should so add to the total external material inheritance that the social world, humanity, and possibly even the cosmos will be richer for his having lived.

In other words, the ideal of perfectly good behavior is to so manipulate the immediate environment as to produce extrinsic goods in persons, institutions and artifacts, and in this way to maximize in the world the total amount of intrinsic good. The end of productivity begins with the means of inquiry and so the activity of inquiry is where the ethical individual begins. But before he can accomplish his aims his feelings and of course his actions are involved. These are as we have seen cumulative. Individual man behaving is man with all his capacities engaged, Entire Man.

Although reason narrowly conceived as functioning apart from feeling and acting cannot make a claim to preeminence over the others, reason more broadly understood certainly can. For the coordination of faculties upon which the integrated activities of entire man depend must be the work of reason. Acting involves the whole man, who must feel what he is doing and must have planned his moves. It is not possible to think without having had that special kind of feeling which consists in groping one's way toward the premises with which thought begins. Thus action is the end product of a process which was started by feeling, but reason is the structure of the process. Reason in human life is supreme.

The end for man is aggrandizement. His goal is a progressive one: from self-realization (hedonism) and the service of society (utilitarianism) to identification with that largest whole of being which is the cosmic universe which alone can assure ultimate survival. We shall see in a later chapter of this Part that what this means for the individual is that he must surpass himself and in so doing give rise to the next evolutionary stage of the organism with its concomitantly increased powers and awareness. The direction of existence is toward an increase in existence. Thus the over-riding need for man is to exceed himself, and his moral obligation to himself is to reduce his needs in order to make this over-riding need possible of reduction. The self is always pointed toward increase, and it is moral of man to work in the direction toward which his nature is pointed.

CHAPTER III

SOCIAL IDEALS

(a) Differences and The Ideal

Here we speak of the obligations of the individual to his society. What does he wish to achieve for it? The end of the individual is the service of society, but not any society and not just his society with all of its defects. That is the actuality, but what is the ideal? The ideal society would be one which furnished a maximum of need-reduction to its individual members. It would be one also which offered the maximum in the way of bonds with neighboring societies. The ideal society faces two ways: toward its individual members and toward the human species.

The moral life is the life best suited to insuring that the society to which the individual belongs shall function in such a way as best to allow the individual to reduce his needs, and, more, to provide the greatest latitude of individual action whereby he may successfully exceed himself without disrupting the social fabric. The moral life, then, is social. The individual moral life is one that satisfies the conscience of the individual both with respect to what he ought to do and what not. But since the conscience is based on the same moral structure as society and indeed derives its moral structure from that of society, it comes to the same thing: that the moral life is social.

The statement of an ideal cannot be ideally made in terms of the result which might normally be expected from applying it in practice. But this is just what Mill did. His moral "ideal," "the greatest happiness for the greatest number," sounds more like what we may have to settle for than what we should wish to achieve. It is an ideal stated in the form of a compromise. But to aim at it might not be to achieve it. To aim at the greatest happiness for the greatest number might result more practically in the unhappiness of a greater number as a concomitant to success in the chosen ideal. In Mill's formulation a totality of happy individuals is admissible but certainly not expected.

It is damaging to practice to confuse theory with it, or to have the actual in mind when framing the ideal. The ideal is if it is anything uncompromising and inflexible. The compromises must be made by those who have chosen an ideal and who encounter actual obstacles while seeking to reach it. That is time enough for flexibility. Ideals imply perfection. The ideal man then is one who will do what is best for his society of his own accord and without restraint. The ideal society is one which is so organized that each citizen will do freely what is needed of him because that will give him the most satisfaction. At the highest social level the ideal is concerned with human individuals and their inter-relations, their bonds. In short, the ideal for man is the perfect individual perfectly organized in the perfect society.

It should be remembered again that human individuals are only the most important parts of society, not the only parts. A society does not consist merely in human individuals. There are the institutions, there are the artifacts, there is the charter, and there is the immediate environment with which the society in all its parts effects an interchange. The ideal morality for society would consist in discovering what is natural under the given conditions. For nature in society is perforce local; the variations from society to society and from immediate environment to immediate environment insure that they must be. Nature is not a total uniformity, for difference is as natural as similarity; it is a uniformity within diversity. The existence of separate societies means that the uniformity must be bound within the limits of the local diversity.

(b) Similarities: The Ideal Morality

With regard to societies, a common theory does not mean a uniform practice. Local conditions differ and such differences must be met. The common theory means the common following of a set of principles. Now morality is culturally conditioned. Every nation has its own culture even though there is some overlap in many cases. There must be, however, a common denominator among the moralities of all culture groups, and it must include the principle that the existence of a difference in moralities is not only tenable but necessary.

Natural morality is the code of the ideal society. The problem is somewhat complicated now that we have the power to design the immediate environment. It is difficult to know whether the search for the ideal society should be in terms of perfect adaptation to a given environment or whether the society just as it is should be rendered ideal by adjusting the immediate environment to it. Moral aims could conceivably be satisfied either way.

Ethics must be founded on the natural society, which, by the way, all of the studies of the theoretical sciences concerned with the social nature of man, from psychology to anthropology are seeking. But the applied sciences also must be counted in. Industrialism, with its adroit use of scientific agriculture and animal husbandry, its tremendously productive manufacture of all articles of utility in numbers which make it possible for everyone to have the materials for leading the good life, is also a method and therefore also one variety of the natural society, for it employs the means made available by nature for ends already provided by nature.

The local conditions prescribe that different societies cannot follow the same path to the ideal though they share the ideal. Cultural uniformity is a threat to cultural progress. The security of humanity depends upon the richness of difference. Those who intend evil, however, sometimes achieve good. And those who intend a lesser good sometimes achieve a greater good. Something must be left to chance because of the occurrence of inadvertent good. Under reason there must be room for the allowable inadvertent good. The tolerance of difference then becomes a necessity. Obligations imposed by the ideal society upon local conditions require essential differences, which must, however, if they are to be ideal, be of the quality of excellence.

The difficulty with monolithic ideals is that they constitute the absolutes of ontology, and when adopted by authority are apt to forbid further inquiry. If they prove wrong there are no available substitutes in the inventory which could be utilized. Nothing is more damaging to the search for the ideal than the supposed possession of the "absolute truth." Unfortunately, the absolute truth is in the possession of rival claimants who do not hesitate to destroy each other by violence in defense of their own candidate. Abate the claims somewhat, however, and the situation becomes more tenable. To be less than fully convinced means to be able to operate and at the same time to entertain proposals for improvement. With new authorities the search may be resumed afresh and so the ideal maintained as a goal. Thus the differences among rival moralities preserve the ideal.

The ideal society will be one constructed by ideal individuals whose zeal does not include merely welfare for themselves. That will be a by-product. What they will want for their society is one which can best help other societies. Not "amity within, enmity without," in

Spencer's phrase, but amity both within and without. Only as much "enmity without" as is required in order to preserve and promote the richness of difference. To say that thus far no such society has existed is only to affirm it as an ideal.

CHAPTER IV

HUMAN IDEALS

The goodness of anything, extrinsically considered, must depend upon its inclusion in a wider system. When we consider the individual in this connection we recognize that his goodness can be measured by whether it is limited to the members of his own society or extends through his affections to the entire human species as Shaftesbury suggested that it should[1]—not the good of these men but of mankind. If this be the case, then what does the individual want for his species, what is his ambition for humanity?

(a) The Evolution of Ethical Superman

The cosmic aspect of the ethics of the human species means that the cosmic good for man is what is conducive to the evolution of the species into moral superman. The ideal for humanity is evolution toward the superman, the effort of man to exceed himself in the direction of the good. It should be at once noted that nothing spectacular is intended by this. The superman is not the superior physical animal of the comic strips and the cinema but moral superman, a being superior in many respects, in which an increase in physical power may or may not be included. Very possibly *Homo sapiens* though larger is also weaker physically than his ancestors *Australopithecus*, *Pithecanthropus*, and Neanderthal Man. But the ideal society is the hope of the future, not a remembrance from the past; not an innocent Adam and Eve living in unaltered nature among the forces they could not understand, but a highly sophisticated moral superman who will have so transformed his environment and himself that the good life in all of its aspects will have been made possible.

The conception of moral superman is not exactly a new one although it is framed here somewhat differently and approached from another perspective. Aristotle discusses what he called "superhuman

[1] *Characteristics* (Indianapolis 1964, Bobbs-Merrill). Cf. A. N. Whitehead, *Process and Reality*, Part III, Chapter I, Section III.

virtue."[1] Nietzsche's "superman" is so named because of his superhuman virtue of self-overcoming. Nietzsche did not envisage the
transformation of the material environment as involved with morality
at all, and he did not mean to suggest any sort of evolution of the
species. Much later Darwin and his followers took up the whole
question of biological evolution as it applies to man. The future evolution of a man-like species which would exceed man in moral qualities as much as he exceeds the apes in intelligence has been discussed
in all except its specifically moral aspects. But these can hardly be
omitted in a full consideration of the properties and relations of the
species of the future which might result from human development.

There are many other ways of course in which man could exceed
himself as a method of giving rise to the next evolutionary stage of the
organism. He could be wiser and more knowledgeable, he could have
more developed sensibilities. The effort of man to exceed himself,
which, as we have noted earlier, is always a feature of his behavior,
has only to be imagined as a successful effort.

There is still another way in which it is possible to make moral
progress, and one perhaps more characteristic of the human species.
This lies through the invention and development of more efficient
artifacts. There are those today who argue that the production of an
artificial environment has frozen the human species in its present form
and serves to prevent any further development. I think the evidence
points in quite another direction. If evolutionary adaptation makes of
the organism a product of its environment, then the new artificial
environment which man has invented for himself will bring about an
entirely new adaptation. There is no reason to suppose that because
man can control his environment that he will design a single one to
last forever. Now that he has found the skill to produce artifacts he
will no doubt wish to improve them. Thus the environment to which
he adapts will be altered through that adaptation to one requiring
further adaptation. It is of course far too early to tell. Civilization,
defined as the settled community made possible by agriculture and
animal husbandry, is not more than 20,000 years old, and only in the
last few centuries has it been brought to that degree of development
whereby most of the environment of the city dweller is artificial, and
this is far too short a period for evolutionary processes to have a visible
effect.

Thus it may well be that in altering his available environment to

[1] *Nico. Eth.*, Book VII.

such an extreme degree man has changed it in a way favorable to the improvement of the species. That he should do so is in any case the ideal of the ethics of humanity. Ethics is the theory of the movement of negative entropy as this occurs in human society. The good life for humanity is that life which relates affirmatively to the largest segment of existence. This measure is certainly intended to estimate human life in terms of its evolutionary consequences. The higher the organism the more complex its structure and the greater its range of feeling and activity, the more, in other words, its life.

Thus the moral precept to increase life means also to increase the higher over the lower species. Man is to our present knowledge already the highest species, but our knowledge is limited to living organisms on the surface of planet earth. It is not hard to imagine that he may have been exceeded elsewhere in some one of the millions of other planets in this and other galaxies which reproduce the conditions favorable to organisms. And so we have both a short-range and a long-range moral obligation: to benefit man just as he is in the contemporary world, but also to help him to evolve into the next higher species, to increase the life of living man but also to hasten the coming of the superman.

(b) Trans-Cultural Ethical Principles

The ideal of the ethics of humanity must include any trans-cultural ethical principles that can be found. There do exist such principles and they have been located among the moralities of societies. Sets of societies share a common culture. Thus for instance all of the societies of western Europe whose moralities overlap (but are by no means identical) share a common culture, usually known as western culture. By comparing cultures it is possible to discover some principles which seem to hold for all of humanity rather than merely for a particular culture, or, narrower still, for a particular society.

(a) The first of these principles is that

Any human individual is able to be a member of any culture provided he is introduced into it at an early age.

An infant transported from central Asia to western Europe will grow up as a typical European in all but physical features. An English infant given to a mother to raise in a village in central India will grow up an Indian in every respect except facial features and coloring. This principle points to the affinity of all human beings prior to cultural conditioning. No doubt cultural conditioning penetrates very deeply, but this takes place at birth and after, not before. The even deeper affinity of all mankind is the first fact that has to be recognized in endeavoring to formulate the ideal ethics of humanity. For what has a common existence also has a common responsibility and a common goal. The ethical ideal of humanity in this respect, then, is given in the following two principles.

(b) *Any member of any culture must consider himself and be considered by all human individuals as an agent for all other members of that culture.*

This is the principle of type responsibility extended as an obligation to the ideal ethics of humanity. To be a member of a particular society or a particular culture does not mean that with the discharge of all the proper obligations to that society or that culture all obligations are ended. The individual has obligations beyond his immediate social organization, and these are represented to him by his type responsibility. What we earlier considered as an individual attitude toward the good is here transformed into an obligation in view of an ideal. The superfluous caring for others has lost its individual intention to transform them, and has become altogether an immersion within an identification sufficient to make of its interior functioning the part of a very large whole which submerges the individual in the immense organization of a common humanity transcending all spaces in which such an individual may exist and all times at which he may have existed. The individual merely in being an individual and human recognizes in himself the living representative, here and now, of a common humanity wherever and whenever.

(c) Ideal moral behavior at the level of the ethics of humanity consists in

Conduct toward the element of any culture, in consideration of the elements of all other cultures.

This is the principle of confrontation extended. Individuals are now to be regarded and treated as members of a culture and as such having trans-cultural responsibilities and affinities. This means that all cultural interactions provide interfaces where there is interposed a type responsibility because there is an encounter. The degree of cultural penetration of the individual is hereby acknowledged and assigned its moral position. What is morally relevant in such a context is not merely the naked animal individual but his habits and dispositions as assigned by the use of artifacts within institutions.

(c) The Ideal Material Culture of Humanity

On the principle discussed much earlier of value as a function of time, what happens to the immortality of human achievements? We are so accustomed to observing the exceptionally gifted man aiming his work at a permanent persistence that we share his hopes for its survival. We think of Homer's epics, of Shakespeare's plays, of Velasquez' paintings, of Plato's dialogues, as being now as much ours as theirs; fully established elements of culture available to all mankind, each a "possession forever." It is then a great lesson that the findings of astronomy predict defeat for these hopes. Nothing, not even galaxies, can last forever; all have their existence-cycles: they come into existence and they go out of existence. If galaxies cease to exist, then certainly so also do any and all constructions on the surface of a rather modest planet, all of the works of man and no doubt eventually man himself. Thus value will have to be a function of a limited time. In this as in everything else, the finite while more complex is also the least demanding and so the more convincing. But the restriction of limited time compels the direction of value toward time in depth; how and in what sense what exists in time has value, how and in what sense value is tied to existence in time.

A certain segment of nature, then, man considered as a special sort of organism together with his works: the alterations that the organism has made in its material environment to suit its own needs, calls out in the individual a special sort of behavior when considered in the context of its totality as a valid isolate. Society is the ideal channel for the individual's efforts to reach toward humanity in a cosmic setting. Not one uniform world culture but rather many "isolated moral communities"[1] operating within a world civilization is the ideal, for it has the advantage of the richness of difference combined with the tolerance of differences.

The ideal requires that morality be identical with nothing less than the human level of nature. Natural morality is the perfect background for functional and ecological morality. Now if we consider the drives to reduce the secondary needs as the leading edge of individual behavior, then the morality of a society, as the least common denominator of behavior within the channels established for reducing the basic organic needs, given the local conditions and the ingrained schemata, is felt as confining, and the individual perforce reaches out

---

[1] See above, Part IV, Chapter 1, Section D.

in his activity toward increased knowledge and increased security toward the ideal culture of humanity.

Such an ideal is at this stage a formulation only. But that is the nature of ideals. Thus far, nothing is empirical beyond culture, but cultures as we have seen are locally limited constructions in which culturally-conditioned individuals are almost totally immersed. It is the efforts made by some individuals to look outside their cultures toward the next higher possible organization: the ideal culture of humanity with *its* trans-cultural arts and sciences, which enables us even to posit such an ideal. The ethical ideal of humanity, then, consists in the perfect material culture of humanity, and the obligations of the individual under such an ideal would be its attainment and establishment. Perhaps this will be the single task of the ethical superman whose future existence we posited as a possibility when we were discussing it at the outset of this chapter.

CHAPTER V

COSMIC IDEALS

(a) Intrinsic Cosmic Goodness

In the previous choice of ideals we have been dealing with behavior within a perspective, one which is individual, social or human. Here we shall try to discover the choice of ideals which gets away from perspectives. This can be done only by using the perspectives which have been occupied at some particular time and place. But the goal of all ethics, the ultimate ethical ideal, is the good of the universe as a whole, the good of the cosmos. This takes us back somewhat to Hegel's position. Nothing is good except as it contributes to the good of the whole universe (Hegel's "Absolute Idea" or the synthesis of the Absolute Idea in the "Spirit" or "Absolute Reality.")

From the point of view of cosmic ideals the good life is the life devoted to the welfare of the cosmos. This is by definition an impossible ideal, for we do not know what is good for the cosmos. If we take the most general principle known to cosmology, which is the principle of entropy, then the end at which the cosmos is aiming is the total unavailability of energy, total disorganization, that absolute uniformity which must result from the "heat death" of the universe. This is the world condition which is most consistent with the Indian *nirvana*. It has not been too well noticed that the moral behavior required by the eastern religions, particularly Hinduism and Mahayana Buddhism, calls for that kind of individual introspective devotion which must lead to the passive nihility of the person, and this is consistent with entropy for the universe. Hinduism in ethics is entropy for the individual.

In the ethics I have been expounding here, however, such passivity by itself is inconsistent with the good life. The ethics of western religion has been much more dynamic but also much more local and uncompromising. Each of the western religions has taken for its ethics one particular set of precepts founded on the morality of the local community and generalized to all of mankind. A price has been paid for the emphasis on activity, and it is the indulgence of violence, the willingness to engage in force in the effort to secure compliance with a doctrine of peace and conformity. How, then, is it possible to achieve the passivity consistent with the eastern religious conception of an ethics in accordance with the doctrine of detachment from the cosmos without sacrificing those lesser goods which have been validated in more limited ways? For the eastern moralist must if he is in earnest give up those lesser goods of individual, social and human worth which he had known and enjoyed. Can an ethics be devised which will serve as a cosmic ideal and have its own methodology?

I will try to describe such a cosmic ideal here and in the last part of this book describe the strategy which is called for by obligations to this ideal. It may be assumed that the greatest good is the universal good. This seems a truism, the universe being the greatest by definition, until we turn the phrase around and speak of the good of the universe. The universal good has the quality of goodness, an intrinsic good which is good in itself and therefore by itself, even though its goodness depends upon its being needed. Of course we know of nothing beyond the universe to need it; what needs it is any part. If the goodness of the universe consists in its being needed by its parts, this accounts for the amount of esthetic beauty involved, for at this point there is no difference between the intrinsic goodness of the universe and the beauty of the universe, except that they represent different aspects. The intrinsic good is the beautiful, and the final good is the beauty of the whole of being. The ethico-esthetic value of the universe is the essential timological value. Nothing less than the universe can be as good because nothing can be as complete. The supreme good would be universally symmetrical, whereas we have been impressed since the second part of this study by the fact that ethical symmetry is more often than not impossible under the circumstances. Thus it must remain an ideal. Consistency lends beauty to lesser organizations, but completeness in any absolute sense belongs to the universe alone.

(b) Cosmic Ethical Principles

The ideal of cosmic ethics, then, is the good of the universe. By comparing individual with social ideals it is possible to extrapolate to the cosmic ideal. For the principles of which we are now in search are not limited to the individual nor to particular societies nor even to the whole of humanity but extend beyond man and his limited environment to the whole of being.

The first of these principles is as follows.

(a) *The human individual has a material being which connects him with everything in the cosmic universe.*

In this sense he is brother to a stone as well as to another man or another organism. Everything in the universe shares the fate of being a visitor to the universe and having in common with contemporary things in the universe an inheritance from all previous things and an ancestry to all coming things. Nothing is alone, not the individual nor his type nor even the whole set of his contemporaries. There have been all those who went before and there will be all those who are coming after. The ethics of the cosmos is represented for the individual by his symbolic value: every part of the universe is a valid part, and looked at from the point of view of the universe is needed in a symmetry which provides the same perspective of goodness from both sides. There is a sense in which everything that is here is here because it was needed; else otherwise why is it here? Generation is never by accident but always from a cause; and this is no less true because the cause may have been accidentally set in operation: causes can be occasioned but when they are they are no less causes.

(b) *The member of any type must consider himself and be considered by all other members of all other types as an agent for all members of all types.*

This is the principle of type responsibility extended as an obligation to the ideal ethics of the cosmos. This comes of the recognition of a common membership in nothing less than existence itself. What exists are individuals, but individuals are related through types not only to other members of the same type but also to other types, since there is a hierarchy of types. Moreover, the relatedness extends beyond relatedness now to relatedness formerly and to future expectations of relatedness. When we talk about "one world" we must not be guilty of excluding from it the absent members, members who because they have gone out of existence or have not yet come into existence could not be present.

(c) *Ideal moral behavior at the level of cosmic ethics consists in conduct toward any existent, in consideration of all being.*

This is the principle of confrontation extended to all possible interactions. This means that all encounters between entities or processes in view of a common existence can be considered as interfaces where there is interposed a type responsibility because there is an encounter: a general state of cosmic confrontation. Every encounter thus symbolizes the matrix of the universe wherein there is contained an activity of encounters leading to a uniformity of values. To be confronted with anything is for anything else an evidence that it exists and has encounters within a framework which provides existence by maintaining being. Whatever affects anything or is affected by something is real. It is likewise good, since there can be nothing real without a quality. And quality at this level is intrinsic goodness without specification. Goodness is what we mean by quality when we are speaking of cosmic goodness and cosmic quality.

The cosmic ethical ideal imposes the ultimate obligation. In his cosmic obligations the individual finds himself again. He has had company on the entire journey through life, but now he stands by himself again, faced toward the universe and released from more detailed concerns. Birth is a social occasion, but every individual dies alone; and it is the fact of death that constitutes the most pressing reminder of his basic ethical status, the ontological good which only he can represent. But until his death and throughout his life the fact that death is coming must be faced and reckoned with in all its reality. To posit an ideal is always to set an obligation, for the ideal is a goal, and a goal requires a strategy. But there are difficulties in the way, resulting from the limitations on everything actual: from bad behavior and its effects at every level of the ethical integrative series. In the next Part we will study the nature of concrete morality with its characteristically bad behavior, and in the final Part we will develop the techniques of strategy, ending with the strategy called out by cosmic ideals.

PART VII

CONCRETE MORALITY

CHAPTER I

BAD BEHAVIOR AND IMMORALITY

In this Part I discuss human conduct as it actually is rather than as it ought to be. A life can be moral only if it is, as Aristotle said, an activity in accordance with reason, but I would add as a necessary codicil, with reason in view of all of the facts, including the ugliest ones. The emphasis here, therefore, will have to be on bad behavior and immorality rather than on good behavior and morality, which was the topic of the previous Part. For we are now concerned not with ideals but with actuality.

In this chapter we have the unwelcome and unsavory, but highly necessary, task of recognizing the existence of bad and even of evil behavior. We shall be dealing with bad behavior under the usual four heads corresponding to the ethical integrative series: individual, social, human and cosmic.

Behavior is morally bad when it is opposed to the self-realization of the individual, the concrete ideal of his society, the welfare of humanity or the order of the cosmos. We shall begin our investigation into this side of morality by looking in general at the sources of the corruption leading to the morally bad.

(a) Corruption of the Four Grades of Obligation

Subjectivity is the outlook characteristic of the morally bad. It is found at its most intense perhaps in certain types of mental illness, running all the way from a concern with the self in simple unfocused anxiety to the solipsism of catatonic schizophrenia. All are characterized by absolute and exclusive concern for the person. An immoral indifference to everything else is implied, and the resultant conduct is consistent with this indifference.

What is true *in extremis* of the mentally ill is true to a lesser degree of the average person. Everyone has to endure a certain amount of pain at some time or other, and pain leads to egotism and excessive subjectivity.[1] Subjectivity in turn gives rise to a corruption of the four grades of obligation. In the case of the individual subjectivity leads to an almost exclusive preoccupation with self-realization, to the exclusion of society, humanity and the cosmos. In each of the next two cases, society and humanity, subjectivity leads to subjectivization, which is to say, an undertaking to constrain society and humanity to the serving of the self-realization of the individual. In the last case, that of the cosmos, subjectivity leads to identification, the supposition that the self-realization of the individual and the ultimate purpose of the cosmos are one and the same.

The behavior which is a consequence of such subjectivity leads to conflicts, as indeed might have been expected. Conflicts when they occur do so between the demands of any two of the four moral obligations. In the case of the individual, exclusive self-realization leads to intentions and actions which go against the conscience. It will be recalled that the retention schemata fall into two more or less separated parts: the private retention schema, consisting of beliefs arising from peculiar experiences, and the public retention schema, consisting of beliefs arising from common social experiences. Now any preoccupation with the self, to the exclusion of society and humanity, is sure to lead to conflicts with some of the contents of the public retention schema.

Another way in which the consequences of subjectivity lead to conflict occurs in connection with society. Every society has laws by means of which its morality is established. The subjectivity of the individual leads him to pursue the reduction of his needs even when this brings him into conflict with the laws. It leads him in short to the commission of illegal acts.

In the case of humanity the subjectivity of the individual leads him to the commission of misanthropic acts, acts which while not necessarily against the laws are still contrary to the welfare of society. This is usually symbolically expressed since it is not possible to take action against humanity at large. It involves aggression against a stranger, or the refusal to give aid and succor under circumstances where they appear imperative.

In the case of the cosmos the subjectivity of the individual leads him to the commission of wantonly destructive acts. Here again the expression can be little more than symbolically expressed. To destroy another species of organism for the sheer fun of destruction, as when

[1] F. Sauerbruch and H. Wenke, *Pain* (trans. E. Fitzgerald, London 1963, Allen & Unwin).

ducks are slaughtered by the use of a cannon without any thought for the market.

The intense subjectivity of the morally bad has as one of its results an indifference to the effect of the subject upon others. Thus there arise many antagonisms and conflicts. Social life is in fact made possible by an equilibrium of antagonisms, ranging all the way from the delicate personal animosities of one individual toward another to the large-scale national hatreds and on to the entire business of wholesale misanthropy. The positive opposition of the contraries involved in human motivation are dramatically clear: man is a fierce animal who preys on his own species and is not averse to causing pain; but he is also essentially a humanitarian given to helping others. He knows that all his goods come to him in some way from others.

The first task of ethics is to determine the range of moral conduct in order to learn with what it is we are dealing. The Nazi extermination of all the Jews who came within their power is certainly evidence for one end of the range, while the behavior of all those exceptional individuals famous or obscure who have been willing to sacrifice their lives to save the lives of their fellows, such as Gandhi, is at the other end. Ambivalence of motivation is a characteristic of human behavior, and the moralization of man must reckon with it. Man wishes both to help and to hurt his fellows, and he does both alternately.

Morally there is little to choose in this regard between the most primitive people living, such as the Bushmen of Southwest Africa or the Guaharibos of the Brazilian rain forests, and the most civilized and cultivated citizens of New York, Paris or London. Men everywhere are angelic pigs or rational lions, capable of both sympathy and unprovoked aggression, of both pity and ferocity. Only those who know something of the depths to which man can sink can understand anything of the heights to which he can rise. It is because he endeavors to embrace the entire range of behavior which is open to him that he produces the ambivalence of motivation with which by now students are so familiar.

What this comes to is that no individual is capable of understanding the nature of the good who has not correctly estimated his own capacity for evil. This holds equally for demotic and heroic man. Consider the plight of demotic man. There are many reasons for antagonism besides the drive to reduce the needs; there is for instance callousness, or mere insensitivity (doing harm without being aware of it), revenge, sadism; absolute belief (in ideas to which some others may

not subscribe), instinctive fear of a potential rival (he is dangerous).
As to heroic man, there is a look of surprise on everyone's face at the
discovery that every genius is also a monster, and no less a monster
because a genius for good. Gandhi saved the lives of many British and
Indians by his campaign of non-violence, but by his own account in
his *Autobiography* he was particularly cruel to his wife and children.
Society often cannot live with a genius even though it lives on him and
by him; and so he is projected outward: he is canonized or ostracized,
he is venerated or condemned to death.

When we look about us at the gains of civilization, we are apt to be
reassured. We have risen, we think, far above the other animals. We
have better organization, greater knowledge because of the sciences,
greater sensitivity through the arts. Yet we are not morally superior
except at times; and there are so many other times: there are wars;
there are the ancient traditions and recent practices of cannibalism.
The prevalence and persistence of wars alone ought to be enough to
convince anyone of the fundamental ferocity of man. As for cannibalism, it would seem to indicate that when we set out to abolish evil
among men we are not dealing with anything simple or superficial.
Cannibalism was Aristotle's example of evil[1] as it is still ours, and as
it has been projected as a definite threat in the future.[2]

(b) The Significance of Bad Behavior

The world man supposes that he lives in is not the one in which he
actually lives. The ingredients of the world of his supposition are
contributed to it by his half recollection of the concrete ideals and his
half recognition of the glossed-over facts. He deludes himself with
respect to his own nature and that of his society, and beyond his
society, with respect to his species and the universe. None of it is as
friendly as he usually imagines or as hopeless as he sometimes supposes.
Inclined toward the good, he encourages the idealist and discourages
the cynic.

Men for the most part operate on the basis of a master illusion. They
suppose that those who are close to them (the members of the in-group)
are like them, and that those who are farthest away (the members of
an out-group) are different. They suppose moreover that those who
are close by are better than they actually are and that those who are
far-away are worse than they actually are. Similarity lends the en-

---

[1] *Nico. Eth.*, VII, 5.
[2] Albert Szent-Gyorgyi, as quoted in *The New York Times* for January 20, 1966, p. 21.

chantment of good quality, while difference always appears in an ugly guise. They deceive themselves as to their true nature and always imagine at least themselves to be predominantly good. That some good exists in each of them, even in the worst, is not to be doubted; yet Hobbes was more right than Rousseau. Men are inherently bad as well as potentially good; and it is the good in them which has invented government in order to actualize this potential, but it is because of the inherent bad that a government was needed.

The ordinary individual lives under the shelter of a wholly artificial and only partly true conception of how things really are in the social world. Evil actions occur under his nose unrecognized because he simply could not accept the facts and continue to live as he does. A challenge to his belief that surface appearances give a true picture of reality is a challenge to his very sanity and to his ability to live as he has been living from day to day. So he tends to reject an unvarnished account as the product of scepticism or of bitterness and to continue with his conventional illusions.

The ideal is no doubt that toward which he aspires, but the actuality is what he faces. The facts are usually ugly, and so they get short shrift. But is this situation adequate for theory construction? Plato erred on the side of idealism and Socrates opposed what the sophists stood for without recognizing that what they brought him was valuable information. For it was the sophists who described the actual world; and though they were in favor of temporizing with it, of compromising for it, and of training the young to be like themselves time servers in it, the fact remains that they did recognize actuality for what it is. This was a service; and although Plato was the greater philosopher, the sophists should be given full credit for their valuable contribution.

In order to approach the ideal, we need to know two things, not one. Knowing what the ideal is (difficult though that may be) is hardly enough. We need to devise a strategy for working toward it. But how can we do that unless we know where we are when we start? In order to climb, it is necessary not only to have the equipment but also to take a purchase. We need to make a stand here, but where and how are things "here"? The facts of concrete morality are rarely described because they are hardly known as effects of the shortcomings of life lived in terms of principles. More often than not men pursue a selfish and tawdry ideal which they do not acknowledge either to others or to themselves while professing the more altruistic one which they and

their fellows officially approve. The ends at which men do in fact aim
are often indefensible. We think we know what is good about the life
we would like to lead, but how bad is the life we do lead and how weak
will we be in pursuit of the good? We can learn much about the conditions requiring strategy if we see how in the past our ideals have been
poorly stated, our efforts to achieve them weak or misled, and the
consequent state of affairs in which we are constantly immersed one
of much confusion.

Thus it is just as important to know the facts of concrete morality
as it is to know the ideals of ethics. If we are to move from the actuality to the ideal, we must know something about the actuality as well
as about the ideal. The most flagrant facts of actuality are those of the
bad and the evil. Moralists have for the most part neglected immorality. They have been too concerned with what-ought-to-be to analyze
the conditions which prevail in ordinary life. The last Part of this book
was devoted to ideal ethics. This Part will be devoted to exploring the
facts of actual practice. And actual practice usually if not always
contains large amounts of bad behavior.

The most important fact about actual life is that (a) it is a mixture of
good and bad; the second most important fact is that (b) goods conflict.

(a) The bad is incompleteness and it fails to bring wholes together,
just as the ugly is inconsistency which fails to bring parts together. A
good thing (or person) is one containing more good than bad. Its (or
his) behavior may therefore have results which are either good or bad.
Hence the actions of anything (or anybody) may have bad as well as
good effects. Elements from the ethical integrative series contain goods
at every level but invariably mixed with the bad.

We can see this illustrated best perhaps in ourselves. Merely material values are hardly available to organisms whose complex for-
malities are so great that they almost put a strain, as it were, upon the
material. The lack of moral considerations we mistakenly ascribe to
pigs is equally true of the human individual who leads what is called
(also mistakenly) a low sensual life. He who insists that when he makes
love to a beautiful girl there is a satisfaction only at the lowest physical
or biological level has inadvertently confessed to his own shortcomings;
to the crudeness of his own sensibilities and the vulgarity of his own
evaluations. He mistakenly supposes that what is good at one level
must be bad at another, as it well may be, for that matter, but not
necessarily.

The most irrefrangible fact in the entire range of concrete morality is that the best and the worst have a mutual affinity. They are drawn toward each other in ways which Aristotle perceived and Hegel proclaimed. This fact limits severely the perfectability of the actually good. Has it not been said that there is more rejoicing in heaven over one sinner who has been saved than there is over one saint? The ambivalence of human behavior is weighty testimony to the affinity of the good and the bad. The individual will act aggressively while admiring those who sacrifice themselves for others. He will perform an altruistic act while secretly admiring those who have the ruthlessness to reduce their primary needs at whatever cost to others.

(b) Perhaps the explanation of the affinity of good and bad is that the goods themselves conflict. If only one good of several can be selected, the others must be rejected; selection involves rejection, and the effect of a rejected good may be morally bad. Leibniz' theory of compossibles is applicable here. If a man has only enough money to buy a painting or a set of books, one of the two must be neglected, but such neglect is morally bad. Other cases may seem stronger. A man who has to choose between supporting his family and defending his country finds himself in this predicament. It is good to do one's duty but what is one's duty, duty to oneself, to one's family, to an institution, to society, to the human species, or to the world? Duties clearly conflict. Hence a certain amount of bad is built into the very nature of existence. The good in a narrow sense may be bad in a larger. A love affair between two persons who may be married to others may give pleasure and yet may hurt more people than it helps. Pleasure is a good in itself but pain is bad, and the degree of each must be ascertained before the event can be classified one way or the other.

The symmetry of relations in which both elements are good is as we have noted earlier rare. In friendship, marriage and barter, each party to the relation is equally good for the other. Two men cannot be friends, a husband and wife in love, or artifacts fairly exchanged, without the relations being good for both the persons involved. But such situations are rare, and often the good is the good for one and not for the other.

In concrete morality we call that behavior good which contains more good than bad, and we call that behavior bad which contains more bad than good. In earlier Parts of the book we talked about the good. Here in discussing actual practice we shall talk more about the bad, understanding always that what we mean is a mixture of the two, but this time with the bad predominating.

We are accustomed to thinking of bad behavior and immorality as being one and the same, and of both as any departure from the accepted morality of a society. This is emphatically not the case. The accepted morality is not identical with morality. Any consistent behavior is the outcome of holding a morality. The individual or group which manifests consistent behavior, though it go against the prescribed behavior of a society, is moral if it be consistent.

Many such cases are known. This is what is meant for instance by saying that "there is honor among thieves." A thieves' compact if adhered to represents a morality, and no less one because for practical reasons it cannot be generalized to the whole society. But there are other moralities which are capable of such generalization. From the point of view of the morality prevailing in a society, any social reformer is "immoral," until such a time, that is, as his program for reform is accepted and his morality becomes the morality of the society. If it does not, then he remains outside and his "morality" continues to be immoral.

Thus "morality" is a captive term. It indicates the approval of a particular morality and the disapproval of all others. Moral behavior is not a special kind of behavior but a moral aspect of all behavior. Thus it makes possible the generic tagging of a particular brand of behavior and indicates that it conforms to a regularity of some established sort, even though it be only the private decision of an individual as to how henceforth he means to live.

Earlier in this book[1] I defined "bad behavior" as action in conformity with a lesser over a greater good, and I pointed out there that evil is the name used for extremely bad behavior as well as for the intrinsic quality of such behavior. Here it will be necessary to explore bad behavior and its consequences at somewhat greater length.

Bad behavior always results from the choice of the lesser good over the greater, of short-range goods over long-range, of the human species over the cosmos, of a particular society over the human species, of an individual over society, of nothing over something. Bad behavior is not merely negative, however; for it has positive results. The positive results of the choice of the lesser good may be positively bad.

"Bad behavior," then, is any behavior which does not lead to the good and which has positive bad results. Whether a specific morality does or does not fall under this classification will depend then upon its effects, and that in turn will depend upon how large a group of

---

[1] Part II, chapter 3, section c.

beings is considered. On this definition, for instance, the "thieves' compact" referred to above is bad because it is too selfish an aim to satisfy even the thieves themselves, and because it will lead to conflict with the authorities of the society and produce punishment for the thieves. Evil is the quality of the bad, and of course absolutely evil behavior, like absolutely bad behavior, is a limiting case, since nothing in actuality is ever absolute.

We know a great deal about good behavior from our study of the ethical "good" at various ethical integrative levels, individual, social, human and cosmic. Our illustrations in those parts were taken chiefly from instances of good behavior. But if we are to understand actual practice as it is rather than as we and others have thought it ought to be, a study of bad behavior is very much in order.

CHAPTER II

BAD INDIVIDUAL BEHAVIOR

I call individual behavior bad when it does not conform to the conscience of the individual. Bad individual behavior can be active or passive, and so it will be well to say a word about each.

(a) Actively Bad Individual Behavior

Actively bad individual behavior is of two kinds, depending upon whether the bad behavior is directed toward the self or toward others. Let us consider them in that order.

First, then, actively bad individual behavior so far as it is directed against the self.

Active individual bad behavior consists first of all and perhaps foremost in the bad behavior of the individual toward himself. Spelling this out is difficult, however, for we have defined bad behavior as behavior that does not lead to the good. And so the bad behavior of the individual toward himself must not lead to the good. But what sort of behavior does that? Foremost, perhaps, we may list direct aggression against the self, consisting of self-abuse, self-laceration, self-betrayal, suicide. But there are some other clear cases, and we have listed a broad catalogue of some of them in the over-reaching of the needs. Care must be exercised in pronouncing judgment, however, as much in the case of bad as of good. How do we know what is bad?

Suppose that an individual has decided to devote himself chiefly to sex or merely does so without having decided. And let us further suppose that he was abnormally endowed for the sexual drive through hormonal activity. Now all that we need to add is that he is unintelligent and in other ways entirely unambitious. Is he not then using himself at his best when he does what he can do best? Provided he keeps within the law and so avoids conflicts with his society, it is difficult to characterize his behavior as bad.

Again, suppose an individual who through no fault of his own has had many disappointments in his life and much pain. Let us further suppose that he has seen clearly that not much in the way of achievement lies ahead of him. Can we condemn his behavior as bad if he becomes a confirmed alcoholic? We may know what bad behavior is in general (and in fact if my definition is correct we do know) but to specify it in an individual case is not without obscurity and much trouble, assuming that this can be done at all.

The best instance on which to test this statement is the case of suicide. It is well known that in some societies suicide is an honorable act, that is to say, one within the allowable limits of approval of the society's established morality; while in others, notably our own, suicide is "immoral," a disgrace to the family, and even a crime under the law. In any case, it is an aggressive act, committed by the individual against himself, and destructive by nature. In this sense it is bad, but whether it is bad or good for the individual will depend upon his private condition as well as upon the morality of his society. If he were well and happy, then suicide would be bad behavior; but would anyone commit suicide under those circumstances? If he were infected with a terminal disease and facing continual pain to the end, then suicide might be justifiable and so good behavior. It would then be designed to provide an end to pain. But how could the patient ever know that at the last minute a remedy might not be discovered by the medical profession or (as sometimes though rarely happens) the disease would remit of its own? Perhaps the right of the individual purely as an individual includes the self-inflicted ending of his existence. But this would be true only if it did not entail any bad for others, and such a situation rarely arises except in societies in which suicide is specifically approved, and then no doubt suicide could under some circumstances be described as good behavior.

Individual behavior is bad when inconsistent beliefs lead to conflicting actions. Conflicts are inevitable both subjectively and objectively.

Let us look at the subjective first. Here is an example. Major premise: schizophrenia is the most prevalent mental illness. Minor premise: pathological conditions are exaggerations of the normal. Conclusion: no individual is less than two people: for instance Jekyl and Hyde.

Conflicts are inevitable on the objective side also because values are not always compossible. An individual may aim at two incompossible goals and so seem to be in an untenable position for subjective reasons, when actually his reasons could as well be objective ones: the situation itself contains inherent difficulties. An individual may tear himself apart emotionally because he is intensely jealous of another and at the same time disgusted with himself for feeling as he does.

The misconceptions from which bad behavior follows are usually those resulting from excess of egotism, inconsiderate need-reductions, or need-reductions socially out of order. It would be deeply satisfying to have both one's neighbor's wife and the esteem of one's neighbor.

A man may subscribe to a religion which is opposed to science, and he may further the interests of the former on Sunday and of the latter on weekdays, never noticing that what he does for the one undermines what he does for the other. And he may be ignorant of the conflict which exists between a belief which he thinks he holds and one which he actually does hold. He may act as though he thought that men are fundamentally bad, while professing that they are fundamentally good; and he will be caught up in the consequences of the latter and compelled to behave accordingly while in his own opinion "knowing better," and so become an unhappy man. For a man whose mind is the arena of conflicts of this sort is sure to be unhappy. The actions which result not from convictions but from irritations are apt to multiply the difficulty and so increase the unhappiness.

Next we must consider actively bad individual behavior so far as it is directed toward others.

The aim of the individual is his own survival through self-surpassing, through self-aggrandizement, or through super-identification, or, failing that, the preservation of his identity through the family, through progeny, or by means of the society through the human species.

The basic need of the human individual is for aggression, and all other needs are species of this one generic need. In order to reduce any need, something in the environment—some material thing or person— has to be altered, and in order to be in the position to do this the individual having the need will have to dominate to that extent. There is in everyone a need for aggression, only in most persons it is curbed or directed into approved channels. When under control and exercised properly, aggression is an essential element in the human individual and may work constructively both for his good and for the good of his society. But it does not always function in this fashion. There is after all the phenomenon of uncontrolled aggression and the left-over drives—what I have earlier called excessive behavior. Naked aggression often takes over, and naked aggression is the fierce, ungoverned will, the urgent need to do something—anything—a frantic grasping at immediate survival. Muscular-need reduction is good, although in a larger context the effect may be bad. Thus destruction for its own sake, wanton destruction and vandalism, often occur. For this reason, crimes of violence can never be altogether eradicated but only held to a minimum.

The aim of the individual in his determination when thwarted can lead to actively bad individual behavior and account for the effects of the wild ungoverned will. Bad behavior is human, not bestial, behavior. Animals kill for food, rarely for other reasons, and never in the wholesale way practiced in wars. The long and melancholy account of human cruelty to animals and men needs no detailing. It is customary to suppose that the kind of ferocity practiced by men in the past is no longer possible, but the facts go against such a supposition. Prisoners are tortured in the wars which are being fought today. Consider the deliberate atrocities of the Viet Cong as practiced against the South Vietnamese and the Americans in the war fought around Saigon in 1965. Not only the systematic ill-treatment of prisoners before their execution, but also cannibalism and rape are still practiced. The well known cruelty of the hordes of Genghis Khan in the twelfth century are matched by sporadic occurrences in almost every decade since, by the "iron maiden" and other instruments specially built for the infliction of bodily pain used in western Europe in the Middle Ages, the festive spectacles of hangings there in the eighteenth century, and the torture and killings of the army generals in the abortive communist coup in Indonesia only yesterday (October 1965).

Evil, as Aristotle said, is natural[1] and "a bad man will accomplish ten thousand times as much evil as a brute."[2] It has been overlooked how well Schopenhauer, and Nietzsche too, recognized the existence in human life of the prevalence of blind irrational force. The aim of the individual is the exercise of power, to dominate the environment, as I have said earlier, and his pleasure comes from achievement. To make the world his, or if not then to make something in it that will be his or will represent him, is what he works to produce in children or in artifacts. What he wishes to do primarily is to use his power to achieve a desirable construction; but if this desire is frustrated, then negatively to use his power to effect an equally large destruction. Witness the prevalence of the illegal power play. Tyrants out of power in ancient Athens were apt to join forces with the enemies of their city. In more recent times, "If I cannot rule Europe I will pull it down,"

[1] *Nico. Eth.*, 1103a19.
[2] *Ibid.*, 1150a7.

Hitler said. Indeed the remarkable fact of our time is the "ideology of brutality"[1] which the Hitler program represented; such organized and planned—and allegedly justified—ferocity seems to have been almost without precedent. The popularity of "murder mysteries" in which both justice and copulation are accomplished only by means of acts of violence is a living witness to the frustrated need for aggression which is the curse of the sedentary.

The generic drive of aggression is often allowed to run unchecked. It then leads directly to overreaching in all of the need-reductions. In the primary needs this is represented by the drive in excess. As Mays has argued, "criminal behavior arises naturally enough out of the ordinary daily affairs in which all of us are engaged."[2] It is possible to drink too much and become an alcoholic, and even the pathological drinking of water is known to psychiatrists. Over-eating is similarly indulged in and can become a disease. As for sex, this exaggeration is common but too well-known to need elaborate treatment here. From the individual who makes sex the end of life and hence its chief occupation, to the rapist, is a large range of abnormal behavior whose effect on the actor as well as on others may be bad. The man who lives to reduce only his primary needs at the expense of the secondary will insure considerable pain for himself. For the secondary needs have their demands, too, and cannot be deprived without penalty and no less so for being self-inflicted.

Aggression also can lead to over-reaching in the secondary need-reductions. The effects of these are more extensive because they are apt to be social as well as individual, and may even be social without being individual. If we recall that the secondary needs are for information, activity and security, and are represented psychologically by thought, action and feeling, then we can see the positive exaggerations in these cases turning negative but remaining forceful. Thought, for example, is represented in bad behavior by error and by extreme conviction, by false knowledge and ignorance; action is represented by violence, destruction and war; and feeling by hatred, envy and malice. Bad behavior in religion (the extreme case because passive by nature) is represented by forced conversions, by compliance enacted on pain of death, by punitive restrictions.

The amount of aggression necessarily involved in the drive to reduce each and all of the organic needs insures that a certain amount of bad

---

[1] *The New York Times*, December 20, 1965.
[2] John Barron Mays, *Crime and the Social Structure* (London 1963, Faber & Faber), p. 16.

behavior will always be involved, if not for the aggressor himself then for the good objects of his needs. The individual who is what he is because of what he inherits from his progenitors and what he encounters in experience is unavoidably susceptible to all four forms of evil: individual, social, human and cosmic, because the drives to reduce his needs are seldom beneficial to the object altered by the drives. We have noted already in an earlier part of this study that good for the cat is bad for the catnip. Rape is no doubt for the rapist a deeply satisfying form of behavior, for it reduces the need for aggression, the need for muscular activity, as well as the need for sexual intercourse. But it is a crime against the person and therefore in many societies justifiably punishable by death. On balance and with the entire involvement of the act in view, rape is no doubt evil: a severely bad form of behavior. But this does not cancel the fact that for the rapist much good is privately involved. The fact of its prevalence despite the known severity of the penalties, would bear this out. Some men risk a great deal for its commitment, and evidently there are always such men in every society.

What we are faced with so often is the fact that individual good conflicts with social bad. What are we to do for example with algolagnia, the sexual pleasure to be derived from the sufferings of others? The psychopath who is sexually aroused only by murder is not an unfamiliar case to the police. The amount of good to be derived by the individual in reducing his sexual needs is so greatly exceeded by the bad effects upon his victims and upon his society that there is no possible compromise.

When bad and good are mixed in such proportions, the bad so greatly predominates that every decent individual is horrified. The moralist must unhesitatingly condemn him. Yet there is no monster who has not in him some good, and for the moralist good is good. The account of an extreme case is reported in *The New York Times* for June 24, 1964. A coprophiliac murderer was apprehended, a man who raped his female victims only after he had murdered them. On the way home late at night after committing one such crime, he stopped to awaken a motorist who had endangered his own life and that of others by falling asleep at the wheel of his car when stopping for a red light.

For the characteristically bad individual, private advantage is his motive, and under it he wishes to impose conformities of all sorts on his fellows. If he is doing something he knows to be socially wrong it will not continue to be so regarded if he can enlist in his support the equally wrong actions of others. Given the structure of social morality, a sufficient number of wrongs do make a right; for when behavior changes and the change becomes in time a custom the laws are changed in conformity with it. Thus the badly behaving individual has a bad effect which tends to spread. The thief feels more secure in the company of other thieves, the alcoholic in the company of other alcoholics.

The bad behavior of the individual is in most cases a result of too limited an objective. The individual always wishes to do good; it is impossible to wish to do bad except in the service of some allegedly supplanting good. But the good which is sought for a limited object may be the source of bad for many other or larger objects; and so on balance the effect is bad. This is another view of excessive behavior. The individual himself is too limited an object, and any purely selfish behavior is sure to produce bad effects upon others. That is in fact what makes it bad. Given a small enough entity, all positive behavior would be good without exception. If as we have noted earlier, construction is good and destruction bad, then all destruction (including self-destruction) is bad. But behavior positively designed to bring about a good is good in itself whatever the other consequences. Thus in judging behavior good or bad we must be sure to remember the size of the consequences.

(b) Passively Bad Individual Behavior

The picture we have been painting is one of extremes. This has in a sense been necessary throughout the length and breadth of this study. In order to show what the good is, an uncompromising portrait has had to be painted in pure colors. Intrinsically, good is good absolutely. And bad is bad. However behavior which does not lead toward some small good is rare. For the fact is that most behavior consist in the mixture of very small amounts of good and equally small amounts of bad. There is nothing either heroically good nor monstrously criminal about the behavior of the average individual citizen.

It is only too often overlooked by writers on ethics that most actions by most individuals in most dates and places are morally very very small. They are small in their physical extent and they are small in their moral effects. They consist in very small goods and they result in very small goods or bads. Most of the actions are discrete actions, tiny in amount and almost not worth bothering about so far as their moral effects are concerned. But the difficulty with such a point is the additive value of small moral actions. The good or the bad accrues in this way. Enough inches will add up to a thousand miles and enough more to a light year. Very small indications of conduct will disclose the weight of a personality if enough of them are collected. A man can be led or can lead himself into very heroic or very anti-social behavior by taking a sufficient number of infinitesimal steps. So they are not for this reason to be discounted.

Most lives are low-level mixtures of small pleasures and equally small pains, averages of experience sufficiently randomized to leave most people when they are miserable with the hope that things will change for the better, although knowing that such ecstasies as they are permitted cannot possibly last and will return if at all only fleetingly. Pleasure and happiness are rare states and seldom destined to last for very long and certainly not forever; while pain and despair have a more certain future: they may not return for a while but return they most assuredly will. However long the individual is able to stave off his fate, it will overcome him in the end, so that we deem him lucky who dies eventually in the most painless fashion. The exception is the action of the individual caught up in a supreme social or cultural effort. Philosophers deal in ideal terms: goodness, the right, etc., but people usually encounter only moderate virtues and vices. The ideal has its correspondence in conduct only in times of crisis. Critical actions illustrate absolute moralities.

But these are rare enough. The analysis of ordinary behavior discloses a very pale spectrum: neither very good nor very bad but only a mild mixture of the two. Life, for most individuals under most circumstances, is very drab. It consists in an apparently endless round of dreariness, of joyless sadness and envy, of anxiety mixed with injured egotism, of resentment expressed in little falsehoods and deceptions. The ambition of most individuals is the barely pragmatic effort to get along from day to day, avoiding trouble and hoping to survive by means of the least amount of effort.

The average person is characterized chiefly by disregard: he did not ask to be born, he does not inquire into the meaning of existence, he does not question anything that happens; he only strives as little as possible to reduce his most pressing needs. He is not very active or very curious or even very anxious about his own security. His characteristically over-riding tone is indifference, indifference to everything: to the things which concern him directly almost as much as to those which concern him only indirectly or not at all. Whatever is for him, is; he never thinks of changing it himself, and for that matter, never dreams it could be changed. He takes his values and his cues from custom, tradition, and the established morality. And if he hears of any others he judges them entirely on the basis of his own experience within his society.

The native nature of aggression makes a difficulty for the individual in his confrontations. How can he alter his environment (which includes the other members of his society) and at the same time conduct himself properly toward those other members? What, in short, does aggression do to confrontation? How then must it be between the individual and his fellows under these circumstances? The command to love his neighbor as himself is a difficult one to obey when the interest of people in such great proximity inevitably clash. It should be easier to love those farther away, but he does not ordinarily do that, either, for then the element of strangeness enters, and he tends to fear what he does not know. Thus the love of all mankind, of humanity, is uncommon. Man can be brought to love his neighbor but only when they have a common enemy and usually not otherwise. And as for those farthest away, he finds loving them quite impossible. All consider themselves his rivals for the love of God.

Now such an attitude is bad because it has bad effects. For he is involved in his society, through it with other societies, and through them with the human species and thence with all other species of individuals in the cosmic universe. All other things in existence have an effect upon him, good or bad, and he on them. There is then an obligation upon him to choose the good over the bad whether he knows it or not. There is a moral obligation to know about obligations; this is perhaps the first obligation. And it is not relaxed through ignorance. The world is an on-going business in which we are all involved with or without awareness. What distinguishes the human individual from other types is the degree of his awareness of involvement. It is an instance of bad behavior not to cultivate as assiduously as possible the awareness and the good behavior. Passivity in such a connection is inherently bad.

I have defined the bad as the substitution of the lesser for the greater good. This would seem to make of bad behavior a kind of familiar and easily recognizable affair, yet it is not. Bad behavior is inseparable from the good and often confused with it in subtle and almost undetectable ways in this mixed-up world. Consider for example the bad aspects of all egoistic efforts at personal salvation, the man who is always good because it is only in this way that he can succeed in controlling an exceedingly bad temper. Doing nothing may under certain circumstances amount to the same thing as doing bad; and there is such a phenomenon as evil inaction.

The selfishness of some saints is often appalling, as for instance when they do good to others chiefly in order to save their own souls. They sacrifice their families to their frantic desire for personal salvation, often ignoring, in their eagerness to do good for themselves and for mankind, what they are doing to those who, like wives, concubines and children, have depended upon them in a previous arrangement when they were not living the lives of saints.

I have been arguing as though the choice of good behavior over bad lay within the provenance of the individual in all respects and at all times and places. Such is by no means the case. There is a certain amount of bad behavior built into the structure of the individual in virtue of his physiology and psychology. The individual is a loosely and poorly organized entity, only at times sufficiently integrated to know the target and to aim at it. The searchlight of attention plays accidentally over the contents of awareness, indifferent sometimes as to its selection and to whether it is a centrally aroused or a peripherally aroused sensation, an abstract thought or an event in the external world. Under such circumstances, the individual is subject to the principle of pragmatic indifference. He is careless of his own welfare in certain of these moods, and almost impartial in the choice between pleasure and pain. Not happiness but a certain numbness is the prevailing and sufficiently satisfying quality of the personality.

The appearance of morality is sought by everyone, even by those guilty of the most heinous crimes. This speaks well for the general opinion concerning the value of morality, and it is in no way diminished by the fact that few agree about the details. As to ideals of conduct, most people feel good about themselves if they make periodic verbal or emotional affirmation of some sort of subscription by rote to a set of moral principles; as though the affirmation would substitute adequately for the concrete accomplishment.

Men do not by ordinary measure themselves against rules nor their behavior against moral codes. For conventional purposes the conscience is kept at a great distance from awareness, and though it is there at all times its effect is in this fashion greatly reduced. What we deliberately refuse to remember hurts us less in this way. Why remind ourselves of our shortcomings if we can find a mechanism for deliberate obfuscation? What the Freudian psychoanalysts call "repression" is

active here. But there is also for the time being at least a substitution
of sufficiently similar material to meet the demands of the conscience
through deception. Reckonings postponed may mean in a longer run punishments cancelled; and this is no less true when the punishment is one
meted out to the individual by himself at the dictates of his own conscience.

(c) The Unsocial Individual

What we are so often faced with in society is the fact that individual
goods often conflict with social goods. This means that individual
goods may have bad effects.

The democratic society is notable for providing the greatest freedom
for the individual. It is a well-organized society and at the same time
a stable one. Let us see how many kinds of actions we can find in it
which is the work of the deliberately unsocial individual.

There are the marginal crimes, such as theft, rape, vandalism. Then
against this there are the organized crimes: gambling, prostitution,
gangsterism, with its "protection," and narcotic rings. There are dis-
honest politicians at all levels of government. In business, felony is
quite common, and is to be found among wealthy and influential
industrialists and bankers as well as in more modest circles. In adver-
tising the misrepresentation of products is well known and common-
place. There are in most religions doctrinaire extremists, each of whom
is fiercely opposed to the others. There are sectional and regional
partisanships, and there are bitter racisms, each of which is keenly felt
and shared by unsocial individuals who do not care at all how much
the society itself is hurt by such conflicts.

Little does the unsocial individual know how much effort is required
on the part of others, how much voluntary social cooperation there
must be, if his own unsocial behavior is to be possible. The immorality
of the few rests on the morality of the many. For if all individuals were
to practice unsocial behavior, the society would break down and the
individuals themselves would not survive. Thus the Jean Lafittes and
the Al Capones are not self-sufficient, and neither is their morality one
which could be generalized to the society in which they practice it.
They are immoral parasites upon a moral society, forever condemned
to an inferior position within it in virtue of the very structure of their
relations with it. Let us look at a few examples of points about unsocial
behavior chosen from the secondary needs.

The tendency to belief which is so prevalent and so facile because
belief is pleasurable and doubt painful has led many times to the quick

acceptance of a proposition as true without examination. The evil man is often one with basic misconceptions. His behavior will exhibit badness because it follows as consequences from false propositions his feelings accept as true. The cheapest commodity in the world is absolute certainty. Its bitter emotional roots insure that it will be defended at all costs. Thus it extends beyond all reason, often beyond the relevant facts, and even beyond the welfare of society. Absolute certainty is common to all types of belief, from theism to atheism, from cannibalism to self-abnegation. It is alien to tolerance and essential to faith. Faith requires blind uncritical acceptance. And since certitudes differ, and more often than not conflict, absolute certainty is responsible for much of the aggression and pain in the social world, and for many of the wars. Thus it backs up and seems to offer some kind of justification for much of the bad behavior that is to be found among individuals. Thus error and false knowledge come to the aid of ignorance in the case of the average individual, and he is apt to try to reinforce his beliefs by imposing them upon others. The behavior of the evil man is in fact twice bad. Not only does he act in ways which have bad effects but often he has considerable power; and since we have noted that the possession of power is good in itself, its misuse is a double betrayal: a betrayal of the use of the good and a betrayal of the power of the good.

In the case of feeling, the evaluation of conduct is more often better than the conduct. Men's judgments are superior to their practice. The feeling of conviction that such a course of action ought to be followed does not necessarily lead to its being followed. Thus where the feelings of the individual support the socially approved morality his conduct will fall short of it. Men who behave in this way demonstrate that they do not really accept the principles they profess to accept, or, worse still, do not believe in the reality of principles.

If actions are guided by thoughts and feelings, and if these can diverge from social morality, how much more so the action itself. What men do in their own interest as they see it is as often detrimental to the interests of the society of which they are members as it as beneficial to those interests. From each only what his society can exact from him, to each something in excess of his needs. How many men would willingly pay their taxes or perform other public services if there were no penalty for infractions nor punishment for defections? Some, certainly, but how many?

(d) The Ambivalence of Aggression

The paradox in man's development is the constancy of his opposite aims. He is at once a maker and a destroyer, and his behavior leads inevitably to both congruence and collision. But despite the conflict involved, there must be some common mechanism. The alternation of war and peace, for example, would seem to point to important relations between them. Wars destroy so much of what was painfully constructed during periods of peace that the two seem at odds. Yet is this entirely the case? Intervals of peace usually last longer than periods of war, probably because men need time in which to rest and recuperate before engaging again in such exhaustive destruction. Yet there must be elements native to the time of peace which accumulate until war becomes inevitable and necessary. Let us see if it is possible to isolate these elements and determine their nature.

Social life always involves for the human individual a certain amount of both cooperation and competition. Cooperation means that competition must be restricted somewhat and conducted strictly in accordance with an established set of ground-rules. But competition by the rules is limited and therefore the occasion for a whole host of frustrations. These can accumulate slowly until the total reaches un-bearable levels. The sedentary life is also a source of frustration which in time must build up to the point where aggression becomes necessary. Thus there arises a need for violent action which the life of civilized man does not reduce except in war.

Peace is a war that nobody wins. The opposing sides stand poised to do battle but neither is strong enough to be sure of victory. Hence it becomes safe (temporarily) for the individual to go routinely about his business, secure in the knowledge that a more open conflict has been postponed.

In this way man finds himself with ambivalent drives and activities. These are: to help and to hurt his fellows. He alternates these drives; and so competition is as common as cooperation, war as common as peace, hatred as common as love, egoism as common as altruism. Thus for example the individual carves out a fortune for himself—and then gives it away, as Carnegie in fact did. Or nations undertake to destroy each other, with the victor helping its ex-enemies to recover, even going so far as to make common cause with them against their ex-allies, as was the case of the United States with Germany and Japan. I am reminded of the Nazi storm trooper who politely assisted the old lady into the van which was to take her to the gas chamber, and of those who resort to the use of force to convince others of the supremacy of brotherly love.

CHAPTER III

BAD SOCIAL BEHAVIOR

The transition from bad individual to bad social behavior is not difficult to discern. It was begun, as a matter of fact, in the last section of the previous chapter, where I discussed the unsocial individual. To speak of society is to speak of the human part of culture. Societies could not exist without the material ingredients of culture any more than cultures could exist without societies.

Civilization, that large agglomerate of culture, depends for its continuance upon learned behavior. Its established institutions, its traditions and customs, must be learned anew by each generation. All children are born primitives, and acquire the rules of behavior from those who have learned them previously and in the same way. It is the external inheritance, not the internal, which is the carrier of the culture. Without such conditioning, behavior would quickly become —or remain—"uncivilized," as it was for instance with those who took part in the Los Angeles riots in the negro slums in the summer of 1965.

I call social behavior bad when there is either the social disapproval of good behavior or the social approval of bad behavior. We need a few words about each of these kinds.

(a) The Social Disapproval of Good Behavior

The morality of a society, the concrete ideal, is an established morality. Despite the ethical relativism inherent in the fact that every valid ethnological unit has its own morality, the universal practice is for members to consider such morality absolute. Probably because of their unswerving subscription, there tends to be something inherently conservative about establishment. Time was required to found a morality and more time is required to gain its acceptance. Once the establishment is complete (for this is what acceptance means) it is so entrenched that it becomes identified with the natural, and its conventional character is either forgotten or denied. Any suggestion of change or improvement is regarded as a threat to it and hence as anti-social behavior. The concrete ideal sets the norm for behavior.

One form of the social disapproval of good behavior is the punishment of the individual whose behavior is good. Another form is the neglect of such individuals. Thus when a genius discovers an improvement or suggests a radical revision which might lead to the betterment of society, he is to that extent disapproved by the members of the society and might suffer punishment as a result, either ostricism or confinement. Both Socrates and Jesus underwent martyrdom for their significant contributions to society. This has only too often been the fate of religious prophets. At first they meet with severe disapproval, and it is no help to them if after their life is over their work is approved and even established. For the individual genius promises an increase of good in the future, but society approves of them only when it can place them in the past.

The hero is as often neglected as he is punished. The story of the artistic genius whose music or poetry is ignored in his lifetime and recognized for its high achievement only after his death, is so common as to become a kind of stock parable. I suppose the archetype is John Keats, but more recently there has been the case of the composer, Bela Bartok who died of neglect in New York. Walt Whitman was not exactly received with enthusiasm in his lifetime, and there are many others who have met the same fate. In science it has been no different sometimes. Consider for example the life of Louis Pasteur, and in technology of Thomas Mitchell. Pasteur wanted the surgeons to wash their hands before performing operations in order to avoid infection, and Mitchell wanted the U.S. Army to fly planes.

(b) The Social Approval of Bad Behavior

Societies though composed of individuals and artifacts often care more for the preservation of artifacts than for the welfare of individuals. This was certainly notoriously true of slave-holding societies. And the story is often told of the plantation owner who said that he took better care of his mules than he did of his slaves because he had to pay more for the mules. Except in recent welfare states, the Platonic ideal in the *Laws* that no man need be poor or hungry has not been carried out in practice. A principle of pragmatic social indifference has operated in more societies than not. There is no social concern for the welfare of the individual. Those who can take care of themselves do so, those who cannot are allowed to starve or rot, or both. This was the case for many years in the crowded countries of Asia. In our own day in India there is seldom enough food to feed the whole population, and travelers report that outside many of the luxury restaurants beggars abound who bear the unmistakeable marks of starvation and want.

There is a side to social morality which differs from and often is opposed to individual morality. Preferred position is so often taken as an opportunity for individual advantage that malversation seems more the rule than the exception. There is no greater bad behavior so far as the welfare of society is concerned than the corruption of those in public office. But in most cases who is to detect their malfeasance, try it and punish it? Although too many individuals doing wrong would dissolve society, it has no gratitude for those who add to it and eagerly acclaims those who subtract from it. This is true for contemporaries, though the values tend to assert themselves through the repetition made possible by time. Thus the acquisitive individual is likely to be more respectable and even glorified during his life, while the productive genius often has to wait until after his death for the proper recognition.

When an individual in performing a certain act knows that he is satisfying the demands of his particular society and yet feels that somehow he is doing something immoral, the chances are that he is going against the demands of the ethics of the human species or of the ethics of the cosmos. No doubt some of the Turkish soldiers who were ordered to dynamite the Parthenon, or some of the early Christians who helped to destroy the Library at Alexandria, must have felt this way. For it is not necessary to be constructive to win the approval of one's society, especially not when destruction is the order of the day.

The leaders who are held in high esteem by societies and remembered with admiration and even affection by history are not the ones who did the most good but those who did the most harm. Men accord great honor to those who have succeeded in getting the most people killed: the war lords, such as Alexander, Caesar, Napoleon, Lincoln. The societies which have done the most harm are those which have existed almost entirely for the purpose of conducting wars. Nearly all societies of course have had their military arm; preparedness or defense, it is usually labelled. But there have been some societies which have openly indulged in aggression and existed only for war; Assyria, Sparta, Nazi Germany, for example. Here bad behavior was socially approved and socially expected behavior. The military hero is the archetype, and his exploits in killing members of other societies extolled.

Unfortunately, human history is a sickening account of wholesale slaughter. Genghis Khan and his hordes killed their millions, and while the use of nuclear weapons is no worse than this it is also no better. *Homo hominis lupus est* is not exactly a new saying, but it is still a true one, no less applicable now than when it was invented. We should decry our nature as much as we do our behavior, and consider that we have the problem of improving both.

It has been noted that history remembers few good women and many bad ones. For every Molly Pitcher or Florence Nightingale there are a thousand Cleopatras. Catherine the Great of Russia left a tarnished record which has not detracted from her fame. The record of influential mistresses is large: Pericles' Aspasia, Cortez' Maria. It would seem that Socrates learned more from Diotima with whom he shared a banquet than from Xanthippe with whom he shared a marriage.

Most large-scale social events are mixed in character. They contain considerable amounts of both good and bad. The bad was the price for the good, yet it was bad; and to the extent to which society has condoned it to obtain the good which resulted, society has to that extent if not approved of the bad at least suffered it. Napoleon was responsible for the death of many men and even had himself crowned Emperor, yet his effect was to bring monarchy to an end in Europe and clear the way for the democratic regimes. The Marxist revolution in Russia has had a similar effect. No doubt many people were killed who were innocent of any wrong-doing, and the call to violence unfortunately is part of the Marxist creed; yet as a result of the change in form of government as well as in its personnel, more people are living under better material conditions now than formerly: they are eating more and wear better clothes under the communists than they did under the Czar, they have more and better medical attention and many other benefits of a like nature.

It often happens that the social attitude toward the behavior of an individual may in one context meet with approval and in another with disapproval. This is true certainly of murder. Murder may be defined as the peacetime infliction of death on a member of the in-group. Thus the wartime murder of a member of an out-group may not only be condoned but highly approved. In most societies during the prevalence of peace severe penalties exist for the murderer. But then suddenly a war breaks out, and that same individual is branded a coward or slacker if he refuses to go into battle in the company of his fellows to murder individuals who are now officially enemies.

Individual actions may meet with the moral approval of the in-group and the moral disapproval of the out-group, or it may be the reverse. Only too often the approval of an action as moral or its disapproval as immoral will depend entirely upon the size of the social group which is responsible for the endorsement or condemnation. For instance, if a white man in the southern part of the United States in 1964 had approved of full civil rights for all citizens including negroes, he would have been condemned as immoral by a majority of the white citizens of his state but he would have been endorsed as highly moral by a majority of citizens of the United States. Thus his actions to suit his conscience might have been in conflict with the smaller in-group and in complete accord with the larger in-group.

The principle of pragmatic social indifference means that societies are primarily concerned with their own internal affairs and do not care about the welfare of other societies. When they do care it is to secure the conformity of the other societies, and this can best be done by dominating them, a condition most easily produced through the practice of warfare. Unprovoked, however, most societies remain indifferent to others. This implies the tacit social approval of the other societies, and, where the other societies include bad practices, the social approval of bad behavior. Morally speaking, the relations between societies never reaches the level of the good which is sometimes at least attained by the relations between individuals within societies. International relations are as a rule notoriously bad. Within a given side, and because of a joint opposition to the same "enemy," war sometimes compels a social approval of bad behavior. The Russian approval of Cuban offenses and European approval of internecine Arab offenses, are examples.

A term has been invented in our time to cover the attitude of disapproval and the activities of antagonism and hostility short of war. It is "the cold war." In some cases at least the cold war must amount to the social disapproval of good behavior from either side.

(c) The Bad Behavior of Institutions

The bad behavior of institutions takes two forms: bad behavior toward individuals and bad behavior toward other institutions.

The bad behavior of institutions toward its individual members takes two forms: inadequate and excessive behavior.

Inadequate behavior occurs when an institution fails to perform its proper function for its individual members. An army which has not paid its soldiers what they were promised or whose officers think and act only for their own welfare, are cases in point.

Excessive behavior occurs when the institutions perform more than their proper function for their individual members. In most societies of the past, religions have authorized a particular morality, and supernatural sanctions have been invoked to compel a certain way of life. The exceptions seem to be Confucianism and Hinayana Buddhism. When a religion claims infallibility and the possession of the truth and uses these to demand and enforce absolute obedience on the part of its adherents, excessive behavior is institutionally in full sway. There are of course smaller examples. A badly run institution, such as the Trujillo government of the Dominican Republic during the second quarter of the twentieth century, is an institution exhibiting excessive behavior.

In a sense, every institution by its very nature exhibits excessive behavior toward its individual members. The individual serves an end with an institution functioning as the means, but only too often the institution becomes an end in itself rather than the means it was intended to be. When the men whose business is the operation of an institution have a vested interest in it, then it and not the purpose it serves becomes the end for them. Thus a university which began as a teaching institution may turn into an institution which exists primarily in order to be run, as was the case with so many large universities in the United States in the second half of the twentieth century; or an army may maintain itself at the expense of the nation it was constructed to serve, as was the case with the "Free Companies" of France which in the latter half of the fourteenth century roamed the French country-side pillaging and looting after their defeat at Poictiers. In such cases the individuals do not serve the end for which the institution was designed but the institution itself, and they are ground down by it as a result. No long-range good for individuals ever results from the self-service of an institution.

The bad behavior of institutions toward other institutions may take two forms: inadequate and excessive behavior.

Inadequate behavior occurs when the institution fails to perform its proper function for other institutions or for the society. When an army fails to defend the country against invading enemies, as when the Roman garrisons crumbled before the invading Germans in the fifth century A.D. or when the French armies surrendered to the Germans almost without a fight at the outbreak of world war II in 1948, we have an instance of inadequate institutional behavior.

Excessive behavior occurs when the institution performs more than its adequate function for other institutions or for the society. This is true whenever an institution preempts the functions of other institutions. We have a good example in the role of the Christian Church during the Middle Ages in Europe when the Church attempted to dictate to government and maintained tight controls over the lives of men in every other institution, thus abrogating its own stipulated edict to "render unto Caesar the things that are Caesar's."

The distinction between secular and religious roles in ethics is a sharp one. In secular philosophy, practical conduct is the means to ethical perfection as the end. In religious philosophy, or theology, moral conduct is the means to religious salvation as the end. Moral behavior is evidently not improved socially through the endorsement and establishment of moralities by religions. What good there is in established religions comes from what they affirm, the bad from what they deny. In the practice of the denial there is much self-interest. Consider the wars of religion, the wars fought by Christians against other Christians, as for instance between Catholic and Protestant in Europe in the sixteenth century, the holy wars fought against Greek Orthodox Christianity by the Moslems in the ninth century, or the wars of more recent date between Hindu and Moslem on the border between the new states of Pakistan and India.

(d) The Bad Behavior of Societies

The bad behavior of societies is bad behavior toward other societies. This takes chiefly the form of war. Here the amount of evil within an institution may be so great that it reaches out beyond the institution and embraces the entire society. Under the Nazi government the Germans were collectively guilty and not merely Hitler and his storm-troopers or the Nazi party. The prevalence of war throughout human history needs no underscoring here. Wars are fought for all sorts of reasons: for territorial gain, for revenge, and for many other reasons. But the chief fact is that they are fought. The character of the society may change but the recurrence of wars does not.

There has been no improvement in human behavior in this direction. The human record recounts that for a million years man's immediate predecessors were hunters and for roughly a hundred thousand he was too. Settled agricultural communities and animal husbandry are only 20 thousand years old, and they are years of hunting, but the hunting in this period was chiefly confined to preying on other men. War is a form of hunting. Thus there has been no progress in motivation. Men always did try to help their own in-group and hurt the out-group, and the extreme form of hurt is war. They do so still. The material efficiency of the invention of tools for helping and hurting has increased to keep pace with the increase in the proportion of population, from the small number of people making up primitive communities to the enormous population of modern industrial metropolitan cities produced by the scientific revolution.

One of the most familiar forms taken by the bad behavior of societies toward other societies is the institutionalizing of such behavior. When cannibalism or slavery is practiced routinely, bad social behavior may be said to have been established. Both are ancient and conventional practices, and neither has been abolished altogether. There are alas modern examples of cannibalism in societies which are primitive still, and examples are not unknown among the great civilizations at war. And there are modern and very much updated versions of slavery, such as is practiced by the Chinese communists in Tibet.

The worst feature perhaps of the bad behavior of societies toward other societies is the moral claim which the stronger make when they prey upon the weaker. The communists of Soviet Russia argue that they are undertaking to "liberate" smaller countries from the oppression of the capitalists, and so feel themselves to be in a very moral position. There are, unfortunately, good precedents. For instance in the last century Whewell, in illustration of the principle "that the members of a Community, organized as a State, have a collective Right to possess Territory," maintained that "a Civilized State, on discovering a country of Savages, may take possession of it; and that the possession of the Savages must be regulated according to the Laws of the Civilized State."[1]

Civilization has the effect of turning hunting into regulated forms of competition. When men seek what they need they find themselves competing with their fellows. Thus opposition and hatred form at the leading edge of activity. Hatred is natural to all encounters of strangers, and in amount tends to greatly exceed the love which occurs earlier in connection with the family. The struggle with strangers does not stop when the needs are reduced but continues on for its own sake. Need becomes greed, contests turn into a series of wars, peace exists only for the purposes of recuperation between wars. These conditions

[1] William Whewell, *The Elements of Morality, Including Polity* (Cambridge 1864, Deighton Bell), p. 401.

have been at their worst in nations which existed for the purposes of fighting wars, such as ancient Assyria, classic Sparta and recent Germany.

The good will not be established until a way has been found for abolishing wars, but there has been no improvement in recent times. The European wars of 1870, 1914 and 1941, to say nothing of lesser conflicts, such as the war in Korea and South Vietnam, and the many wars smaller still, such as the one fought against Yemen by the Egyptians in 1964, give no indication that war has been abandoned as an instrument of national policy. A third conflict, which would be world-wide in extent and led by Soviet Russia or China on one side and the United States on the other, hangs over everyone even as I write these words, a threat under which most of us now alive will live for the remainder of our lives. On the definition of "the good" advanced here, war is an unmitigated evil the consequences of which man must suffer by his sacrifice, unless a way can be found to abolish it.

CHAPTER IV

BAD SPECIES BEHAVIOR

I call human behavior bad when the species *Homo sapiens* has a deleterious effect upon its own or any other organic species.

First, then, we will look at some of the evidence of inter-specific aggression. We have noted earlier how subjectivity leads to the commission of misanthropic acts. Wanton aggression against segments of the human race by individual members of it is not an uncommon phenomenon. The individual shifts all his frustrations, his defeats and his shortcomings to others, blames them for his own misery, and subsequently attacks them, as though eliminating them would help him. Bad inter-specific behavior is thus one characteristic weakness of humanity, one of many ways in which man proves himself to be no better than other organic species. The hero who sacrifices his first-born is no different from the sow who eats her young. Fortunately, humanity has not yet been able to destroy itself in this way, for it did not have the power; but now it has, and what the result will be none can yet say. Bad inter-specific behavior may yet account for the destruction of the human species.

But chiefly here we have to examine the evidence of intra-specific aggression. Bad species behavior has already accounted for the destruction of some of the other species. Animals which have been hunted so fiercely that an entire species has been destroyed, is a good example. The soilless agriculture practiced by some primitive tribes, for instance by the Baiga of central India, in which entire forests were burned down so that a single crop could be planted in the ashes, is so wasteful of plants as to constitute an instance of bad species behavior.

There is a sense in which bad species behavior is unavoidable to some extent. Nature is cruel. Men are born in pain and usually die in pain, and there is much pain in their lives which can clearly not be traced to their own decisions or actions. The last cruelty, perhaps, is a painful death. When a hawk eats a sparrow or a lion a wildebeest, it can hardly feel good to the sparrow or the wildebeest. The eating hierarchy, based on the food-chain, with plants at the bottom, animals at the top, and humans pyramided over both, insures that all but the lowest species shall exist by courtesy of its ability to prey on the lower. Man is the greatest predator of all, for there are few species on which he has not preyed. Almost anything edible has been eaten by man, who is neither exclusively an herbivore nor a carnivore but usually both. This includes his own species, for cannibalism is among the oldest and at times the most prevalent of practices. No doubt it can be included as an uncompromising example of bad human behavior.

The general point here is that diet defeats all moral theory. How can there be a moral confrontation or a justification of need which destroys the object needed? How can there be a good which of necessity includes a monstrous bad? This is what Whitehead meant when he wrote about societies which destroy other societies as their food.[1]

The defense which is usually made rests on the superior value of the higher species. A man is higher than a peanut or a cow, and so if he eats them they are serving a higher purpose and he is using them for a good end. It may be so. But we must be very sure of our own super-terrestrial importance if we dare to use brutally and destructively everything on the surface of the earth which can contribute to our advantage without feeling the slightest compunction in the process.

At the very least this points to a complete absence of the virtue of humility, but there are other difficulties. By our very acceptance of the existence of a hierarchy of the integrative levels and consequently also of the organismic sublevels, are we not placed under an obligation at least to destroy the lower in preference to the higher even though both are lower in the scale than ourselves? In short, if we can derive the same sufficient nourishment from both cow and peanut, are we not under a moral obligation to eat the peanut rather than the cow? And if morality requires the pursuit of pleasure and the avoidance of pain not only for ourselves but for all creatures capable of feeling pain, should not our diet consist for moral purposes of peanuts and milk rather than steaks?

Inter-specific and intra-specific human behavior are intimately connected. There is no decisive break between them. Men who are cruel to other species cannot be expected to be kind to each other. There are exceptions, but there is also the rule. It has been affirmed that no western man understands his own culture unless he has visited a slaughterhouse and a children's hospital. The former is a species

---

[1] *Process and Reality*, Part II, chapter III, Section X.

problem, the latter more general, since no human can be held responsible for the fact that children do sometimes contract fatal and painful diseases a few of which have remained incurable. We shall come to the latter point in the next chapter. Here I wish merely to emphasize that what the human species has to answer for in the way of bad behavior is considerable, especially where there has been no power to say the human nay.

The heights to which man can rise are matched only by the depths to which he can sink. At his most human the ferocity of his aggression still has its reason for being deep down in his organic needs. He cannot survive as an animal without altering organisms in the external world in ways which are productive of pain. It comes to this, I suppose, that we have reached an impasse with the human species where we regard as morally wrong what can easily be accounted for biologically.

CHAPTER V

BAD COSMIC BEHAVIOR

I call cosmic behavior bad when any species of existent has a deleterious effect upon another species.

Cosmic behavior can be bad for reasons of inadequacy or of excess.

Inadequate cosmic behavior is exemplified by the lack of environmental conditions which will enable a species to survive. The destruction of any species of existent is bad if it contained any good, and
who can say that there is an existent which was destroyed and contained no good? Anything that is, is good, at least to a minimal extent.
Thus the dinosaur and the dodo contained some good but one died
out millions of years ago and the other in our lifetime, so the process
of the destruction of the good has a long history and is continuing.

Excessive cosmic behavior is exemplified by large destructive effects,
as for instance it is possible to detect in astronomical observations the
destruction of large bodies. The Crab nebula looks like a star that
exploded, and it is correlated with Chinese observations from the year
1001 A.D. Could such a vast cataclysm have failed to destroy with it
many complex forms of matter, including perhaps organisms of one
sort or another on neighboring satellites? The account of the career of
any actual thing has as one of its stages a period when through its
enlarging efforts it seeks to include too much and thus commits hubris.
That this can be true for planets, solar systems and galaxies as well as
for plants, animals and men, would seem to be logical.

The concatenation of a large number of very special circumstances
had to happen before organic life in general and human life in particular could occur. This is remarkable; and yet the principle of pragmatic cosmic indifference means that every species is concerned with
its own affairs and is not concerned with those of other species. As for
the human species and its welfare, the cosmos seems wholly uncon-
cerned. Human existence is almost an accident and could be snuffed
out by any puff of cosmic change, by a deviation in the sun's parallax
for instance. Individuals live or they die with astonishing casualness,

and, on the part of larger organizations of whatever size, from a small society to the cosmic universe, with overwhelming indifference.

Since everything in the universe is bound up to some extent with every other thing, any indifference on the part of anything to the fate of anything else is bad. But the individual is so small and the universe so large that the individual hardly appears to count, and certainly no group of individuals however many if it is short of the whole cosmos counts for very much. Granted an involvement, any indifference is bad. All such speculation is of course predicated on the ignorance of a grand design, whether there is such a thing, and if so, what it is. That we know little if anything about these matters it is unnecessary to emphasize; and that what we project by extrapolation from what we do know is, as in the present case, intellectually venturesome and to that extent unreliable, is obvious.

PART VIII

MORAL STRATEGY

CHAPTER I

THE USES OF STRATEGY

In the sixth Part of this study we looked at the area of ideal ethics. In the seventh Part we surveyed some of the more sordid aspects of concrete morality. Ideal ethics undertakes to study what-ought-to-be, concrete morality describes what-is. Between them lies the largest gap possible. It presents the problem of bridging: how does one get from where one-is to where one-ought-to-be, from concrete morality to ideal ethics? An entirely new and almost completely neglected area of ethical strivings thus presents itself. Its existence has rarely been acknowledged.

Although writers like Machiavelli have treated politics in this way, and Whitehead has recognized the wisdom of Ulysses as distinct from the wisdom of Plato, the existence of strategy as a speculative field devoted to the techniques of moral methodology remains uncultivated. In this, the final part of this study, I undertake to answer the question of how by means of a grand strategy the task of the moralization of entire man can be undertaken.

(a) The Ideal, the Actual and the Strategic

It is certain in any case that any writer who proposes to deal with a topic involving conduct is committed to distinguishing between three separate domains: the ideal, the actual and the strategic. Once having by means of an ideal set the goal for morality, he must realize that he starts from an awkward place. The predicament of the individual with respect to morality is that he finds himself irrevocably involved in the field of the mixed. He stands in the concrete world of good and bad as it exists both within himself and within society, there to be confronted at once with the ideal as he sees it and with the obligation it imposes on him of working toward it from wherever he finds himself. Thus his chosen ideal has associated with it the compulsion of a duty. For to be human is to operate to some extent according to the dictates of reason, and reason however poor holds before itself a model of conduct.

We have to comprehend full well exactly where it is that we are, and then, in the light of where we want to go, design the appropriate steps which must be taken to get there. Strategy is the study of destiny, for it is under the category of destiny that we find ethical strivings, the life that is lived in the field of compulsions arising in the domain of aims, and moving from the chronological order of material existence toward the logical order of essences. To study the structure of strategy is therefore a necessity for the understanding of the moral life. This will be our task in the present, and last, Part of this book. Theoretical ethics can in this way be justified empirically, and the pursuit of ideals be demonstrated good policy.

The program as I have thus set it forth is not one which will immediately appeal to partisans. Most individuals are either exclusively idealists or positivists with respect to moral action.

The idealist prefers to think that ideals can be not only formulated but emulated without regard to the actual state of affairs. He thinks that his ideal can be attained or at least aimed at without strategy or compromise. It is an all-or-nothing gamble, and one in which he usually loses. The idealist tends to withdraw from action to contemplation because actuality disappoints him by forever falling short of the ideal. But he has not given proper due to the size of the problems involved. To go from 999 to 1,000 is not after all likely to involve great planning or an extensive campaign, but to go from 9 to 1,000 may.

The positivist, on the other hand, thinks that he can safely dispense with ideals. He holds them to be the hopeless blueprints of cloud-cuckooland, and not useful to a practical man of affairs. Social adjustment on his view should be enough. Or else he thinks he can reach the ideal working purely with and for the actual and coping only with day-to-day exigencies, eliciting such improvements as will be forced upon him by practical experience. But his advances will be small, and while he is making them in one quarter things may be slipping back in another. No matter how careful he is to repair an old house, it never will be new. No one can deny the urgency of keeping the individual or society afloat and in good working order, but this aim will go very far in the direction of improvement. Perfection was never approached very closely by repairs and patches made on the imperfect.

The quarrel between the idealist and the positivist is a false one. It assumes that one is right and the other wrong, and this is a mistake they have in common, for neither is. It is insufficiently recognized that both the ideal and the actual are speculative fields in which investigators are hard put to discover the truth. We sometimes think we know what we ought to do, but we always think we know what we are doing. Wrong in both instances: what-ought-to-be suffers from inadequate discrimination; what-is suffers from inadequate description. Needed then: a theory to reconcile the two through appropriate action. The study of teleology confirms the necessity of keeping the ideal in view as an end of action; the study of deontology confirms the obligation to act in such a way as to conform to a chosen ideal. But these studies are not enough. We are very much in need also of moral tactics and moral strategy; moral tactics as the technique of designing conduct, and moral strategy as the technique of directing conduct: how to deploy one's moral force and how to perform moral manoeuvres.

Thus we have in strategy a theory and a practice. The theory consists in the design of the strategy, and the practice in putting it into effect here and now. We have always to consider not only what is best for a first step but what is best under the circumstances. This yields two goals rather than one: a short-range and a long-range. The short-range goal is necessary in order to maintain what good there is while planning something better. Such considerations require the development of a full-scale theory but a theory which can be sharply distinguished from other theories in ethics, the theory of the ideal, for example. The theory of practical strategy is a theory, not a practice; the practice consists in the actual operations involved in putting the theoretical strategy into effect. It too has its theoretical side, since we must know exactly the nature and strength of the forces with which we are to be dealing. Thus the theory leads us to practice and the practice compels us to appeal to theory.

Ethics is devoted to the theory of how to avoid the disastrous consequences of error, the rectification of behavior against the sanction of false knowledge by bringing it into greater conformity with morals—if necessary by changing the morals. This is negative morality a description of the states to be avoided, for instance as Aristotle said, "vice, incontinence and brutishness."[1] But the negative side alone will not do, for in a given concrete situation corresponding to every good there are many possible errors, and even when there is more than one good there are still more potential errors.

(b) The Four Grades of Obligation

We have noted that the individual has moral commitments which

[1] *Nico. Eth.*, Book VII.

are individual, social human and cosmic. For the individual, self-transcendence, super-identification; for society, to embrace all of humanity; for humanity, to develop a higher species; and for the cosmos, to order all species. We have seen how thanks to their corruption these may be in open conflict and often are, but meeting one commitment may mean neglect of the others. To over-emphasize a particular aspect would be to distort the ultimate nature of reality and so to produce a limited and incomplete person. How the individual is to deal with this situation is a delicate and subtle problem in attention and timing. It is as though a composer were to score a concerto for all of the instruments of the orchestra playing the entire time, or as though a juggler could keep in the air more than he could receive and toss upward.

Before the individual stands the choice of ethical ideals, an open, speculative domain. Behind him stands the rich world of fact, a bewildering collection. Upon him is the necessity of acting against the background of the latter and in the direction of the former. He acts, in short, by manipulating the facts in terms of some ideal. All three domains, the ideal, the actual and the strategic, are insecure, tempestuous and approximative. They represent the best anyone can do at the time and under the circumstances. But they do not prove that no absolute exists. For we may assume from the very evidence of our search and speculation that there is an absolute for each domain. It is the one we are looking for among the debris of fact, among our choice of ideals, at which the preparation for our action aims.

In moral strategy there is the need for a criterion. How is the actor to know what is ethically true (in terms of long-range ethics) and at the same time morally strategic (in terms of short-range morality)? What moral values would an individual hold who proposed to improve the established morality of his own society, those of the next higher integrative level? Evidently moral strategy always looks up one moral integrative level.

Moral action involves selecting a level, for moral behavior is not a stage process, activity being usually singular and one-dimensional. The principle of selection in moral action may be stated somewhat as follows.

Try to act so that the effects of your actions satisfy the ethical demands on a given level in such a way as to reach upward toward higher levels.

The higher an individual is able to rise with his majority confrontations in the moral integrative series, the more of an individual he becomes, that is to say, the closer he approximates to entire man. Thus the moral integrative series serves as a value scale on which it is possible for an individual to measure his own worth. It is in this way perhaps that a reconciliation can be effected between obligation and privilege. The distinction between them points to something out of order. Thus perfection is reached for each grade when obligation merges with privilege; when, that is to say, what the individual thinks, feels and does is precisely what he may think, feel and do.

Curiously, the reconciliation cannot be accomplished by means of any compromise. Here we invoke the use of excessive behavior in moral strategy, and the argument in favor of its introduction is simple. Only the best is good enough, but the best is not a mean but an extreme. For the extremes the method of over-reaching is required; over-reaching alone will reach the best. Here Max Weber's choice between an ethics of ultimate ends and an ethics of responsibility is dissipated by the fact that responsibility, with its necessity of committing small evils in order to attain to great goods, is actually aimed at those ultimate ends which have in fact dictated the decisions. What is in the background always, conditioning the moves at the practical level, is the definition of excellence as the quality of perfection, for such a quality can be experienced in little and need not be put off to ultimates. There are, as Plato correctly saw, goods of substance and property,[1] even though he put them third after goods of the soul and the body. Every act in some way integrates the four grades of obligation, the lowest as well as the highest, but also the highest as well as the lowest. Effects reverberate throughout and suffer no confinement.

---

[1] *Laws*, 697B.

CHAPTER II

THE STRATEGY OF INDIVIDUAL OBLIGATION

(a) Individual Moral Methodology

Everything in the universe bears in some way on the individual. Forces are at work on him of which in most cases he is unaware. At the present time it would be altogether impossible to make a computer analysis of all the elements which could and should be brought to bear on the making of any single moral decision. It is difficult to evaluate any given situation; for the values involved are many in every case and they all belong to a value-system the dimensions of which still remain largely unknown. Thus moral decisions must be left for the time being to other means. Some progress, however, can be made. It is only by increasing his knowledge that he can hope to think about the extent of his involvement and if possible to choose the preferred course of action. In this sense Socrates is right that knowledge is virtue, since increased knowledge leads at least to the possibility of increased virtue; and Dewey is right that leading the moral life presupposes an activity of inquiry. The requisite for the solution of any problem, then, is understanding. We must first know what the problem is and then consider the proper method of solving it. What should we do and what tools do we have at hand for doing it?

The ultimate moral fact about each individual is, "How large a confrontation does his nature demand?" The ultimate moral question for each individual is, "How much of an enlargement in confrontation can he bring himself to support?"

The problem as we have been disclosing it in the last two Parts of this book is a simple one. The ideals set before human behavior as models are remote and they are exacting and demanding. The facts of the moral life as we live it contain almost as much bad as good; I say "almost," because if they as much as balanced, life would not be worth living. But since life is worthwhile for most people most of the time, we must conclude that on balance there is more good than bad. Yet we must deal also with the bad in our efforts to emulate the ideal. This can be done in only one of two ways: by ignoring the facts which contribute to badness or by circumventing them. The former method will not do. Facts are among the things that will not go away simply because we ignore them. To suppose that they will is a familiar approach—and a disastrous one. Only by recognizing how bad the bad often is can we hope to construct a program for its reduction. Then, too, it is sometimes the case that a bad thing will have good effects. A monstrous crime may shock a community into instituting a needed reform, a bad painter may free the art from restrictions which were too confining. Not that a man should behave dialectically by aiming at the bad in order to effect a good; for reactions are not that mechanical or reliable, and such behavior often achieves only the bad.

Facts must be faced, and the bad and even the evil nature of some facts is inescapable. By common consent the bad is not mentioned in polite society. This may be a contributing cause to the further fact that polite societies disintegrate and have to be replaced by societies which are reconstituted on an altogether different basis. No; the best method is bravely to face the facts, on the assumption that recognition in no wise carries approval with it. The proper way lies *through* the facts, not *around* them. We must learn how to use the facts whether we approve them or not in order to transcend them.

In the actual world effects follow from causes, and that is the hope of all rationality, at least on the side of consistency. But rationality has another side, and the theory of probability supplies all the information which is available about it. Probability is the hope of rationality on the side of completeness. Given the doctrine of objective chance, then no matter how much we know, an absolute prediction as to what anyone will do under such and such circumstances becomes impossible. But a conjecture can be provided, for every situation contains a number of variables, and the determination of their rank-order must precede the decision as to what is moral in a proposed course of action.

Yet rationality is only a preparation for action, not a substitute for it or a guarantee of its success. When the moment for action is upon us it is too late to think. Reason prepares for action but does not conduct it. The time for reason will by then be past. But there was a time for reason, and reason is the only hope. Thus the method of achieving morality is a relatively simple one. *Equip a man with a maximum of reason, set him down in a society in which his legitimate needs can be reduced, then leave him to act on his impulses.* This is the procedure which reason itself recommends. For the impulses of a rational man will be more rational than those of an irrational man; that is the hope of rationality.

Casuistry is the reverse of this method. Casuistry endeavors to discern particular duties as decided by established ethical principles; it is the application of moral rules to individual cases. But the function of reason in ethics is to decide about moral principles, leaving it to the intuition of rationalists to work out the application of those rules. Something must be left to character, which has been entirely overlooked by the casuists. A man who, as we say, "knows what is right" will "do what is right" only if he has sufficient strength of character; and no number of questions and answers relating to moral questions will put him on the correct path if he has elected an incorrect one.

The individual wishes, let us say, to prepare himself for moral conduct. A posture is required, but postures must recognize situations. The posture is the one required by the knowledge that existence contains both the perishable and the imperishable. The things that change, and the classes and properties of things that do not change, are to be sought in the facts about himself and his situation. The individual tends to seek first his own welfare; in terms not of pleasure exclusively but of the avoidance of pain. The comforting thought is that there is a limit to pain. Beyond a certain point what is guaranteed is loss of consciousness. Yet if he conceive it entirely in selfish terms it can be self-defeating. Therefore the positing of a Principle of Self-Advantage is needed. It reads as follows.

An individual ought to be suspicious of the morality of anything from which he stands to benefit personally.

It would follow that he ought to suspect the validity or the truth of any argument from which he would appear to gain. If for example he maintains that his country is the best ever, his city the best in the country, his neighborhood the best in the city, his house the best in the neighborhood, and he the best person in the house, is it because the evidence supports him or merely because he is emotionally convinced? He may in effect be externalizing a belief and pretending to himself that it is independent evidence. His behavior will be such as it must be in view of his knowledge, giving way half to exigencies and retaining the other half for ideals.

Individual moral methodology, then, can be resolved into a formula. The method is one which can be characterized in two ways.

The first way is the method of alternation: advance when possible, retreat when necessary; a periodic procedure in which advances and pauses and even retreats are combined. Havelock Ellis once described it as the fine art of holding on and letting go. It is a method of giving and taking, of backing and filling, of moving and stopping. This part of the method is the opposite of Aristotle's method of the mean. Virtue may be a compromise but it is a compromise found not by finding the median but rather by combining extremes in a system of alternations. Movement toward the good is a dialectical progress in the modulation of excessive behavior. William Blake wrote, "The road of excess leads to the palace of wisdom." Prohibitions and permissions, opposable goods, must be neatly fitted together in a way which makes slow but inevitable progress toward the good possible.

The second way is the method which consists in the moral art of indirection. The good cannot always be pursued directly, indeed it seldom can. There is for instance something self-defeating about the professional do-gooders. The "harm that good men do" has been eloquently noted by Bertrand Russell. Values move obliquely in an atmosphere of values, and the situation is always more complex than it appears to be. When qualities are the leading edge of a movement, decisions concerning its direction have to be made intuitively. As Benjamin Franklin observed, painters have difficulty in distinguishing between a rising and a setting sun.

Consider a pair of opposite cases, for instance. The saint and the sinner are in a sense both professionals. They have committed themselves to a certain uncompromising course of action, the saint to do absolute good and the sinner to do absolute bad (i.e. evil). The saint pursues the absolute good directly, but it is his own narrow good alone which can be pursued in this way. As we have noted already in a previous part of this study, when he does good to others it sometimes appears that he does so only to gain moral credit for himself. Yet the sinner is equally uncompromising; he will do no good at all (if that is possible) because of his unswerving consistency, but he always fails, for under the circumstances he is certain to fall short of such an absolute goal.

Thus the pursuit of the good is an art, the art of indirection, and the indirection is made necessary by the fact that the external environment is partly friendly and partly hostile. The most important steps in an individual's life are those which he must take indirectly. There is nothing that can be done deliberately to further the ultimate good. Efficient causes are always tiny steps, but no less important because they lead toward final results.

Thus for instance it has been recognized since Aristotle that it is possible to live the good life only if provided with a moderate degree of material goods. A good life is hardly possible under conditions of grinding poverty. Thus a man would want to direct his steps toward the accumulation of a certain amount of material wealth as one efficient cause of the good life. Again, few things are more important in a man's life than the girl he falls in love with and marries, yet this is not a goal at which he can aim directly. He will not meet a girl and fall in love with her by design. But we know that if he meets no girls he will never fall in love with one. He may meet many girls and not fall in love, but meeting girls is certainly the necessary though not the sufficient cause of falling in love. Thus as a youth all he can do about it is to put himself in the way of meeting girls.

In both these instances efficient causes and indirection could lead to enormous moral results. It is in the choosing of axioms that the great value of a deductive system lies, and by analogy the action premises of a man's life are often determined subtly and indirectly. These may later prove to have been the most important steps toward the good life for him.

The moral art of indirection is best spelled out by the Chinese sage, Lao-tse. The *Way of Life* of Lao-tse is doubtless a manual on how to achieve moral aims by the method of indirection. "The best way to do is to be" is the major premise, the minor premise is the recommendation of "water-like behavior." Demotic man is committed by his nature to a slow approach to good behavior, based on the fact that at his level the amount of the good and the amount of the bad are both small and tend to approach each other. Only heroic man need be without such severity in the matter of compromise, and I propose to deal with him before we are done, but not here.

The Asian wisdom was devoted to the control of the internal environment, the European wisdom is devoted to the control of the external environment and treats the control of the internal environment only in pathological cases. I am recommending water-like behavior but not only for the internal environment. The skilful European use of it could be applied also to the external environment. Professional politicians are those who instinctively understand and use the strategy. Others could learn how to imitate the virtue.

(b) Practical Moral Conduct

The practical moral conduct of the individual is a result of the individual's behavior and therefore must be considered both as its affects himself and as it affects his fellows. The two results of his behavior cannot be so simply separated; the distinction between integrative levels is involved but not two different worlds. The individual lives in a public world, and he lives also within himself. There are social elements within him, but ultimately every man is alone with his own solitariness. And so he must come to terms with himself. He must be good for his own person, and this means quietly to settle for whatever it is that he is—whatever his own parts and capacities have made of him.

For the individual the problem is all but impossible of solution. Complete self-understanding is perhaps unattainable. The individual is a self, a point of self-consciousness floating within an internal environment, and aware both of it and of the external environment, sometimes confusing them. When the self undertakes to become aware of the internal environment alone, it finds that the elements of the external environment prove distracting; when it undertakes to become aware of the external environment alone, it finds that its awareness is conditioned by the structure and moving readjustments of elements in the internal environment. In this way it becomes impossible to succeed in approaching directly the experience of the self or in conveying self-observation directly to its results. Since internal goods, like external goods, conflict, the individual has before him the necessity of at least partly circumventing himself.

The individual finds himself with a number of organic needs. Through their activation the corresponding drives often conflict. I think of the human individual as a kind of loose English type of democracy in which now one and now another party gets the upper hand and in which the sovereign reigns but does not rule. Here individual morality must make the decision when it cannot be made on the basis of exigent importunity. Thus motivation largely determines intentions or dispositions; and if not modified by reason to legislate a rank order and preference, may run wild and cause injury to the individual himself as well as to his society. In performing such a function, therefore, reason must not only regard the act but also look to its foreseeable consequences, which may lie in the immediate present or the remote future and may be local or global.

The task then is one of modulation; what needs are to be reduced and what repressed, and in what order; for all of the needs must be reduced if the individual is to live a good life. A good life is most certainly a full life. Many things happen when one drive is substituted for another or preferred to another, but this is the rule, not the exception. The way toward the attainment of the secondary needs lies through the prior partial reduction of the lower, in moderation. Moderately reduced primary needs are facilitating. There is nothing half so pleasurable or liberating as insisting on participating in occasions when "the world, the flesh and the devil" are invited to take their toll. The individual who meets the importunate on its own grounds will find that he has made his way toward the important. He should always consider long-range goals before taking short-range steps but then he should take the short-range steps.

This is a chapter on individual moral strategy and I am under an obligation to spell out the procedure in sufficient detail to render conduct practical. Sooner or later every reader asks of a book on ethics, "Yes, but given my desire to pursue the moral life, tell me exactly what I should do in every concrete situation!" A legitimate demand. And I am prepared to answer it.

At this point I humbly ask the reader to hearken back to the discussion of the ethics of the individual as set forth in the second Part of this study. There I defined good behavior as conduct toward another, in consideration of all others. Then there is no harm, I suppose, if in the instant before action I ask the actor to call up before himself the image of all his fellows, of the whole of humanity, including all people past and future as well as living, for the effect such a preparation will have upon him in what he is about to do. It would be perhaps an occasion resembling the appeal to the conscience but without specific moral precepts; a little like the still, small voice but consisting instead in a picture of all those among whom he belongs and who not only might be helped or hurt by his behavior but upon whom as upon an image he could cast the reflection of honor or dishonor.

In the end it is species-responsible behavior which counts. A man is responsible for his conduct not only to himself and to the other members of his society but to all of his fellows, living, dead and unborn. It is the universal which governs the particular, though to be sure the particular has to survive *as* a particular in order to represent the species. But how far should his actions take him in this direction, how much of an advantage can he gain without hurting his fellows? Distinctions come in two definite forms: those that help and those that hurt humanity. The seizure of power may hurt, while a medical discovery may help (though the opposite is sometimes true, as for instance the defeat of Hitler helped while the poliomyelitis vaccine may keep more people alive than can be fed). But the decision must be made on the basis of the recognition of the existence of confrontation as defining the immediate situation.

Such is the maxim of immediate moral action. I have ruled out the appeal to reason and principles at this critical stage in the instant before action on the grounds that it is by then already too late. Reason is an indispensable ingredient but should occupy the large foreground of anticipatory preparation for all actions in general. Should there be however a second instant before the instant preceding critical action, then there is another maxim which might without loss be inserted. This is the application of the Principle of Detachment in Moral Reasoning.

The Principle itself may be stated as follows.

If an individual alone stands to gain from a proposed course of action, then the proposed course is too narrow and should be modified or abandoned.

The Principle follows as a corollary to the Self-Advantage Principle.[1] It may be employed as a maxim, and it calls for the following procedure. The individual is called on to consider before embarking upon a certain course of action whether others stand to lose from it more than he personally stands to gain. If they do, then he should ask himself whether that is the reason he proposes to act in this way. If it is, then he should abandon the action.

The application of the Principle is difficult to illustrate, for who knows what actions have been considered and then abandoned by morally-inclined individuals? But, unfortunately, illustrations of violations are all too common. Stalin had many men murdered when their only offense was that they had made some minor criticism of some of his decisions. This is an extreme case. The deliberately misleading statements intended to sell products which, if not harmful, are at least not beneficial in the way which is claimed for them, as in the advertisements for patented drugs, is another and more modest illustration. If Stalin in Soviet Russia and some members of the drug industry in the United States had been following the Principle of Detachment in Moral Reasoning, they would have behaved differently.

(c) The Formula for Happiness

The goal for the individual is the service of society. Happiness is to be found only in fulfilling that end. It is a by-product of the service of

---

[1] See p. 282, above.

society. But moderation in the pursuit of that end is not always efficient. Against Aristotle, it is necessary to claim that virtue is not always a mean. Extreme actions are often called for and may be the most socially beneficial. A happy man is one who uses himself well. Ideally speaking, he should move straight toward his goal, and all his energies should be directed toward it. But this is more often than not impossible, and society may be served indirectly. Any other kind of activity: struggle, opposition, conflict, is permitted only to the extent to which adversaries get in the way. Once they are out of the way they are not to be pursued, for that would mean to lose sight of the goal by accepting a substitute. Nietzsche wrote, "Where one can no longer love, there should one—pass by."

Happiness is extensive, pleasure intensive. Neither, however, is the direct goal of moral effort. The aim of man is perfect suitability; a fitting of the form to the facts, a harmony of parts in the whole. When things are and do what they ought to be and do (and "things" here includes men), then a sense of well-being results, and the sense of well-being of this sort is in man called happiness. Happiness then is what so many moralists have said it is: the state which is desirable for man. It is attained not by aiming at it directly but by aiming at what produces it. *Happiness is a by-product of the search for perfection.* The aim of man is perfection, individual and social perfection, the perfect man in the perfect society.

The good life is the full life, but there are many varieties and degrees of it. Moral virtue consists in fulfilling the highest grade of obligation and enjoying the highest consequent grade of privilege to which a man by his equipment is prepared to attain. The full life calls for the use of all his capacities. That is why both the ascetic and the libertine are from one point of view immoral; they overuse one capacity at the expense of the others. They deny too much when all they should do is affirm.

The two dimensions of moral conduct are just what we would expect them to be if they were drives: direction and intensity. Teleology is the older name for direction and deontology for intensity; these are felt extrinsically as utilitarian and intrinsically as hedonic, respectively. Are you working toward the good which is the highest attainable under the circumstances (extrinsic and utilitarian)? How *good* do you feel while you are actively engaged in the effort (intrinsic and hedonic)?

The intrinsic good is absolute. The individual good is intrinsic: only the individual is able to feel. Therefore only through feeling is the individual able to attain the absolute good. But what is it? The most he can hope to do with life is live it intensely. This life is the life, and to live it more fully is to participate more in existence. Sufficient for existence is existence. What came before, he has forgotten; what follows after, is hidden from him. Even if it be in both cases no more than oblivion, he cannot even know that because he can neither remember nor anticipate. Hence the wisdom of living this life as completely as possible.

Yet the most intense form of feeling can be obtained only by participating in social life. Of course such participation is not to be read naively as meaning rubbing shoulders with other people. It is often necessary to withdraw from society in order to make a valuable contribution to it, as many artists and scientists have discovered. Social, life must be, however. Utilitarianism means that the individual endeavors to attain to the good by cooperating as much as possible with other members of his society. To this end the hard core of selfishness and egotism must be broken up. The social nature of the individual is once more affirmed by the fact that he cannot live for himself alone. To wish to do so is an illness; and a man is proved healthy only to the extent to which he chooses to live for the welfare of his fellows. Altruism is a necessary prerequisite for well-being.

He cannot live *for* himself no; yet he must live always *in* himself, and the two are often confused though they are not the same. It is within himself that he knows and feels and has the impulses or makes the plans to do whatever it is that he does. He may have his successes in the external environment but he has his failures in the internal environment, in himself. And so it is there that he must make the last stand in the struggle for happiness.

The chief problem for the individual perhaps is how to deal with that ambivalence of motivation which is native to him. When it issues in action it tends to destroy his effects on the world. It should be shifted if possible to an outward bound program of subjective feelings, which have so much more to do with the external world directly than mere thoughts can possibly achieve. Thus the individual can find comfort in his similarity to his fellows and hope in his differences from them.

I have said that happiness cannot be pursued directly. This is true. The happy man is the man who pursues his appropriate ends. The pursuit cannot always be successful but the happiness can always be continued. How can a man be unhappy if he have the intelligence to recognize that effects follow from causes? The rational man is happy, for he occupies himself with finding nature in the human field. For this he need have character, which consists, as we have noted, in the ability to lead the good life irrespective of events in the external environment. A kind of[1] psychological homeostasis is possible, a standing fast in the face of events. The last confrontation is that which takes place when the self is faced with disturbances in the internal environment as a result of disorder precipitated by frustrations in the external environment. It is then a question of how successfully the unreduced needs are handled, and whether the individual can call on a certain resilience to the frustrations, as for instance by "making the best of circumstances."

(d) The Rational and the Good

In (a) we discussed the individual and his needs when confronted with a partly friendly and partly hostile outer environment, in which the art of indirection has to be practiced. In (b) we discussed the happiness of the individual within his inner environment in which the good is pursued directly. Here, with the consideration of reason the two methods can be combined, and indirection itself shown to alternate with direction.

We have noted earlier that a rational man is not in need of principles to govern his conduct when the moment comes to make decisions and to act. By then it is already too late to think and by then the impulse itself must be enough. The impulses of a truly rational man are through and through rational. Thus the ground for impulsive action (and this is, as we have noted, the preferred kind) must be laid well in advance not only by a study of principles but also by their acceptance into belief. Reason enters into the training whereby a man learns to feel what is right and good; he can thereafter be permitted to act from his feelings without explicit reference to what first dictated them. For the feelings of a rational man will be rational. As a guide to action didactic reason is not much better than irrational or unconsidered impulse or feeling.

We should think about what we might do or be called on to do well in advance of the event. Decisions and actions in this way can be taken through feelings, feelings which were however anteriorly dictated by adequate reasoning.[1] Actions are always rational—provided we have thought them out first. What men mean by a reasonable course of

---

[1] Cf. P. B. Medawar, *The Uniqueness of the Individual* (New York 1958, Basic Books), p. 138.

action is one for which the decisions have been reached by means of reason. However, the results of reasoning may be false in at least one of three ways: they may follow from erroneous deduction, from inconsistent axioms, or from incomplete axiom-sets. The axioms must be chosen in such a way that the deduced theorems when applied in practice will be adequate and will not lead to conflict. The truth of axioms in abstract deductive structures, such as those of mathematics, may be irrelevant but become relevant when the theorems are applied in practice.

Reason enters into moral strategy for the individual through decision and its rational background in the retention schemata, for society through the individual act and its consequences, and for humanity through the attempt to find and establish by means of legal enactment an international morality.

So much for reason in society; but what is rational? The answer is that everything is rational. Emotions for example, are often considered opposed to the reason, but emotions as such are not. We never consider irrational the passion of a man for his wife or of a mother for her child. But when emotions lead to anti-personal or anti-social actions we consider them irrational. But are they? A man may destroy himself in a fit of passion or he may act contrary to the best interests of his society; but it is perfectly rational to expect that some men will do so under some circumstances. Reason in some quarters has somehow got confused with the good and the right. What we call "irrational" is simply what has not yet been included in any rational system. Values, then, are not irrational; we cannot yet measure them and so we suspect them of possessing the property of incommensurability.

Ethics is primarily rational, but since no ethical system is complete its rationality does not include all reason, and therefore the individual is always reaching out toward a greater rationality which he can sometimes dimly envisage. He encounters reason directly only when it is limited; what is rational about his life is the concrete ideal of an integrated personality within an integrated society. But applied rationality requires completeness as well as consistency, and for completeness subordinate or remote elements of "irrationality" must be included.

The danger of rationality issues from the risk involved in an inflexible commitment to the axioms. If the axioms are false then because of the necessity of logic they will lead to monstrous theorems and these to even more diastrous applications. The preparation for any master strategy, then, must include the elaborate construction and testing of rational systems and the agility to abandon them the moment faults begin to appear. Rationality requires that in practice we only half hold on to any rational system.

Abstract reasoning is man's natural advantage. To some extent the higher animals other than man can think, too, but all other animals are locked up in the present, the here-now. Only man has found a device for partly freeing himself so that he can reach beyond the present. By means of abstractions he is able to range over other spaces and times. Universals are the symbols representing absent objects in distant space and remote time, deep space in the past and in the future. In other epochs past and future, as well as elsewhere, things and events have meaning for him here and now.

Cosmic ethics ranges the farthest in rationality, human ethics not as far, social ethics only a little farther than individual ethics. But the increased range of his perspective is qualitative as well as quantitative. I have said earlier that the aim of the human individual is his own survival through self-surpassing, through self-aggrandizement, and through super-identification. Although calling for an interim suspension in the reduction of his other needs, the urge to exceed himself which is very fundamental to his nature can result in an extension not only of his understanding but also of his sympathy by extending both to absent objects. Rationality when the axioms are true, represents the skilful use of overreaching.

CHAPTER III

THE STRATEGY OF SOCIAL OBLIGATION

(a) Social Strategy Toward the Individual

A comprehensive survey of history, which is after all the chronological study of cultures, discloses the immense range of human behavior. So many alternative paths are open to the individual that he cannot be helped in choosing by any simple formula. Man is capable of a very diverse range of actions and if left to himself will run the entire range. Just as everything edible has in some culture been eaten, so also in some culture probably everything has been forbidden as food for religious reasons; and in a wider context everything it is possible for man to do has been done—or been prohibited.

The range itself so far as morality is concerned consists in a spectrum, with absolute good at one end and absolute evil at the other. The morals of most persons fall within the center, in the usual Gaussian distribution. But it does not follow from this that man can be "left to himself" with his unprepared impulses. By the very fact that no individual lives an entirely individual life he requires principles to guide his actions. Indeed the opposite is true: individuals lead an almost entirely social life.

On what do such principles rest? Supernatural sanctions apart (for such sanctions have no place in a book devoted to ethics in which humanity rather than merely society or culture is considered), the principles respecting conduct can be shown to rest upon the conduct itself. For this purpose, and for the individual in his daily life of strategy, his society must be considered the good at which the individuals separately and collectively aim. The bad as a social principle is simply not practical. Negative aggression (i.e. cruelty) may be workable individually for a short run but it is unworkable socially. Socially there is no "short run"; the social short run is from the individual viewpoint a long one. Any society which does not aim at the greatest good of the greatest number of individuals will fail of sufficient organization to enable it to function as a society.

Given that ambivalence of aggression which is so much a part of human nature, how is a society to exist or survive? One thing is sure: societies can be neither constructed nor maintained on the basis of pure love or pure hate alone. On the basis of pure love there would be insufficient competition to insure that the individual would exert himself sufficiently to do his best and so contribute the most of which he was capable. Love tends to be more passive than active. On the basis of pure hate, only total destruction could possibly be the final outcome. There must be a combination of love and hate, but how much of each? Clearly the principle of pragmatic justification requires that love must be dominant over hate, if the fabric of a society is to hold; but that the most strategic arrangement is to include as much hate as is consistent with the dominant, integrating force of love.

This principle of pragmatic justification allows for an unconscionable degree of variation. A society such as that of the ancient Egyptians whose emphasis on the future life of the dead and the divinity of the Pharaoh led them to sacrifice the lives of the living in great masses to unremitting labor on giant tombs certainly had in mind the greatest good of the greatest number. So does the welfare state of today. Thus the question of ideals is important to strategy, but here our task is the discussion of the strategy itself. So whatever the ideal the problem is how to get people to behave in the way that they already think they know will lead them to the good.

How to counter the weakness between aim and accomplishment, is the question. Evidently, only by showing the individual that a selfish aim is a self-defeating one, and that although the individual is a good such an aim does not accomplish the most good. No amount of argument or persuasion will convince a man bent on selfish advantage that the money he was about to steal, the girl he was about to rape, is not worth the immediate advantage involved, and he is amenable only to the threat of severe sanctions.

Strategy depends, then, very much upon the current social situation. What are the values and rules current in his established society which the individual can approve and is therefore willing to work for or which he must disapprove and therefore be willing to work against? Immorality leads to social chaos. There is always some immorality abroad, but we must behave as though there were not—at least so long as we accept the prevailing social morality. Our efforts to change it should not be by example where we stand to gain personally by the change, but permitted only where we do not.

There is another question to be asked. Is it for the society a beginning or an end, an establishment and a looking foward or a decline and a looking past, a time of troubles and of revolution or one of peace and harmony? Utilitarianism is expediency based on the prevailing establishment, whatever it happens to be, and calls for coming to terms with exigent problems by whatever means are available.

Such at least is the nature of short-range strategy. In the event the society itself is flourishing it does not present any critical or peculiar personal problems for the individual. He has only to go along with others in continuing to promote the establishment and its concrete ideals. But what if the social situation is otherwise? What if the society is in decline, the morality severely tested and questioned, the establishment breaking up? Such a social situation calls out a kind of basic strategy. It forces the individual back upon himself; and since it does so for all individuals, this too is a social movement. The problem for each and every individual becomes a strenuous affair: how is he to maintain himself *as* an individual in a state of moral health in the face of a disintegrating society?

This is a confrontation of an altogether different sort from the one discussed in the second Part of this book. We noted there that Kierkegaard and his followers sought to study how, by means of a minimum morality and in the midst of the disorderly elements of a fragmented social order, the individual could successfully maintain himself *as* an individual. Here the problem is, how the individual can maintain himself as a socially-oriented individual, with all of the individual benefits this entails, when there is no immediate social support for the posture?

Christianity as a "slave morality" is not the only alternative to Nietzsche's "master morality." Then, too, each implies the other. Consider for example the possibility of a society of political and economic equals, in which there is a hierarchy of obligation to justify privilege. The greater the capacity of the individual the greater his obligations to serve society. The ideal of Marx and Engels, "From each according to his ability, to each according to his needs" can hardly be surpassed as an ideal, and it is partly their own fault that socialist countries take steps which are so far removed from this ideal as to seem almost wholly unrelated to it. The ruthless use of force. the strategic use of falsehoods, torture to extract confessions and to effect conversions, these are hardly the correct instruments for bringing about the kind of society the stated maxim indicates. For to have good societies there must first be good individuals. If the end of the individual is the service of society then each can accomplish this only according to his abilities, for in an individual sense we all have the same needs. But coercion is not the best way to lead us to them.

One way which is often taken by the individual in his efforts to reinforce his personal convictions and so insure confidence in his own self-maintenance is to extend his control to others by securing their compliance through compulsion. But can the individual ever be sure that such control is the best thing in *their* interest? If not, it may be curtailing life instead of extending it. Thus persuasion rather than force should be employed. Extending power over inanimate nature is less dangerous, although even here morality can be controverted unless care is taken to be constructive.

(b) Demotic and Heroic Strategy

Societies come into existence, they grow and flourish, then decline and die. Each of these periods would have to be specified in a different and characteristic way if it was to be viewed from the moral perspective which is the subject matter of this work. Another work of equal length would be required to treat of each of these periods thoroughly. The readiness of the individual to accept authority means that we have underestimated the social roles of original minds. We need two concrete moralities and a strategy appropriate to each: the morality of those who discover ethical systems and the morality of those who live by them. These will need to be discussed in the reverse order, for discoverers emerge from the morality which had been inherited from previous discoverers and established for all to live by.

I will only say a few words in outline about the perspective of a typical period, say the period when the society is flourishing, and then try to indicate the strategy for the majority: demotic strategy; and for the specially-gifted minority, heroic strategy. Then, in the final chapters of this Part of the book, I will turn exclusively to the model of heroic morality and show it *in extremis*.

First, then, demotic strategy. Demotic man supposes that his own way of doing things is the one and only natural way prescribed for that particular kind of occasion. He is forever finding nature in the social field as though it were a common sort of enterprise. Social differences of course occur from society to society, but the discovery of cultural relativism has not impressed demotic man. He is sure that he *knows* right from wrong. Thus demotic man is culturally confined and limited, unable to see even a little way outside of the confines of his own peculiar perspective. And so within each culture there is a special kind of demotic man, a vast majority absolutely committed to the culture. The typical demotic man looks to a better day in the future which will be more like the immediate past when, he falsely supposes, nothing had ever been altered. On such shoulders the continuance and the solidity of the culture depends.

Thus we have in demotic man the true picture of the conservative, who does not think anything should be changed very much but grudgingly gives in to change provided only it is cautious and gradual. For demotic man, except on those rare occasions when he is in a high state of arousal, moral virtue consists in a disposition to choose the mean. The conservatives always feel and act like the owners of the values they wish to preserve. These values are of course the customary and traditional ones. They are to be neither increased nor lessened.

Heroic strategy rests on the assumption that heroic man has to be risked in the effort to obtain newer and more powerful values. There is nothing in human culture that did not have its point of origin in the waking dream of some one among the few men of genius. Heroic man is progressive; he is more interested in adding to the sum of values than he is in their preservation. That is why he is ordinarily—and quite calmly—able to maintain himself in a frame of mind analogous to that of demotic man in that high state of arousal which keeps him prepared for extreme and critical action. Heroic man looks ahead to a day when the human situation will be better than it is now, and he is willing to sacrifice what he has that is good in order to help a better future in coming to birth. Heroic man is venturesome man. There are very few of him, but his value to the society, and, as we shall presently note, to humanity and beyond, is far out of proportion to his numbers.

Every society consists for the most part in demotic man. Whether society rewards or punishes, recognizes or neglects, heroic man is partly a result of merit, partly a matter of circumstance. So many social factors enter into the calculation that chance has a large role to play in it. Thus heroic man may be elevated, but usually he is not. Considered in terms of growth potential and long-range social investment, the ivory tower may be the most important building in the market-place, but the bandwagon does not customarily stop there.

Women and children, very young men and very old ones, are essentially conservative. They wish to pursue the good as (they fancy) it has always been pursued. It is for the most part a few men and they only in their vigorous years who envisage and plan cultural improvement in the pursuit of the good; for ordinarily it is they who have the strength to seek another and a greater good.

Most societies consist in a small proportion of heroic men and a large preponderance of demotic men. But there may be an exclusive population of demotic men: heroic representation is always small if it exists at all. Perhaps this must be the case, for a society has the exigent task of maintaining itself while better things are being prepared for it. Heroic behavior is a species of excessive behavior, and no society can survive while maintaining more than a small percentage of heroic men in its midst.

Thus no strategy is required to transform demotic man into heroic man. What is needed instead is a technique for securing the moral obligation of existing society to accommodate itself to heroic man. Toleration is necessary, and it is all that is usually obtained, and often it is enough; but preferably there would be facilitation as well.

(c) Institutional Strategy

The individual does not serve society directly but indirectly through the medium of social institutions. What is transmitted institutionally from generation to generation is the external inheritance: the artifacts of tools and languages, and cooperative behavior. We see this in the detritus of behavioral patterns, where an agglomerate collection of fossils consist not only in traditions and customs but also in material artifacts. This process often involves the temporary frustration of particular individual needs. Step-wise behavior is the rule for the individual on his way to the fulfillment of his proper end, and the institution constitutes the first step after the individual's own self. The institutions are the same in kind in every society but their arrangement varies, and it is the order of institutions which determines the character of the society. The institution which enjoys the greatest prestige in terms of reality and accomplishment is the leading institution of the society.

An illustration from our own society in the period in which this book is being written might be the most helpful. The three institutions which stand near the top of the society are those which run it. A coalition of government, applied science and heavy industry certainly dominates. Since World War II applied science has risen in the hierarchy of institutions to join the others. One good test of the power of an institution is the amount of money (representing available social energy) which is devoted to each, and on this criterion these three stand up well.

Applied science is the latest institutional arrival on the scene, and its elevation has been accomplished mainly through the discovery of nuclear energy. The morality suggested by science in its period of growth and development is that human social behavior must be ranged as conveniently as possible around the enterprise of inquiry: the investigation of nature according to the scientific method. The strategy of the society is to so use its new power as to effect the greatest improvement in the human condition. But who is to determine what this is and how it is to be done?

The task of the scientist is to employ the scientific method in the discovery of natural law. The task of the applied scientist is to employ natural law and technology to discover practical applications. Now the scientist is not only a scientist; he is many other things. He is a husband and father, a citizen, an institutional man, a biological organism, and so on. In his capacity as a scientist he behaves in a manner which is ethically neutral with regard to the uses to which his discoveries shall be put. In his capacity as a citizen he may wish to influence those uses. But he should not do so as a scientist, for instance by refusing to develop the rigged cobalt bomb for fear that it may be misused. This would be to mix up his roles in society and to substitute one role for another in an unjustifiable way. As a mere citizen he cannot influence the use of his products to any great extent. This function properly belongs to the government and the politician. Social good results from proper social functioning and social bad from improper social functioning.

Social gains toward the good life are not necessarily the result of deliberate efforts toward that end. Industrial production, which has done so much to provide ample goods for everyone, was developed by the profit motive, not by the desire to raise general living standards. But it did raise them, and that is what matters. Doing good for the wrong reasons at best does only psychological harm. In the above example, a few are confirmed in their selfishness while a great many more receive benefits.

The problem of human ethics is not a simple one. Let us elaborate our example to an inter-cultural comparison. The Buddhist ethics is one of infinite compassion. A Buddhist could not be a good Buddhist and be happy so long as a single person went hungry. Yet Buddhism is essentially passive and lacks the kind of dynamism which in the west has developed scientific agriculture and with it a greater abundance of food than was ever produced by any other method. Thus it is science and not Buddhism which is the most capable of preventing hunger; yet that same science has also produced terribly efficient weapons of war. Thus ethically speaking we are here at the moral cross-roads; one ethical movement wants to eliminate pain, the other eliminates one pain: hunger, but also aids and abets other pains through the increased efficiency of war.

Institutional strategy consists in the discovery and installation in a society of those new institutions and of those new elements of old institutions which will best enable the individual to serve his society in a way which enables that society to serve humanity and beyond it the cosmos. The occurrence of a new institution is rare; but it may be dynamic when it occurs and it may, as in the recent advent of science, cause an enormous rearrangement of other institutions. But the discovery and installation of new beliefs and artifacts is more common. That new beliefs call out new patterns of behavior is not exactly a startlingly fresh truth, but that new artifacts do so also is not as well known. New tools, however, demand and receive new patterns of behavior. We shall all be somewhat changed by the computer, as we have been already by the automobile, the airplane, and the television set.

Moral strategy, then, must reckon at the institutional level with all of its entities and processes. What we have to use, as well as how we use what we have, is a moral question. We need good institutional elements with which we can have good relations, and the one is as important morally as the other. For if society is, as we have already noted, the fundamental level for the establishment of morality, then institutions which go to make up society can hardly be omitted from issues of moral strategy. It is at the institutional level that the strategy of social obligation begins.

CHAPTER IV

THE STRATEGY OF HUMAN OBLIGATION

Civilization, the life of human beings under the conditions imposed by cities, with agriculture a prerequisite, is not much more than 20,000 years old. In terms of the length of human life in pre-history it is a mere moment. In short civilization may be regarded as an experiment, and the time has been far too brief for anyone to be able to say whether or not it will work. The motivations of an earlier million years have not been changed. We have noted that men still wish ambivalently to help and hurt their neighbors, and we may still watch them do both with dependable alternation. Neighbor-love exists, but rivalry and competition of both the violent and peaceful varieties are so common in human life that the only justification for the continuance of the species is the hope that it may evolve into something better.

The good in terms of the strategy of the human species has two branches. In the first branch, that action is good which carries the greatest number of individuals forward to a future participation in existence; in the second, that action is good which contributes to the evolutionary improvement in the human stock. Of the first, there are many religious examples, as for instance the saying of Jesus, "I am come that ye may have life and that ye may have it more abundantly." Of the second there has been the example of the universal morality which consists not in the pursuit of pleasure but in the avoidance of pain. We have the evidence for this that the only ground on which it is possible to unite all of the world religions is in their common pursuit of the avoidance of pain, which is the same for all despite the differences in methods. But religion, alas, treats of the present and future in terms of events in the past, not in terms of reason and fact governing the future. All of the western religions look back to a golden age in the past and so do many of the eastern ones. Those eastern religions which do not look back look forward to the end of all existence, to a total extinction. The ethics of the human species has not yet been embodied in a religion that looks forward to a golden age of moral superman.

Can man assist in promoting the evolution of the next species higher than the human? There is reason for hope. Certainly it is safe to say that he has taken the first step. On the principle that natural selection is environmentally affected he has constructed his own artificial environment. Not content with what already existed because non-adapted to living in an unaltered environment of forest or savanna (as is the gorilla or the lion), he has constructed his own ecological niche. Adaptation to it permits the interaction of internal and external environments to achieve the alternating states of instability and stability on which progress is based. It may be expected to produce genetic alterations given a sufficient number of generations. Man is in this way at least trying to make his own life better. The construction of material civilization is the greatest step ever taken in applied ethics. It conditions man in a way that ties him to his fellows and makes him interdependent with them for his and their well-being.

The new note in the human species, then, as compared with all lower, is that man has taken a hand in his own development. He has not changed his biological nature through the deliberate application of the principles of genetics (though this may come) but he has changed his environment in a serious way. He has in effect made it over. There is very little in the environment of civilized man that has not been altered through human agency. His artificial surroundings constitutes an altogether new environment, and if we take seriously the Darwinian version of evolution, then natural selection operates in terms of the environment that we can reasonably expect to change as a result of the novelty involved in the artificially produced ecological niche.

The moral philosopher as I see him has two tasks. He has to reconcile man to the sorrier aspects of things-as-they-are. This does not mean accepting as final the worst of the natural order. For the natural order is not all bad, and he has in addition another and entirely opposite task, which is to point the way toward change and improvement. We shall see in the closing pages of this work how these two seemingly contradictory enterprises both have their legitimate places in human existence.

To make an ethical point of nature's inevitable order does not necessarily mean accepting as conventional the more harmful aspects of existence. Things cannot be used against their nature without penalty. And this is true whether the "things" are human or non-human, and from whatever moral level. But routine can be elevated into ritual with the provision of a foundation of evidence compelling belief. With the institution of science in the lead, we refuse to accept natural developments like cancer, tuberculosis or the traditional death-rate; instead we endeavor to change them. Morality itself may prove to be an accident of existence, a shortcoming from whose grasp we can learn how to escape as we seek to escape from getting run over by large trucks or from being struck by lightning. The effects of applied science are capable of altering all the traditional considerations made classic in conventional fields.

The making of plans for the destruction of everything bad is good. Yet the ontological status of future evil remains a problem. That there will be a murder tomorrow is a moral problem today. It is a variety of the quality of conflict, a positive effect of a negative occasion. Organizations will be damaged or destroyed inevitably, and we must be prepared for it even while not approving or accepting it. What is bad is always the destruction of organizations, since all organizations contain some good. An organization which exists today and therefore contains some good contains also the prospect of its destruction tomorrow and the consequent loss of such good as it contains. If it contains a predominance of bad its destruction must be hastened, even though harm is done in destroying whatever minimum of good it contains. How are we ever to reconcile ourselves to the status of future evil which is involved in the inevitability of the destruction of organizations tomorrow?

Strategy involves duty, but duty to what, to whom? Duty to the individual himself? But this is too limited, for the individual is hardly his own end. Duty to his society? But this may be in need of revision in comparison with other societies. Duty, then, to humanity as to an ideal, provided the individual is successful in discovering a conception of humanity corresponding to the ideal. Grotius was right in insisting that all men accept certain rules in recognition of a common life; but which rules and whose formulation? A few principles can be discerned.

Strategy commits us all to the establishment of those minimal conditions under which the maximum individual contribution to the whole of humanity can be made possible. This would have to include the similar contributions of the majority of individuals and the different contributions of the minority of productive individuals—the contributions of demotic man in preserving while awaiting the contributions of heroic man in advancing.

The highest personal lives, the greatest cultures, are those which bring into existence some improvement in the pattern which without them might never have been known. Few societies can afford many heroic men, for these need the kind of purchase which is provided by the others holding still. That is why ancient Greece has been such a valuable possession. It stands as a model but it perished as an existent because its few were so many, its heroes numerically out of proportion to the amount of support which could be provided by the demes.

Human life is cumulative, however, and along with it the knowledge of the good. There is a positive feedback operating. Man not only knows, he also knows that he knows. Self-consciousness means the awareness of knowing. Such an awareness carries with it a certain effect, for it tends sometimes to accelerate the processes known. If shares on a stock exchange are known to be dropping in value because of a decline in business, this very knowledge will increase the steepness of the decline.

Now let us see how this principle works in the case of the influence of the human species over its own future. If human individuals think that they can control to some extent the fate of their own progeny by improving the material conditions of existence, by treating more rationally and with less violence their own inter-social problems, for instance by abolishing war, then this should help them to do it; and by doing it they will see that human life is made better, and so this will encourage them again to make it better at a faster rate. Positive feedback of this sort tends to accelerate any process to which it is applied. Thus while Aristotle was right in criticizing Socrates for his principle that knowledge is virtue and that to know the good is to follow it, since men often know the good without following it, still Aristotle was wrong and Socrates right for men will *tend* to follow it, and this tendency given a long enough run will accelerate. Thus if the knowledge of the good is repeated a sufficient number of times, its tendency to produce a following will be effective; and the greater the repetition the stronger the following.

To think that abolishing war would be a good thing theoretically should help mankind to do it. But there are many attendant practical difficulties which delay such an achievement. It is wise to hope for peace but not to expect it, for history is largely an account of wars. The human race has developed as an aggressive species, the most aggressive, in fact; and the same forces which account for destruction account also for the magnificent constructions which have made civilization possible. Without aggression there would have been no cultures: no cities built, no books written, no music played. The construction of culture results from a studied assault upon the non-human environment, in an effort to change it. We need the aggression to get the construction, but we must learn how to avoid the destruction. How can we preserve the one and dispense with the other?

Perhaps we can do better with this argument by getting down to the most flagrant of contemporary cases. The opposition to the manufacture and military use of nuclear weapons is understandable but only as part of a total picture of pacifism. There is no difference except a numerical one between killing a million people with an atomic bomb and a single man with a bullet. If one is morally wrong the other is also. But neither can be defended any more than the other.

We cannot leave the discussion of the concrete morality of the species without raising the question of whether war is an instrument of evolutionary survival. This is not an easy question to settle. Wars have always been fought, and they have always been opposed by men of good will. They wipe out the healthiest and youngest males of the population, and this would seem to be a backward step; but they also enable the strongest to survive. Rome only became a viable empire and a civilization after its destruction of Carthage following a series of disastrous wars. But when the legions weakened toward the end, that same empire was destroyed by the German barbarians.

The problem is, can we retain the strength of constructiveness without the weakness which results from abandoning destructiveness?

CHAPTER V

THE STRATEGY OF COSMIC OBLIGATION

The individual is small and the cosmos large, how large we do not at present know. For when we say "the cosmos" we are talking, remember, about all material orders, which is to say, about all species of actual organizations. The cosmos is, then, for all existing things the ground-state, and in considering the whole of the cosmos we are bound to encounter difficulties. We shall consider a few of these which arise from the paradoxes and which are inevitably involved in any kind of ultimate confrontation.

(a) The Paradoxes of Ultimate Explanation

The final encounter of strategy is with the paradoxes of ultimate explanation. I will state them in this section and then in the following sections propose a strategy for dealing with them.

The paradox of final good and total beauty. The final good, we learned in ideal ethics, is the good of the whole of being. Now the good of the whole of being, like all good, has its intrinsic and extrinsic aspects.

Its intrinsic aspect is identical with total beauty, for if we talk about the intrinsic good of the whole of being or the total beauty of that whole, we seem to be saying the same thing. At the level of final good and total beauty, beauty is goodness and goodness beauty.

So much for the intrinsic good; now we must talk about the extrinsic good. But since extrinsic good means good *for* something, what can there be outside of the whole of being for what it can be a good? God, perhaps; but this takes our inquiry outside its natural bounds. We can say no more in this direction about the good.

What lessons if any are we to draw from the paradox of final good and total beauty? One, at least. The only truth about the whole universe that we are privileged to know may prove to be the feeling of the beauty of the parts as they fit together to make the good of the whole.

The double paradox of ultimate explanation.

First paradox: nature cannot be completely explained on its own terms, but any supernatural explanation is limited in its expression to terms derived from nature.

Second paradox: from the outcome of the first paradox it would seem natural to turn away from the search for an explanation, were it not for the natural curiosity which urges us toward it. Hence we seem called upon both to turn away and not to turn away. We can neither know with any certainty nor cease to inquire.

What lessons if any are we to draw from the double paradox? We can, I think, point to at least two.

The first lesson is the derivation of the principle of ultimate diremption. There is no answer to the question of which is the preferred way of life. Those who do evil prosper in this world as much as, if not more than, those who do good. It is not true that the good are rewarded and the evil punished, not, that is, from the perspective of the natural world. The members of one religion do not live longer or better lives than those of any other. God, it seems, is not the exclusive member of any particular religion, and indeed—judging by events—often prefers to take the side of the atheists. He is unaffiliated, and to this extent at least he has, so to speak, turned away from the world. In an act of ultimate diremption, He has indicated that we are on our own, for He gives no sign that one morality is to be preferred to another except as the negative answer of nature makes the choice pragmatically: this morality does not work, that one does.

The second lesson is the principle of ultimate self-reliance. Freud may have been right in his theory that God is a father figure, and that continued dependence upon Him indicates a lack of maturity. The evidence I have cited above indicates that we are justified in taking the next step. What God wants (assuming there is a God) is the independence of His children. If God exists, the best we can hope to do for His sake is to turn away from the limited and finite conceptions of deity which men have designed to comfort themselves and instead seek to improve the world, which is to say improve all that exists in the world so far as lies within our power. And just what the limits of our power are it is too early to say, for with every improvement in artifacts and the techniques of their use we continue to increase our power, which is to say, increase our ability to lead the good life. And the good life in this sense may be all that there is left to us of the holy life.

The strategy of cosmic obligation has two phases: active and passive. The active phase may be named "the unlimited community" and the passive phase "standpointlessness." We shall discuss them in that order.

(b) Toward the Unlimited Community

In a famous essay on "The Doctrine of Chances"[1] Peirce propounded his ethics of the unlimited community. I will first state his thesis and then comment on it.

If man were immortal he would live to see everything in which he had trusted fail. Death saves him from such misery. For first of all if he examines the facts he will discover that human individuals are too short lived for him safely to confine his identification of interests to himself. But for the same reason he will find in turn that neither can he identify his interests with his family, his institution, his community, his nation, humanity, or with anything less than the cosmos. The only proper object with which he can logically identify his interests is the "unlimited community" which "reaches out beyond all limits, beyond all bounds."

The first point to notice in this conception is the stepwise hierarchy of ends, which requires of the individual that he should ascend the ladder of morality one step at a time, and no less so because all the while his gaze is fixed at the top. For the hierarchy of ends is also a hierarchy of concerns, and what every individual is dealing with is a hierarchy of concerns. Each level of concern has its own authenticity of being. Skipping steps, which is such a familiar feature of the behavior of absolutists, does moral damage to any steps which are skipped. The hero who at a single leap hopes to move from himself to the cosmos may in the process injure his family as Gandhi and Buddha no doubt did and as Jesus recommended; or he may hurt his and other communities, as Mohammed did; or indeed turn against humanity as so many saints by their actions implied. The way to the top is slow, painful and intricate, and to identify one's interests with those of the whole world cannot be properly done except by moving carefully through the intermediate stages of organization.

The second point to notice is the emphasis on the future. This is consistent with evolution, whose golden age does in fact lie in the future; but it is not consistent with the existing religions which tend to place the golden age in the past. The theory of evolution promises the future to those organisms best fitted to survive, that is to say, those which manage to adapt to changes in the environment. There is, however, no equating value with survival so that the ability to survive is proof of a higher value. If this were so, the cockroach and the horseshoe

---

[1] Charles S. Peirce, *Chance, Love and Logic* (ed. Morris R. Cohen, London 1923, Kegan Paul Trench, Trubner & Co.), Part I, ch. 3.

crab would be vastly superior to man for they have survived for millions of years longer. What evolution promises is the opportunity for the development of higher organic forms, not a guarantee of their eventuality. Man may in the future evolve into moral superman.

The third point to notice is the program for strenuous action which the concept of the unlimited community engenders. The unlimited community is not to be interpreted as a static set of relations but as a dynamic program for action. It can be construed as implying a simple imperative: widen the community; and this means in effect, manage all conduct in such a way as to enable each increase in the level of personal concern to lead to the next. Efforts are being made already in that direction, feeble in some respects no doubt, nevertheless plainly indicated ones. I will mention two in their chronological order. The first, is the League of Nations, founded after world war I, and the United Nations, founded after world war II, which were attempts to construct a global society. The second is exploration of deep space, in artificial earth satellites and rockets sent to the moon and other planets, which are undertakings made in a quite different way to widen the scope of human society by enlarging its available environment.

The fourth point to notice is the immediate practical aspect. Consider the predicament of man who, thanks to applied science and technology, is able now for the first time to control his own destiny but who lacks the knowledge of the direction in which he should propel it. In the past he has lacked the means but fallen a prey to every claimant to super-natural knowledge. Now he has the means, yet his knowledge must come from the natural domain. The conception of the unlimited community points toward the climbing of the moral integrative levels without omitting any steps.

The direction of enlargement through definite steps none of which is to be omitted lies through the kind of transfer of reliability which has taken place long ago from the individual to society. It must now be extended to greater units of organization. What formerly was left to the individual conscience now has the support of the establishment of a society, for instance as contained in the Constitution of the United States, and after that in the charter of the United Nations. Personal integrity is thus supported by social establishment, and social establishment is supported by a formal charter of human cohesion. There is a step beyond, and it remains to be taken in the same empirical terms: the formal recognition of cosmic solidarity.

(c) Standpointlessness

Confrontations of the order dictated by cosmic obligation have their passive as well as active phases. At the cosmic level the passive phase plays a greater role than it does at any other level. In the last section I have been discussing the active phase of cosmic obligation. Now I propose to enter upon a discussion of the passive phase. I shall name it standpointlessness. The unlimited community was a direction toward the future. Standpointlessness is neutral and timeless.

The general conception of standpointlessness refers to the technique of employing empirical knowledge to rise to a more extended view of existence in order to understand and feel at one with as much of it as possible. Standpointlessness involves a natural explanation rather than a supernatural one. In this sense it is an overview. Every effort at generality may be interpreted as an attempt to rise to an extended view of the world and so to achieve something similar to standpoint-lessness; the arts through intuition, the religions through feeling, the sciences through activity, the philosophies through understanding, are all aimed at the same goal.

Standpointlessness is the ultimate strategy of cosmic obligation. The method of standpointlessness consists in obtaining, and then improving on, the widest possible context for any particular position. If we consider the self as an imaginary point necessary for locating a set of perspectives on the environment, then standpointlessness becomes a measure of the dimensions of the extensity and intensity of the environment. How large is the entire environment and what are its terms and conditions?

There are four stages to the process of arriving at standpointlessness. The first is that of preferring the good over the bad; the second that of acceptance, the bad as well as the good; the third that of the love of difference; and the fourth that of progressive detachment.

The first stage in the strategy of cosmic good is to work for the good and against the bad, and this is a necessary stage in which all predominantly good men are engaged. But it presupposes a knowledge of the good, and here the sceptics begin to drop off: to know what is good is not as easy as we might suppose. Still, there is always the call to action, which cannot be put off until the good has been finally determined.

And so the actor falls back meanwhile upon the second stage in the strategy, which is that of acceptance. This involves leaving the world as it is. In reaching this stage there is a kind of moral acquiescence.

But moral acquiescence is not merely negative, nor is it readily available to those who know nothing of ethics. It is a conscious step and has to be taken deliberately. It is the natural ethics of productive artists; others must strive to attain it. As Pope said in his *Essay on Man*
"One truth is clear, whatever is, is right"
and as he was careful to point out in the line preceding, if reason did not agree it was not in spite of correct reasoning but only "in erring reason's spite." The attitude calls neither for a denial of the world nor for a preoccupation with it. To use each thing in the world for what it is: a means—that is the right use of the world.

The third stage in the strategy is the love of difference. And the love of difference is a test of love. In the love of difference there is the true condition of toleration. The individual tends to love things which are similar to himself because he can find in them a variety of self-love; to love what is like himself is in another way to love himself. But the truest form of love is love which has nothing personal to gain and this consists in the love of what is different from himself, because this kind of love presupposes a self-overcoming in favor of a love without exception, embracing as it then must the entire cosmos. To so overcome the influences of one's own narrow interests and those of one's culture that there remains only that half influence which is necessary for continued survival is the task. The other half can then be devoted to the position of generality. Ultimate love is cosmic love, love without exception of similarity or difference.

The fourth and last stage in the strategy is that of progressive detachment. Progressive detachment consists in following the graded stages of the unlimited community with an increasing separation from interest in it; not selfishness nor the aloofness of self-isolation but a kind of generalized concern combined with freedom. Progressive detachment reverses the inclusiveness of the unlimited community by substituting a uniformity about its parts as they relate to the whole. The ultimate object of identification for the long-range self is the universe—all of it, the whole of being. This is the individual's only hope for permanence for himself and for the reality to which because of its equality he belongs. When the interests of the short-range self are indistinguishable from those of the long-range self, then complete realization will have been achieved.

Before achievement, however, here is a model for the imitation of virtue. But then what about standpointlessness in morality? It exists on analogy to the definition of reality as equality of being. Cosmic morality is equality of goodness. In it all quality is reducible to the same quality. That is why all of the great philosophers from Plato to Spinoza have counselled contemplation as the best way of life; it constitutes total immersion in equality. Is there a trans-cultural morality which could stand as the ideal for every particular culturally-conditioned morality and in terms of striving toward which an appropriate strategy would have to be locally devised?

What exactly does standpointlessness mean here? An averaging of ethical standpoints? A reaching beyond one's own type to a higher responsibility? To what then? To being as such? What does it call for if anything? Standpointlessness is the last moral attitude, and it is appropriate to cosmic ethics only; and then only if supported by other viewpoints, from other, and lesser, moral integrative levels. What is required is a sharpening of the power of choice in the matter of abstractions; keeping essentially unaffiliated.[1]

Standpointlessness involves cosmic solidarity, which is felt as pan-provincial caring, the recognition that from the point of view of the largest and most enduring object, which is the metagalaxy, one position is much the same as another, and all are dear. Security is ultimately found to rest on this identification. The metagalaxy is a whole such that everything is some part of it, the human individual no more but also no less than any other part. The metagalaxy is the object of the good; but to see the nearest good as its representative, this is the proper kind of moral mysticism. For the ultimate begins at home, and no steps may be omitted in working from the nearest good, which is perhaps the smallest, to the farthest and largest.

Why is it that like all animals we live in the present, but unlike them we have glimpses of the past and the future and are able to observe over enormous distances and speculate about vast times? Yet this does not fit altogether the mind of the man of action, which is peculiarly composed. It needs to have a strong central theory, and to have this theory surrounded by a large area of ignorance. For the man of action to be able to take vigorous and forceful action requires not only a powerful conviction but also an inability to see the weakness of his own side and the strength of his opponent's. Action is direct and it can issue only from a single truth. Thus it may represent more good than harm if the truth is wide enough, or more harm than good if it is not, but always in any case some harm.

To the rescue of the individual who aspires to the fourth stage of

[1] See Aristotle, *Nico. Eth.*, 1103a9 and 1106b36.

obligation, a certain liberation from harm-doing is provided by freedom. Intellectual freedom consists of high levels of abstraction: his ability to rise from the practical to the theoretical, to be faced with many alternatives and to be aware of the system of ideas within which he operates, that there is a world of material things and of abstract ideas beyond it and containing elements which it does not include.

Moral freedom is the same as intellectual freedom but in terms of the values. A free man's knowledge means that he is free to see himself as he can imagine from his knowledge of the world others might see him, or, more broadly still, as he might be regarded from some cosmic perspective. The achievement of standpointlessness, however briefly it is attained and held, carries with it the virtue of intellectual freedom. The alternatives to freedom are either to live on impulse, as now one, now another idea takes possession, or to live by the narrow reasons, those say consistent with some one of the gray, monolithic structures in which all is ordered by deduction from a set of axioms which are too few and which have never been adequately questioned.

To see such alternatives with the proper detachment is to wish to stand apart. To be independent of all close moral systems in order to enable the individual to choose his own proper morality (which may lie outside all established systems, but, if not, may lie outside the moral system of the society to which by his presence he is committed) is a highly desirable goal. In the event that there are no equals competing for choice (if this should indeed be the case), the alternatives lie on a scale from better to worse. Then freedom must be freedom to choose only the lesser good, for the best is also the most compelling if it is understood by the mind and apprehended by the feelings.

The choice of the best, then, does not involve or require freedom but exists as a matter of compulsion. One should seek not freedom necessarily but comprehension, for to understand what is the best is to be compelled by it. And to seek the best is after all the most one could ask from freedom. Freedom means of course the opportunity to choose a determinism. The three freedoms of thought, feeling and action referred to earlier here come up again, but this time fused into one. The individual who has achieved occasional glimpses of standpointlessness is free for the moment from commitment to any rational system; he feels free in this way, and all of his responses are neatly balanced between the stimuli of what-is and those of what-ought-to-be.

In formulating the ideal it is necessary to have shared the analogical glimpse of sidereal duration which is given to those who are able to detach themselves sufficiently from the exclusiveness of the affairs of their own limited neighborhood. It begins perhaps with self-consciousness conceived in a certain way; namely, as the view of the self as a dimensionless point, a perspective from which it appears that the body is an object in the world.

Standpointlessness, then, is the ultimate philosophy, moved to from the last position at a single point. The dimensionless point, the widest perspective possible in existence, is based on knowledge, not ignorance. Hence it is not the Asian way, not the way of the religious saint. It requires considerable information and the occupancy of a considerable number of limited perspectives before these can be assimilated to an unlimited perspective. Thus the larger the knowledge the greater the probability of achieving standpointlessness, provided only—and it is an important provision—the knowledge can be properly organized and utilized as a whole.

Individual ethics is the view from the actor; standpointlessness is the view from the spectator. In human strategy, aggression reaches its outermost limits. In cosmic strategy, the strategy of the unlimited community and of standpointlessness, the movement is the opposite of aggression and issues from an ultimate appeal of assimilation: belonging to the cosmos. The art of ethics at this stage consists in comprehending without wishing to change. When there is no more energy for action then the perspective of moral conduct must be shifted around to that of standpointlessness. Strategy at the level of cosmic ethics calls for superfluous action, just as esthetics calls for superfluous caring. There is an ascendency of completeness over consistency in the case of the good, and an ascendency of consistency over completeness only in the case of the beautiful. Human dignity subdivides into high seriousness and the attitude of cosmic waiting; the maintenance of a kind of indifference to the vicissitudes of pleasure and pain, of suffering and enjoyment.

The designing of a strategy of standpointlessness is not without its attendant difficulties. The most obvious of these is presented by the spectacle of religion. What are the consequences of that ultimate diremption which we have already declared to exist?[1] Put otherwise how is it possible to rise to an extended view of the world without slipping into supernaturalism? If the Platonic Ideas be understood as the occupants of the second story of a two-story world, then naturalism can be saved without sacrificing the values of supernaturalism and yet

[1] See above Section (a).

also without making unwarranted supernatural claims. What is usually meant by a belief in God (or gods) is faith in the essential rightness of things, that there truly is a cosmic ethics. This rightness is necessary to the individual when his efforts to probe into the meaning of his possibly brief and largely painful existence fails.

The most common difficulty stems from the limitations of language. Standpointlessness is not a system but a distillation; all languages are at least partially-ordered systems; therefore standpointlessness cannot be entirely expressed in language. Yet it can be worked toward through language, it can be pointed out in language, even though at the last stage the language will have to be left behind.

Standpointlessness implies the concept of cosmic solidarity. But we are not yet ready with the degree of understanding requisite to embody it in an institution. The direct action which results from the functioning of men in institutions is inimical to the kind of insight which standpointlessness allows.

Standpointlessness is the final product of the art of ethics, and sublimity the moral feeling of standpointlessness. The beauty of the whole as it is always can be seen from the perspectiveless dimension, but only by viewing the moral with the detachment of the artist. The requirements for axiom-sets are precisely those corresponding to the values, namely, consistency for beauty, completeness for goodness, and independence for holiness. Total completeness, as in cosmic solidarity, is indistinguishable from total consistency, since in both cases we have the entire scale and we are merely looking at it from opposite ends.

By making us feel the sublime through works of art which symbolize cosmic solidarity, the artists remind us reassuringly that all things, both those things that are wholes and those that are parts, are equally themselves parts of that larger whole which is the cosmic universe: the value of the greatest whole to every one of its parts. In this approach to sublimity the cosmic plays a considerable role. Thus the reassurance of cosmic solidarity is furnished by appreciating being through the help of the greatest works of art, which is therefore one of the techniques for achieving standpointlessness. Here, however, we encounter our final difficulty. For the work of art viewed as the literal truth is always the concrete expression of a false proposition. For the eliciting of value we need to know how we can distinguish the valuable side of the false proposition from that side on which it is lacking in value. We avoid this difficulty if we feel through it rather than at it, with it rather than from it, by means of a kind of super-identification. For within the context of standpointlessness it is the quality of the largest of all good objects[1] that is the true object of our longing.

(d) Dual Attachment

We have noted that the strategy of cosmic obligation has its active and passive phases. We have studied the active phase as the approach to the unlimited community, and the passive phase as the end attitude of standpointlessness. Can these two be harmonized?

One difficulty seems to constitute an obstacle to such an accord. I said earlier[2] that the end of man was to increase the precious store of material artifacts together with the principles of their management as part of the external inheritance. I say here it is the subjective and psychological attitude of standpointlessness. How can these two statements be reconciled?

Every action is accompanied by an attitude: the proper attitude produces the appropriate action. To achieve the proper understanding of the proportions of things it is necessary to recognize the inevitability of conflict. So long as the world falls short of perfection there will be activity, and so long as there is activity there will be opposition and struggle, a surrender but also an overcoming. What there is, is natural, whatever it is, the bad as well as the good, and activity is productive of both. The individual who has attained to standpointlessness does not discriminate; in it he has reached the overview from which the detached contemplation of action is possible. He acts, it is true, from his convictions; yet he has convictions extending beyond the actions; and it is in that extension in which total comprehension is undertaken that the assumption of standpointlessness occurs.

Let us revert here to a point we made in discussing the unlimited community. The individual is a whole consisting of parts but as a whole he seems ultimate in virtue of a much tighter organization than exists at most other and higher levels. Each level upward above the human individual does seem looser than the lower. Thus a man is more dependent upon his particular kidneys than upon his particular society. Both can be changed, but not with equal efforts and not without equally disastrous results. Thus rising to a higher confrontation in the moral integrative series stands always as a possibility, while confrontation at the lower levels remain always a necessity. This is the ground for dual attachment.

---

[1] A. N. Whitehead, *Science and the Modern World*, chapter II.
[2] Part IV, chapter 2, Section *c*.

The dualism is one not of methods but of the double nature of that at which the moral individual aims. It is difficult to know persons and things, and difficult, too, to comprehend the moral principles governing their use. But some knowledge of them we do have else we could not act toward them with any consistency and hence with any effectiveness; there are principles in our possession which we intend to apply. But our conceptions of both persons and things on the one hand and of principles on the other keep changing, and so the concept of dual attachment applies so long as we have them both despite the shifting nature of our conceptions of just what they are.

Dual attachment: to the activity of the unlimited community and to the inactivity of standpointlessness, that is to say, to the two stories of a two-story world, to the order of matter and to the order of logic above it. The practicality of the second story of the two-story world is that it makes one integrated structure out of the two sets of elements which must provide the balance necessary for making the proper decisions concerning action. Dual attachment is a moveable division which can take up its position at any cleavage.

It is not advisable to live alternately in two worlds, the actual and the ideal. For this would call at one time for an exclusive attachment to the ideal, from which the exigencies of the actual were regarded as illicit; and at another time for an exclusive attachment to the actual, from which the perfections of the ideal were regarded as dream-like irrelevancies.

In place of this division we need a dual attachment, since each of the domains has its legitimate demands. Just as logical elements have an order among themselves, which is not the same as the order in which they occur in matter; just as experimental science requires equally both mathematics and material instruments; so morality requires its own version of dual attachment, of rules tempered by expediency and of practice mediated by principles. This makes of the moral life a delicate business of walking a tightrope, and makes of every action, however slight it may be, a quivering drama. Thus dual attachment calls for continual balance, compromise, unification. It is a nice judgment to make the decision driven by the organization of entire man, and it must be made every time and immediately on those moral grounds which are deeply imbedded in him and are made up by his whole being.

In an earlier work[1] I set forth the articles of a creed which involves

---

[1] *The Pious Scientist* (New York, 1958).

no more than the ethical yet manages somehow to effect the reconciliation we are seeking. The ethical portions, with certain changes and emendations, read as follows.

Look for the unaffiliated truth.
Balance attachment with non-attachment.
Practice active non-interference.
Stay on the positive side.
Reduce the amount of harm done to others.
Have faith only in inquiry.
Find dogma only in fallibilism.
Maintain half belief.
Respect the existence of everything.
Extend altruism to stones.

These ethical admonitions bring out the practical side of dual attachment. They show clearly that reconciliation of its passive and active aspects by calling for a balance between attachment and non-attachment: never more than half participation, and at the same time never less than half. But man thinks and feels as well as acts, and so through the reason and the feelings as well as in the way stipulated above for activity, the integration of entire man with his entire environment is implemented. Nothing less could be acceptable as a final description of the meaning of ethics.

NAME INDEX

TOPIC INDEX